PUBLIC SERVICES AND THE 1990s:
ISSUES IN PUBLIC SERVICE FINANCE
AND MANAGEMENT

PUBLIC SERVICES AND THE 1990s: ISSUES IN PUBLIC SERVICE FINANCE AND MANAGEMENT

Edited by

JOHN WILSON and PETER HINTON

TUDOR

© John Wilson and Peter Hinton 1993

First published in Great Britain by Tudor Business
Publishing Limited. Sole distributors worldwide,
Hodder and Stoughton (Publishers) Ltd, Mill Road,
Dunton Green, Sevenoaks, Kent, TN13 2XX.

British Library Cataloguing in Publication Data

Public Services in the 1990's: Issues in Public Services Finance and Management. –
(Management Series)
I. Wilson, John II. Hinton, Peter
III. Series
363.0941

ISBN 1–872807–75–5

Typeset by Deltatype Ltd, Ellesmere Port, Cheshire
Printed and bound in Great Britain by
Athenaeum Press Ltd, Newcastle upon Tyne

CONTENTS

Notes on Contributors

JOHN WILSON is Head of Accountancy and Financial Management at Liverpool Business School. He is a qualified member of the Chartered Institute of Public Finance and Accountancy (CIPFA) with an academic background in politics and economics. His main research interests concern the management and economics of public service provision in the UK. He currently acts as an academic adviser to CIPFA.

PETER HINTON is Director of Professional Programmes at Liverpool Business School. He is a qualified member of CIPFA with considerable experience in the provision of public service accounting and management courses. He has a Master's degree in public service management from the University of Aston, to which he has been a visiting lecturer teaching MSc and MBA public service modules. He is extensively involved in CIPFA education and training. He has undertaken research in specialty costing in the NHS and is currently researching the appropriateness and application of Total Quality Management in public service organisations.

ANITA CARROLL is a Senior Lecturer in the Liverpool Business School. She is a qualified member of CIPFA and an associate member of the Institute of Marketing. She has an academic background in business studies. Her main research interests concern the National Health Service and strategic management in the public services.

DAVID GARDNER is a Principal Lecturer in the Liverpool Business School. He is a qualified member of CIPFA with an academic background in economics. His main research interests are local taxation and economic regulation. He acts as academic adviser to CIPFA and is a member of its Education and Training Executive.

DR DENIS SMITH is Professor of Management and Director of the Liverpool Business School and the Business School's Centre for Risk and Crisis Management. Prior to this he taught at the Universities of Manchester and Sheffield, the Open University and both Nottingham and Leicester Polytechnics. In addition, he has been a visiting Professor of Business Administration at the University of Kobe, Japan. His main research interests are in the areas of risk assesment, business policy and crisis management. He has published widely in the area of crisis management and his more recent publications include Business and the Environment: Implications of the New Environmentalism (Paul Chapman Publishing) and Waste Location (edited with M Clark and A Blowers, Routledge).

ELISABETH WILSON is a Senior Lecturer in the Liverpool Business School. She is a qualified social worker with considerable experience at a senior level of social work management in a number of local authorities. She has an academic background in philosophy and is a Master of Business Administration. Her main research interest is the rationale, impact and implications of decentralisation and devolution in local government.

Foreword

Public service provision will be one of the most important issues debated in the UK throughout the 1990s. Politically, it was the subject of considerable debate in the period leading to the general election in April 1992 but, given the nature of the issues involved and their constant impact upon the population, the relevance of the topic will extend to future election campaigns.

The quality and extent of public service provision raises political, economic, financial and managerial issues which themselves encompass a multiplicity of questions which may be more or less relevant to different public services but which cut across all.

The central aim of this book is to identify the major finance and organisational management issues confronting the public services and to explain their background and present and future relevance. Particular emphasis is placed on local government and the National Health Service.

The publication will serve as an invaluable teaching text for undergraduate, postgraduate and professional courses. It will prove useful to students and to public service managers as a means of placing in context issues with which they will already be familiar, but it is also accessible in terms of style and presentation to those who are newly-concerned with public service provision.

The publication presents in a coherent and readable way a thorough discussion of the major issues and does so by means of an appropriate combination of theoretical argument and practical application. The issues relevant to the public services are identified, explained and placed within the context of the political environment within which they can expect to operate throughout the 1990s. The thematic approach is supplemented by consideration of the practical implications and consequences of the issues for two sectors: local government and the National Health Service.

The book contains contributions from staff of the Accountancy and Financial Management (AFM) Unit of Liverpool Business School and from specialists outside the Unit.

Staff within the AFM Unit have a national reputation for the training of financial managers, notably through course provision relating to the Chartered Institute of Public Finance and Accountancy (CIPFA). They also have an active professional involvement in the activities of CIPFA where they are often engaged in a consultancy capacity.

The book has both academic and professional appeal. However, it is aimed primarily at actual and potential public service employees, particularly those who are studying for financial and/or management qualifications eg registered students of CIPFA, students registered for the Diploma in Management Studies, public service personnel undertaking a Master of Business Administration degree and final year undergraduate students undertaking public finance and management options.

Chapter One introduces the reader to the scope and magnitude of public service activity in the UK. Current service provision is placed in a historical context and contrasted with levels and scope in previous years.

Chapter Two deals with the policies pursued in particular by the Conservative Governments since 1979, but the political environment within which public services can expect to operate in the 1990s is also critically considered.

Chapter Three considers the cultural changes which have taken place in the public services. Factors influencing the cultural change are considered and the concept of new managerialism explored.

Chapter Four considers the issue of quality. Public service organisations are developing quality policies in three main areas as purchasers of products and services; in delivery of services to external customers; in respect of internal operations. Increased compulsory competitive tendering and customer charters have added to the pressures on public service organisations to assess the relevance of the theories and practices of quality assurance and total quality management established in the business and manufacturing sectors. The chapter considers the applicability of quality concepts to the public sector, the ways of implementing quality programmes and the benefits to be derived.

Chapter Five examines the meaning and extent of privatisation. This involves consideration of denationalisation and competitive tendering. The focus is placed on the rationale underpinning both policies and an analysis of its practical significance. The theoretical arguments will be considered by reference to empirical evidence.

Chapter Six examines the economic case for regulation *per se* and as an alternative to public ownership. The validity and relevance of the economic theories of regulatory origin and the various forms of economic regulation are critically evaluated. Regulatory practice pre- and post-1979 are also considered and the chapter concludes by assessing likely domestic and European regulatory policies throughout the 1990s.

Chapter Seven examines accountability, its meaning and types in public service organizations. The impact of consumerism for accountability and the significance of recent developments in accountable management in the Civil Service and Next Step agencies are described. Particular attention is then given to the use of a market approach for accountability and the influence of *The Citizen's Charter*, the changing character of professional accountability and the growing emphasis on individual accountability. The chapter concludes by assessing the prospects for improved accountability in the public sector in the rest of the 1990s.

Chapter Eight considers the process of crisis management which has attracted considerable attention within the media during the last decade. In particular the public services, especially the Prison Service, have been portrayed as in a state of crisis. The prevention and management of crisis events are of particular importance to those who are managing within a dynamic and hostile environment. The questions of whether an organization is crisis-prone or -prepared take on a new dynamic when it is as complex and diverse as, for instance, the Prison Service. Drawing upon recent research, this chapter explores the issue of crisis management and develops the thesis that the culture, structure and communication and control systems of an organisation are important in determining its ability to respond to crises.

Chapter Nine analyses the economic issues relevant to local government. The economic rationale of local government is considered, followed by an analysis of the alternative ways by which expenditure can be funded.

Chapter Ten discusses Conservative policy towards the National Health Service. Conservative policy is briefly placed in an historical context, leading to a critical consideration of the main features of the Government's reforms.

This book is dedicated to Chris and Hannah, Beverley and Jennifer

Acknowledgements

The editors are grateful for the support they received from staff within Liverpool Business School and from colleagues, both academic and practitioners, in other organisations. Particular thanks go to Tina McLoughlin for preparing so expertly the drafts of the chapters. Needless to say, any errors are entirely the fault of the editors.

J. Wilson
P. Hinton
March 1993.

CHAPTER ONE

PUBLIC SERVICES IN THE UK

John Wilson

Introduction

It is true to say that the condition of the public services in the United Kingdom will, directly or indirectly, affect every inhabitant of the country. The range and quality of public service activity are issues in which everyone has a legitimate vested interest irrespective of age or social background. Whether affluent or indigent, young or old, healthy or ill, pedestrian or commuter, the impact of public service activity is all-pervasive. It is so because although there are varying degrees of dependency no individual can live life entirely isolated from the public services. Even the wealthiest individual cannot lead a life which is hermetically-sealed from the existence of all others. This is true for two reasons.

First, even though use of services may be minimised it cannot be eliminated. Certain services may be used directly, *eg* roads and public utilities, whilst others may be used indirectly, *eg* environmental regulation, police. In either case, they are used by all members of the community. Secondly, even where an individual may be sufficiently wealthy to be able to avoid direct use of certain public services, he or she will not legally be able to avoid contributing towards the cost of their provision. Taxes have to be paid.

Consequently, either as a direct or indirect user of the services or as an individual helping to finance them, all persons are affected. This fact is predictably, and rightly, sufficient to ensure that there is an overtly political dimension to the debate about the extent and quality of the public services. To make sense of the political debate it is important to establish a factual base. This allows for interpretative and predictive comments to be made. To do this, the chapter will be divided into four sections: definition of public services; scale of public services in the UK; trends in public sector expenditure and, finally, conclusions.

Public services defined

There is no universally accepted definition of a 'public service'. An initial distinction can be made between the public sector and the private sector but not all public sector activity – which ranges from the armed forces to the commercialised state-owned industries – can be classed as a public service. Nonetheless, the distinction is a starting point and hinges on the related questions of ownership and purpose (see Perrin 1985 for a discussion of differences in organisational categorisation). Where an organisation is owned by and operated on behalf of private sector individuals and institutions (*eg* shareholders) it is said to be part of the private sector; where ownership is public, *ie* not confined to specific individuals, and exercised through, for instance, central government on behalf of society, the organisation is said to form part of the public sector. Ownership will largely determine purpose. Private sector and public sector organisations can be crudely categorised as being concerned with profit maximisation and service provision respectively.

The public sector has three component parts – central government, local government and public corporations. These three sub-sectors provide a multiplicity of services including the National Health Service, education, law and order, defence, social services, public utilities, broadcasting *etc*. However, the distinction between public and private sector was never clear-cut and obscured the fact that parts of the public sector, *viz* certain nationalised industries, sought to achieve a profit even though this was not the prime consideration.

This definitional imprecision increased as a result of the policies pursued by Conservative governments since 1979. Particularly relevant here is the policy of 'privatisation' (see Chapter Five) which has led, *inter alia*, to a change in ownership and the relocation of certain organisations including public utilities such as gas and electricity from the public to the private sector. This in turn has led to the increased use of the expression 'public service'.

This expression reflects a greater sectoral overlap and emphasises similarities. However, the principles governing public service provision and which distinguish such activity from the private sector have perhaps not changed at all. In fact, it could be contended that policies pursued since 1979 have sharpened the distinction between public and private service provision rather than blurred them. This contention is based on the assumption that 'indigenous' private sector organisations can rightly and properly aim for profit maximisation whereas public services, whether located in the public or private sector, must consider to a far greater degree the social costs and benefits of their decisions.

Scale of Public Service Provision in the UK
Any assessment of the scale of activity requires an analysis of the relevant statistical data. This allows the *status quo* to be placed into both historical and international perspective by the use of comparators. For analytical ease, public service provision will be measured by aggregating those activities undertaken by the public sector plus those which have recently been transferred from the public to the private sector. This facilitates historical comparisons.

Because the final output of the public sector is not sold at market prices, the scale of its output must be measured by the volume of its input. Two measures are available: employment levels and the cost of service provision.

The scale of activity is apparent by considering the numbers of people employed in the public sector, as shown in Table 1.1. Figures for 1978–79 are included for comparative purposes and also to indicate the impact of privatisation. Excluding armed forces personnel, civil servants working in the Ministry of Defence (141,000), and employees of British Coal and British Steel, there were almost 4.5m people working in the public services in 1990–91. Privatisation has reduced the number of people employed within the public sector – civil service manpower has fallen by 24% in the period and the public corporations (including nationalised industries) have witnessed a 62% fall – but they are now engaged in public service activity within the private sector. Local authority staffing has declined by 2%. Contributing to this has been the fall in numbers of staff in education, reflecting the fall in school rolls and the transfer of Polytechnics and other Higher Education Institutions from the local government sector. Important within the total is the NHS, with a little under one million employees in 1990–91.

The scale and scope of public service activity is clearly substantial and this is further illustrated by referring to levels of public expenditure. This is the second measure of the volume of inputs. Public expenditure is usually defined as 'general government expenditure' (GGE) of central and local government, excluding public corporations and privatisation proceeds. Definitions of public expenditure are subject to change but provided appropriate adjustments are made for such changes its level represents the cost of public sector provision of

Table 1.1

**Public Sector Manpower 1978–79 and 1990–91
(thousands: whole time equivalents)**

	1978–79	1990–91
Civil Service	734	560
Armed Forces	326	311
National Health Service	923	970
Other central government	211	213
Total Central Government	2194	2054
Local Government	2325	2280
Nationalised industries	1843	665
Public Corporations	203	108
Total Public Sector	6565	5107

Source: *Public Expenditure Analyses to 1994–95: Statistical Supplement to the 1991 Autumn Statement*, HM Treasury 1992, Table 8.6

certain goods and services. Details are given in Tables 1.2 and 1.3.

In deciding the level of public expenditure, the Government previously determined an annual 'planning total' of expenditure for control purposes. However, at its meeting in July 1992, at which public expenditure plans for three financial years beginning April 1993 were considered, the Cabinet approved a new system whereby a 'control total' was to be introduced in the next spending round *ie* in 1993. It is designed to increase control over public spending by granting greater authority to the Chief Secretary to the Treasury (the Cabinet member with responsibility for planning and controlling public expenditure *vis-a-vis* departmental ministers).

On the basis of 1991–92 estimated outturn, GGE excluding privatisation proceeds (which, by the adoption of a rather eccentric accounting policy, were then treated as negative expenditure) amounted to 41.5% of Gross Domestic Product (GDP) *ie* the annual value of goods and services produced by UK residents. Table 1.4 provides a breakdown of the relevant figures and the basis of the ratio *ie* £244.4bn as a ratio of £588bn.

Table 1.2

Expenditure by spending authority, 1991–92 (estimated outturn)

	£bn	%
Central Govt (1)	156.7	70.2
Local Authorities	63.8	28.6
Nationalised Industries (2)	2.7	1.2
Total	223.2	100.0

1 Includes finance for public corporations
2 Includes actual and planned privatisations

Source: *Public Expenditure Analyses to 1994–95: Statistical Supplement to the 1991 Autumn Statement*, HM Treasury 1992, Tables 4.8, 4.15, 5.11 & 6.5.

The GGE to GDP ratio can be placed in context by considering historical figures (see below: *Trends in UK Public Expenditure*) and also by distinguishing between expenditure on goods and services and transfer payments.

Expenditure on goods and services, known as exhaustive expenditure, reflects the state's decisions about how money should be spent, in terms both of level and purpose. For instance the state decides how many schools, hospitals, roads, houses *etc* should be constructed and how many teachers, nurses, police and army personnel *etc* should be employed. The level and composition of exhaustive expenditure are determined by these decisions which constitute a claim by the state on the nation's finite resources. Transfer payments, however, are simply redistributions of cash from one section of the community to another. They include pensions, child benefit, unemployment benefit, disability benefit *etc* – transfers effected by the state acting as an intermediary. These payments are largely demand-led and inevitably fluctuate with economic activity (unemployment benefit, for example) and demographic trends (pensions, for instance).

Table 1.3

Central Govt expenditure by department and Local Authority expenditure by economic category and function, 1991–92 (estimated outturn)

Central Govt	£bn	%
Defence	22.9	14.6
Overseas aid	3.0	1.9
Agriculture, fisheries, food & forestry	3.1	2.0
Trade, industry, energy & employment	5.9	3.8
Transport	3.0	1.9
Housing	3.7	2.4
Other environmental services	1.8	1.1
Law, order & protective services	5.0	3.2
Education and Science	6.1	3.9
Arts and Libraries	0.6	0.4
Health and personal social services	31.7	20.2
Social Security	63.4	40.5
Miscellaneous	6.5	4.1
Total	156.7	100.0
Local Authorities:		
Capital expenditure	5.9	9.2
Debt interest	5.6	8.8
Current expenditure	52.3	82.0
Sub-total	63.8	100.0
Current expenditure:		
Agriculture, fisheries, food & forestry	0.1	0.2
Trade, industry, energy & employment	0.3	0.6
Roads and Transport	2.9	5.5
Housing	0.4	0.8
Other environmental services	5.1	9.8
Law, order and protective services	7.5	14.3
Education	23.8	45.5
Arts and Libraries	0.8	1.5
Personal social services	5.5	10.5
Social Security	5.9	11.3
Total current expenditure	52.3	100.0

Source: *Public Expenditure Analyses to 1994–95: Statistical Supplement to the 1991 Autumn Statement*, HM Treasury 1992, Tables 4.4 & 5.8.

Table 1.4

The planning total and general government expenditure 1991–92 (estimated outturn)

	£bn
Central govt expenditure	156.7
Central govt support for local authorities (1)	53.3
Nationalised industries – financing requirements	2.7
Privatisation proceeds	− 8.0
Adjustment	0.3
Planning Total	205.0
Local authority self-financed expenditure (1)	10.5
Central govt debt interest	16.7
Accounting Adjustments	4.3
General government expenditure (GGE) (2)	236.4
GGE excluding privatisation proceeds	244.4
Gross Domestic Product (GDP)	588.0
GGE as a percentage of GDP	41.5

1 Aggregating central govt support for local authorities and local authority self-financed expenditure (£53.3bn and £10.5bn gives the figure included in Table 1.2 above).
2 Total reflects roundings as in the original.

Source: *Public Expenditure Analyses to 1994–95: Statistical Supplement to the 1991 Autumn Statement*, HM Treasury 1992, Table 1.1.

Table 1.5 shows that in 1990–91 general government expenditure excluding privatisation proceeds was 39.9% of GDP, of which exhaustive expenditure and transfer payments constituted 22.3% and 17.6% of GDP respectively. It is now necessary to place public expenditure figures into context by considering trends.

Trends in UK Public Expenditure
Conservative policy towards public expenditure has been inconsistent (see Johnson 1991 Ch 3). However, the objective since 1987 has been to

Table 1.5
Public Expenditure 1970–71 to 1992–93
Year General Govt Expenditure (GGE) – excluding privatisation proceeds

	Goods & Services bn	% GDP	Transfer Payments bn	% GDP	Total GGE bn	GGE Real terms bn	GGE per cent of GDP	Money GDP bn	Privatisation proceeds bn
1970–71	11.9	22.4	9.7	18.2	21.6	148.1	40.6	53.2	
1971–72	13.4	22.6	11.0	18.5	24.4	153.6	41.1	59.3	
1972–73	15.2	22.5	12.4	18.3	27.6	161.1	40.8	67.6	
1973–74	17.9	23.9	14.1	18.8	32.0	174.3	42.7	75.0	
1974–75	22.9	25.6	20.0	22.4	42.9	195.3	48.0	89.4	
1975–76	29.4	26.4	24.4	21.9	53.8	195.3	48.4	111.2	
1976–77	32.9	25.3	26.7	20.5	59.6	190.5	45.8	130.1	
1977–78	35.2	23.2	29.2	19.3	64.4	181.1	42.5	151.4	0.5
1978–79	39.1	22.5	35.9	20.7	75.0	190.1	43.2	173.7	
1979–80	46.6	22.3	43.8	21.0	90.4	196.4	43.3	208.6	0.4
1980–81	56.8	23.9	52.0	21.9	108.8	199.9	45.8	237.7	0.2
1981–82	61.1	23.4	59.9	23.0	121.0	202.6	46.4	260.9	0.5
1982–83	67.5	23.6	65.6	23.0	133.1	208.1	46.6	285.6	0.5
1983–84	73.0	23.6	68.7	22.2	141.7	211.7	45.8	309.7	1.1
1984–85	78.6	23.7	4.3	22.4	152.9	217.5	46.1	331.5	2.0
1985–86	82.6	22.8	78.5	20.9	161.1	217.2	44.4	363.0	2.7
1986–87	87.4	22.4	81.7	20.9	169.1	220.8	43.3	390.6	4.5
1987–88	94.5	21.9	83.9	19.4	178.4	220.9	41.3	432.3	5.1
1988–89	99.7	20.7	87.0	18.1	186.7	215.6	38.8	480.9	7.1
1989–90	112.6	21.6	92.2	17.7	204.8	222.1	39.3	521.5	4.2
1990–91	123.8	22.3	97.7	17.6	221.5	221.5	39.9	555.1	5.3
1991–92					244.4	228.4	41.6	588.0	
1992–93					264.4	236.5	41.9	631.0	

Note: 1 Real term figures are cash figures adjusted to 1990–91 price levels
2 Privatisation proceeds have been added to transfer payments but are shown in extreme right-hand column for information
3 Figures are available on a consistent basis for out-turn years only

Source: *Public Expenditure Analyses to 1994–95: Statistical Supplement to the 1991 Autumn Statement*, HM Treasury 1992, Table 2.1.

reduce public expenditure, usually defined as General Government Expenditure (GGE), as a percentage of Gross Domestic Product (GDP).

Attainment of this objective permits increases in public expenditure as long as the rate of increase is less than that of GDP. Conservative policy, therefore, is to reduce GGE as a percentage of GDP. This is consistent with the Government's desire to reduce the relative scale of public sector activity in the economy thereby increasing resources available to the private sector.

In considering the impact of governmental policy on public expenditure it is useful to place the figures into a historical context and to differentiate between exhaustive expenditure and transfer payments. Table 1.5 reveals how exhaustive expenditure, as a ratio of GDP, was at its highest in 1975–76 (26.4%) but subsequently declined, constituting 22.3% in 1990–91. Transfer payments peaked at 23% in 1982 but were down to 17.6% in 1990–91.

In analysing the figures it is important to remember that the changing ratios may actually be the result of changes in GDP rather than fluctuating spending levels. The mid-1970s, for instance, was a period of economic recession caused by dramatic increases in the price of oil. Such exogenous occurrences are likely adversely to affect the rate of growth of GDP but simultaneously perhaps increase the level of public expenditure (increased heating costs of public sector buildings and fuel costs for public sector vehicles, for example) and can lead to erroneous conclusions concerning governmental expenditure. Similarly, the impact on transfer expenditure exerted by domestic economic conditions (*eg* increased expenditure on unemployment benefits) and underlying demographic trends (*eg* increased expenditure on state pensions) needs to be considered in assessing the public spending to GDP ratio.

Also relevant in assessing the ratio is the importance of economic forecasting as a determinant of public spending decisions. As Thain and Wright (1991 p26) state: 'The relationship between these two variables reveals little of the government's "success" in controlling the aggregate of spending. Fluctuations from year to year make the relationship an unstable one; while errors in estimating GDP may mean that public spending could absorb a larger share of it, if later GDP statistics reveal over-estimation. The "success" of a falling profile due to rapid growth may have as little to do with Treasury performance as "failure" due to recession.'

Nonetheless, the figures show that public expenditure fell below 40% of GDP in 1988–89 – the first time in over 20 years (the last time was 1966–67 – see Treasury HM 1992a Table 2.1).

Although there is actually nothing economically significant about a ratio of 40% it enabled the Conservatives to claim that public expenditure was under control and that the reducing ratio not only provided the opportunity for enhanced private sector activity but also facilitated phased reductions in direct taxation. This was emphasised in 1991 (Treasury HM 1991, p14, paras 2.24 and 2.27):

'The Government intends that public spending should continue to take a declining share of national income over time . . . recent increases in the GGE ratio have taken place around a continued underlying downward trend. . . . The Government's objective . . . is to bring down the tax burden . . . and in particular to reduce the basic rate of income tax. Given the medium-term balanced budget objective this requires continued public expenditure restraint.'

The policy was re-emphasised in 1992 when the Chancellor announced a new 20% band of income taxation and reiterated his aim to reduce the standard rate to that level. However, the attainment of this objective has been made much more difficult by the recent increases in public expenditure which are themselves the indirect result of poor economic forecasting. The recession has proved to be deeper and longer than initially forecast and the result has been increased public expenditure, particularly social security payments, and in-creased borrowing. In addition, the fact that 1992 was an election year also predictably led to increased spending on certain programmes, including health and transport.

The magnitude of the increase in expenditure is shown below:

	£bn
planning total 1991–92 (Autumn Statement 1990)	200.3
planning total 1992–93 (Autumn Statement 1991)	226.6

This 13% increase was greeted by the *Financial Times* (7 Nov 1991 p23) as heralding a 'break with Thatcherism'. Johnson (1992 p27) com-mented that 'Such an increase . . . from one year to the next, is remarkable for any government let alone one claiming to be the inheritor of the substance, if not the style, of the Thatcher revolution.'

This point is reinforced by considering the changes in fiscal stance *ie* the relationship between expenditure, revenue and borrowing. When expenditure exceeds revenue there is a Public Sector Borrowing Requirement (PSBR); when revenue exceeds expenditure debt can be repaid and there is a Public Sector Debt Repayment (PSDR):

	£bn
PSDR 1990–91 (Budget 1990)	7
PSBR 1991–92 (Budget 1991)	8
PSBR 1992–93 (Budget 1992)	28

This sharp deterioration in public finances, £35bn in two years, again reflects the expenditure decisions taken in the run-up to the general election but, critically, it reflects the depth and duration of the recession and the inaccuracy of official forecasts. This point is reinforced by the revised PSBR figure for 1992–93 announced in the Autumn Statement on 12 Nov 1992, *ie* increased by 32% from £28bn to £37bn (see Treasury HM 1992b). The possibility, therefore, that 'the fiscal frontiers of the state will stand where they were when Labour was last in office' (Rogaly 1992), has not only occurred but actually been exceeded. The revised estimated out-turn for GGE in 1992–93, as given in the 1992 Autumn Statement, is £257.8bn (1991–92 price base) which represents 44.75% of GDP.

There has not, however, been a decisive break with the policies of Mrs Thatcher. The Government's intention is to regain control of public expenditure and public borrowing and to reduce each as a proportion of GDP, consistent with the requirements of the Maastricht agreement designed to lead to European economic and monetary union. This means that there will have to be a squeeze on public spending over the next three years. This need to tighten control explains the change in the system of planning public expenditure. However, the recession will continue to exert upwards pressure on public expenditure which means that, if control totals are not to be breached, cuts will have to be made in spending on departmental programmes. In addition, the Chancellor announced in the Autumn Statement (Nov 1992) that an incomes policy is to operate within the public sector. Although this does represent a break with Thatcherism, the objective it is designed to attain is consistent with it. The Conservatives remain committed to reducing expenditure and borrowing. This has been the case in principle, if not always in practice, since 1979.

Their commitment to reducing public spending can be illustrated by comparing public spending growth over the last 30 years. Thain and Wright (1991 p34) reveal that the annual average percentage growth in GGE in real terms was 1.4% in the period 1978–79 to 1990–91. This contrasts with:

	%
1973–74 to 1978–79	1.8
1969–70 to 1973–74	5.3
1963–64 to 1969–70	3.2

However, they also point out that the figures conceal distinct phases within the periods given. For instance, the first years of the first Thatcher Government – 1978–79 to 1983–84 – saw public spending increasing at an average annual rate of 2.3% which contrasts with the previous Labour Government's record of 1.8%. Nonetheless, during the period 1983–84 to 1990–91, real growth has averaged less than 1%.

The UK experience over the last 30 years can also be placed in an international context. By the end of the 1970s there was general concern in the member countries of the OECD (Organisation for Economic Cooperation and Development) over the seemingly inexorable growth of the public sector – as reflected by the increase in general government outlays from 28.0% of GDP in 1960 to over 39% in 1980 – and, concomitantly, over the general level of public sector budget deficits. This concern was particularly evident in the USA, with the election of Ronald Reagan in 1980, and the UK, with the election of the Conservatives in 1979 and both events 'accelerated the process of trying out new solutions' (OECD *Economic Outlook* Dec 1991 p7) to the economic problems prevalent at the time, *viz* inflation. A central feature of the 'new solutions' was to reduce the size of the public sector, involving a reduction in public expenditure.

Table 1.6 shows that, of the G7 (Group of Seven) countries, the UK in 1970 had the highest ratio of government spending to GDP but by 1989 only two countries had a smaller ratio. The ratio now is much the same as it was twenty years ago, unlike all other G7 countries (including the USA). The exceptional nature and extent of the UK trend is even more apparent if all other economies in the western world are included (OECD *Economic Outlook* 1991 Table R15).

Table 1.6

Total outlays of general government. Per cent of nominal GDP

	1960	1970	1980	1989
USA	27.0	31.7	33.7	36.1
Japan (1)	17.5	19.4	32.6	33.0
Germany	32.4	38.6	48.3	45.1
France	34.6	38.5	46.1	49.7
Italy	30.1	34.2	41.7	51.7
UK	32.2	38.8	44.7	40.9
Canada	28.6	34.8	40.5	44.3
Other OECD countries	26.8	32.6	44.0	49.0
Total OECD	28.0	32.3	39.3	41.6

Note: 1 1988

Source: 'Economic policy making since the mid-1960s', *Economic Outlook* December 1991, OECD, Table 3

Under the Conservatives, public expenditure has grown by 16.5% in real terms during the period 1978–79 to 1990–91 (see Table 1.5). It is apparent from the detail in Table 1.7 below, however, that this increase disguises significant variations in different spending programmes.

Table 1.7 suggests dramatic variations in governmental priorities have occurred over the years and between spending programmes. There is *prima facie* evidence to show favourable treatment of certain services (health, law and order) and extremely unfavourable treatment of others (*viz* housing). (See Likierman 1988 Chapter 3 for a discussion on the determination of public expenditure priorities).

However, the figures require further investigation because at the outset there are several important reasons for exercising extreme care when interpreting the statistics. Public expenditure is presented in terms of current prices and conversion into real terms is problematic, resulting in figures which are at best ambiguous. First, real terms figures are calculated by adjusting the initial data so as to take account of inflation and this is achieved by using the GDP deflator – an index which allows fluctuations in money values caused by price changes to be isolated from those caused by physical changes in output.

However, the real terms figures do not precisely reveal the volume of goods and services which the cash buys. The absence of accurate information concerning volume makes it extremely difficult to establish what is actually happening to the level of service provision. For instance, suppose that of £35bn spent on health, £25bn relates to wages and salaries and the following happens:

Expenditure	£35.0bn
Govt announces increase	£2.45bn
% increase	7.0
Inflation forecast – % increase	4.0
Real terms % increase	3.0
Actual pay award – % increase	10.0
Cost of pay award	£2.5bn

In the above example, the cost of the pay settlement has exceeded the increased allocation. This means that there is actually less money available to spend on beds, equipment *etc*. The result is that only £9.95bn (*ie* £37.45bn minus £27.5bn) is available for non-labour expenditure when £10.4bn is actually needed just to maintain the same level of service. In this example, the result is a reduction in the volume of service in excess of 4% even though the government has announced a cash increase of 7% and a 'real terms' increase of 3%.

A second reason for caution in assessing the statistics for 'real' expenditure concerns the Relative Price Effect (RPE). Different services experience different rates of inflation which must be measured by a dedicated index. The difference between a specific index or deflator and the GDP deflator is known as the 'relative price effect'. In the case of a service where there is a tendency for the prices of inputs to increase by more than the average, any increased expenditure may simply reflect these increased costs rather than indicate a 'real terms' increase in the level of service. It is also the case, however, that the RPE may be negative *ie* inflation relevant to a specific service is actually less than that in the economy as a whole. Johnson (1991 Ch 3) provides examples of both negative RPE, *eg* transport spending, and positive RPE, *eg* health, and shows clearly the importance of quantifying them and relating them to volume.

Table 1.7
Total expenditure on services in real terms (1990–91 price levels)
1978–79 to 1991–92 and percentage distribution of total
expenditure by function (figures given in brackets)

Service	1978–79 outturn £bn	1991–92 estimated outturn £bn	%
Defence	19.0 (11.5)	21.4 (10.5)	+ 12.6
Overseas services	2.7 (1.6)	2.8 (1.4)	+ 3.7
Agriculture etc	2.6 (1.6)	3.0 (1.4)	+ 15.4
Trade, industry etc	10.5 (6.4)	6.8 (3.3)	− 35.2
Transport	7.6 (4.6)	9.1 (4.5)	+ 19.7
Housing	11.6 (7.0)	5.5 (2.7)	− 52.6
Environmental servcs	6.2 (3.7)	7.6 (3.7)	+ 22.6
Law, order etc	6.4 (3.9)	12.0 (5.9)	+ 87.5
Education & science	24.7 (14.9)	29.0 (14.2)	+ 17.4
Arts & libraries	1.0 (0.6)	1.4 (0.7)	+ 40.0
Health & social services	23.4 (14.1)	34.9 (17.1)	+ 49.1
Social security	43.0 (26.0)	64.8 (31.7)	+ 50.7
Miscellaneous	6.8 (4.1)	6.0 (2.9)	− 11.8
Total	165.5	204.3	+ 23.4

Source: *Public Expenditure Analyses to 1994–95: Statistical Supplement to the 1991 Autumn Statement*, HM Treasury 1992, Tables 2.3 & 2.4

This is illustrated by the examples given in Table 1.8. The figures confirm the importance of the RPE when assessing the impact of governmental policy on services and can demonstrate the contradiction which may exist between political rhetoric and actuality. There are marked contrasts between real terms and volume changes in the cases of both education and health and the difference will affect the ability of schools, hospitals *etc* to satisfy existing and future demand.

The impact of RPE on health is particularly important given the cost of medical technology. Technological costs combined with the rapidity of medical advances place ever-greater pressure on central government to increase funding to the NHS. Increased resources are required to accommodate the inflation rates applicable to health service provision and also the increased demands resulting from medical breakthroughs, increased societal expectations and changes in the composition of the population.

Table 1.8

Expenditure on defence, education and health: percentage real terms and volume changes 1979–80 - 1989–90

	Real terms changes %	Volume changes %
Defence	9.2	7.5
Education	13.7	− 0.5
Health	31.8	11.6

Note: Volume changes relate to equivalent calendar years. *Source*: Johnson C (1991), *The Economy Under Mrs Thatcher: 1979–1990* Table 20 p287

A third factor, therefore, is that of demography. This, again, is particularly relevant to the NHS. Many conflicting claims have been made about the level and adequacy of resources devoted to the NHS but to make sense of the figures it is important not only to measure the RPE but also to quantify the impact of demographic changes. This caveat is necessary because where the elderly account for an increasing proportion of the population there are concomitant pressures upon the health service as the demand for treatment increases. The total demand for health care is a function of the age profile of the population. Demographic trends constitute an important determinant of total demand and need to be analysed when assessing the real increase or decrease in the level of resources devoted to the NHS.

A final reason for caution when interpreting real terms increases is that often no distinction is made between capital and current expenditure. Capital expenditure – or investment – is as important for the public sector as it is for the private sector. In fact, the traditional Keynesian argument would be that they should complement each other *ie* public investment, considered solely from a macroeconomic viewpoint, should be counter-cyclical in that it should be increased as private sector investment declines or is forecast to do so. It is also immensely important for the country's future economic well-being. This is true across a range of services from the nation's transport and infrastructure to the education and training of the workforce.

However, Johnson (1991 p99) states that in fourteen of the twenty years between 1971 and 1991 there have been cuts in public capital expenditure, including a 40% cut by the Labour Government between 1974–79 and a further 40% cut by the Conservative Government between 1980–83. Such cuts have long-term implications and any assessment of expenditure must isolate capital and current components in order to ascertain more accurately and realistically the present situation in the context of past and anticipated trends.

The reasons for exercising caution when interpreting statistics can be illustrated by further analysis. For instance, a study on the effects of inflation, medical advances and demography was undertaken by the Nuffield Institute for Health Service Studies on behalf of *The Guardian* which reported (*The Guardian* 25 March 1992 p11):

'The Institute has analysed the Government's health spending record since 1979 [adjusting] cash increases by allowing for NHS inflation . . . and by providing for essential demographic, medical and policy demands. The result is that real growth in NHS funding is shown to have been virtually non-existent during the 1980s. Only since 1990 . . . has there been significant expansion of funding.'

This finding demonstrates the need to avoid simplistic conclusions from figures relating to health service expenditure but also illustrates the need to do likewise in respect of all figures included in Table 1.7. Particularly relevant is the case of education. The figures show an increase of 17.4% over the period but, compared with health and on the basis of international comparisons, education has fared badly. The real terms increase of 13.7% (Table 1.8) is entirely explained by increases in salaries of teachers and other employees. Taking this into account, the result is an actual reduction of 0.5% in volume terms. It should also be noted that compared with other groups within the public sector and as compared with the private sector, teachers' salaries fell considerably throughout the 1980s.

Rowthorn (1992 p272) states: 'Over the period 1981–1990 the real earnings of the average school teacher rose by 12% as compared to 26% for the average nonmanual worker in the economy at large. Teachers in further and higher education fared as badly or even worse.' (see Rowthorn 1992 p273 Table 12.3)

International measures also show that health and, in particular, education have not been generously treated. Between 1979 and 1988 *per capita* expenditure on health in the UK rose at an annual rate of 0.9%, one of the lowest rates of growth in the European Community. Education, however, suffered a fall in real expenditure per student compared to an increase in most other European countries. This is shown in Table 1.9.

Table 1.7 also indicates that housing has been particularly badly affected, law and order has been treated favourably and expenditure on social security has risen considerably.

The figures for housing reflect the constraints placed upon local authorities which have been discouraged from building new houses despite the significant sales of council houses which have taken place since 1980 – 1.4 million in the period 1980–89 (see Johnson 1991 Table 30 p297). Between 1984 and 1989 public sector housing completions in Great Britain were reduced from 51000 to 28400 – a decrease of 44.3% (Terry and Queen 1991 Table 8.1 p119).

The main influences on social security expenditure were the levels of unemployment throughout the 1980s, the increasing proportion of the elderly within the population and the increased number of people in receipt of long-term sick and disability benefits.

With regard to law, order and protective services the main expenditure relates to the police service, expenditure on which accounts for approximately 50% of total estimated outturn expenditure for 1991–92.

Table 1.9
Education and Health: real *per capita* spending in the European Community (average annual rates of growth)

Country	Education (1) 1980–88 %	Health (2) 1979–88 %
Belgium	4.3	2.3
Denmark	− 1.4	0.8
France	1.9	3.7
Germany	4.8	1.3
Greece	0.8	6.0
Ireland	− 0.8	− 2.0
Italy	3.2	2.5
Netherlands	0.2	4.9
UK	− 1.8	0.9

Note: 1 Average spending per student
        2 Spending per head of population covered by the public health insurance system

Source: Oxley, H *et al* (1990) *The Public Sector: Issues for the 1990s* OECD as given in Rowthorn (1992 p274)

Conclusion

The nature of public service activity within any society demands political and economic debate concerning its scale, scope and means of provision. Such a debate is continuous given the dynamic nature of the external and internal environment. Political decisions have to be made about the size of the public sector *vis-a-vis* the private sector and priorities have to be established across and within the public services (should education be prioritised over defence, should nursery education be prioritised over higher education *etc*?) Professionals within the services, economists, consumers and, most importantly, the population generally all have an input to the debate but ultimately the decisions are political.

The outcome of the 1992 general election has determined the domestic environment within which the public services can expect to operate over the next four to five years (see Chapter Two). Conservative policy will be implemented within the constraints of global economic conditions, the requirements of European convergence criteria (limiting individual governments' fiscal as well as monetary autonomy) and their own economic objectives. Conservative policy is to reduce public expenditure as a proportion of GDP (Conservative Party 1992 p14) and to realise a commitment to reduce direct taxation (Conservative Party 1992 p16). Both commitments, particularly when set against the exigencies of the current (1993) and projected state of public finances, not only effectively preclude public service expansion but also undermine the ability of the public services to maintain existing levels of service provision.

In order to effect a relative reduction in the scale of public sector activity there will be continued emphasis on privatisation (see Chapter Five) and securing value for money. There are likely to be profound implications for central and local government and the NHS as a result of measures which include devolving executive functions from White-hall, extending compulsory competitive tendering and contracting out, local management of schools, internal market in the NHS, trust status for hospitals *etc*. Against this background it is unlikely that the 1990s will be remembered as a decade devoted to promoting, improving and expanding UK public services.

References

Conservative Party (1992), *The Conservative Manifesto*, Conservative Central Office

Johnson, C (1992) 'Public Expenditure' *Public Domain: The Public Services Yearbook*, Terry F & Jackson P (Eds), Public Finance Foundation pp27-

Johnson, C (1991) *The Economy Under Mrs Thatcher: 1979–1990*, Penguin

Likierman, A (1988) *Public Expenditure: Who Really Controls It And How*, Penguin

Perrin, J R (1985) 'Differentiating Financial Accountability and Management in Governments, Public Services and Charities' *Financial Accountability & Management* Vol 1 No 1 pp11–32

Rogaly, J (1992) 'The reins tighten on public spending' *Financial Times* 24 July 1992

Rowthorn R (1992) 'Government Spending and Taxation in the Thatcher Era' in *The Economic Legacy 1979–1992*, Michie J (Ed) Academic Press: Harcourt Brace Jovanovich pp261–293

Terry, R & Queen, B (1991) 'Housing', *Public Domain*, Terry F & Roberts H (Eds), Public Finance Foundation pp109–125

Thain, C & Wright, M (1991) 'Public Expenditure', *Public Domain*, Terry F & Roberts H (Eds), Public Finance Foundation pp23–40

Treasury HM (1992a) *Public Expenditure Analyses to 1994–95: Statistical Supplement to 1991 Autumn Statement*, HMSO

Treasury HM (1992b) *Financial Statement and Budget Report 1992–93*, HMSO

Treasury HM (1991) *Financial Statement and Budget Report 1991–92*, HMSO

Acknowledgements

The author would like to thank Dr John Thompson of The Liverpool Business School for his comments on an earlier draft of this chapter.

CHAPTER TWO

POLITICAL ENVIRONMENT AND PUBLIC SERVICE ACTIVITY

John Wilson

Introduction

The Conservative Party's fourth consecutive election victory determined the political environment within which public services can expect to operate over the next five years. This environment is unlikely to differ in any fundamental sense from that which has prevailed for the last thirteen years. Three main factors underpin this assertion. First, the direction of Governmental policy was made clear in the Conservative manifesto (Conservative Party 1992); second, the level of resources allocated to the public services will be subject to considerable constraint, as evidenced by the Cabinet meeting in July 1992 which agreed to a new system for controlling public expenditure. Finally, the economic prerequisites for continued progress to economic and monetary union, agreed at Maastricht in 1991, necessitate considerable reductions in current levels of borrowing (£37bn for 1992–93 as per the Autumn Statement Nov 1992). This will inevitably involve stringent control of public expenditure and probable increases in indirect taxation given the Government's commitment to reducing direct taxation. In short, the climate for the public services does not appear propitious.

This chapter will consider the background to the present situation before analysing current policy towards the public services. Comments will then be made as to the environment in which they can expect to operate throughout the remainder of the 1990s. Finally, a number of conclusions will be drawn.

Political environment: background

The domestic political environment changed as a result of the replacement of Margaret Thatcher by John Major. The change, however, was essentially one of style rather than substance. In some respects it would be surprising if the substance of policy were to change given that they are successive leaders of the same party and considering Major's route and rapidity of ascent to the premiership. He is very much a Thatcher prodigy, rising from backbench obscurity in 1979 to Prime Minister in 1990.

A continuation of policy, therefore, could be expected but with two exceptions both of which related to the immediate cause of Thatcher's downfall: the Community Charge (poll tax) and Europe. However, even on these two issues there is no real evidence that Major wished to dissociate himself from the past and pursue alternative policies.

The announcement of the abolition of the poll tax was not accompanied by a repudiation of the principles upon which it was based. It is recognised that such a repudiation by Major would have been self-incriminating but it may also be reasonably contended that the decision to abolish the poll tax primarily reflected electoral considerations. Similarly, with regard to Europe, Thatcher had already signed the Single European Act and the key economic decision to join the Exchange Rate Mechanism (ERM) of the European Monetary System (EMS) had been taken, albeit reluctantly, under her premiership. In addition, Major cannot be said to be a Europhile. Like Wilson and the Labour Party in the 1970s, his main consideration in negotiations may be said to be balancing factional views within the party. This has become even more problematic since the UK suspended its involvement in the ERM (16 Sept 1992). However, although this was a total U-turn in economic policy it was not one which Major wished to make. In short, there has not been an ideological *volte face* nor was there likely to be one after the general election even though, at that time, Major had considerably strengthened his position within the Conservative party. After this victory Thatcher declared 'There isn't such a thing as Majorism' and went on to state 'Thatcherism will live. It will live long after Thatcher has died . . .' (Thatcher 1992 p15). She does not specify the period for which her eponymous ideology will survive her own death but she clearly believes that it embraces 'great principles' (Thatcher 1992 p15) which will guarantee longevity and which, importantly, distinguish it from Conservatism (and, of course, Majorism which she claims does not exist at the moment).

This raises numerous questions which, though not actually relevant here (*eg* what is Thatcherism? What is Conservatism? How do they differ? *etc.* See Leach 1991 pp88–116), in general are worthy of consideration if the role and future direction of public services are to be understood.

Whether 'Thatcherism' can be said to mean anything and whether it can be accommodated within the mainstream of Conservative tradition are debatable. To some Conservatives (*eg* Gilmour 1977) the claim that there is a Conservative ideology is almost to adopt an oxymoron. Conservatives seek gradual change; to improve rather than innovate. Policy is based on the lessons of experience and not *a priori* principles. By its very nature, therefore, conservatism has traditionally been unconcerned with long-term intellectual coherence or doctrinal consistency. Its rationale is to improve the *status quo* whilst conserving certain features of our society and constitution (*eg* monarchy). Conservatism is synonomous with pragmatism not dogmatism.

None of this, however, mattered to Thatcher. She intended to exorcise the memory of Conservative acceptance of previous socialist measures and craven accommodation of over-powerful vested interests. In retrospect it can be said that she sought to effect an economic and attitudinal transformation in the UK, although such an ambition was not evident in 1979.

The 1979 manifesto was not a particularly ambitious document. It was consistent with the shift in thinking which had occurred within and outside the Conservative party but was hardly 'revolutionary' in its content. It identified the enhanced role of the state as a contributory factor to UK economic decline (see Conservative Party 1979 p6) and included a commitment to economic policies which amounted to monetarism (see Conservative Party 1979 p8; Smith 1987) but a revolutionary assault on the *status quo* was not really possible given the policies pursued by Labour since 1976 (see Britton 1991). The ideological ground had shifted to the right. However, it could also be argued that the changing consensus allowed the opportunity for the Conservatives to produce their most radical electoral document to date. This they failed to do.

Perhaps the main reason for this was that many senior Conservatives were extremely sceptical of the types of policies in which Thatcher now appeared to believe. Their scepticism continued after the election and extended to their view of Thatcher personally (see Young 1990). Although this situation was in time to change completely it is important to remember that in 1979 the objectives the Government sought to attain were reasonably clear but the means by which they were to be attained were not.

This did not seem to matter to many rank and file Conservatives nor were they concerned with the intellectual consistency of Conservative objectives with the tradition of conservatism. Esoteric debates concerning the true meaning of conservatism could be left to the academic cognescenti. They wanted someone who could win power and articulate and address their grievances. Thatcher was naturally able to meet their needs. Her Manichean view of the world was at one with their own but also had a wider appeal and reached well into the traditional Labour constituency, particularly the skilled working class. Thatcher believed that successive Labour governments had expanded their own activities to the extent that they had 'crippled the enterprise and effort on which a prosperous country . . . depends' (Conservative Party 1979 p6) and had simultaneously allowed trades unions to become too powerful *vis-a-vis* the elected government and individuals. In short, the state was too active economically but too weak politically. She claimed that her policies were not based on dogma or political theory but on reason, commonsense and the liberty of the people under the law (Conservative Party 1979 p5).

A central feature of Conservative policy throughout the 1980s was an ideological commitment to reducing the scope of public sector activity and increasing that of the private sector. This policy followed logically from the assumptions which formed the intellectual substructure of the strand of Conservative thinking which prevailed throughout the decade. The kernel of the orthodoxy was a belief in the efficacy of market forces as a mechanism for achieving a socially-efficient allocation of resources. This belief has a long tradition in political and economic theory but its acceptance and attempted application by a governing party in an advanced, industrialised economy marked a watershed in post-1945 economic policy particularly with respect to the objective of full employment. The post-War consensus had been broken (see Kavanagh 1990).

This consensus had been largely based on the acceptance of the welfare state and the application of Keynesian economics but the problems of the 1960s and 1970s led increasing numbers of politicians and economists to question the efficacy of this policy. Against a background of acute industrial unrest and high levels of unemployment and inflation there was a growing consensus that the policies pursued in the post-War period – *viz* Keynesian demand management designed to achieve full-employment – were not only inappropriate to the modern era but in fact contributed to the seemingly intractable problems with which it was beset. Keynesian economics, it was said, was the product of the 1930s and as such was concerned almost exclusively with unemployment; the work and ideas of Keynes were not simply irrelevant to the 1970s, their implementation actually exacerbated the problems with which they were meant to deal. The policy dilemma resulting from this assault on the post-War economic paradigm was soon, however, to be resolved. The theoretical lacuna resulting from the rejection of Keynesianism was filled by monetarism (Smith 1987) and a rediscovery in the merits of *laisser-faire ie* market forces.

The emphasis on the market was not new to the UK. The Heath Government 1970–74 was initially ardently pro-market and contrasted sharply with the planning bias of the previous Labour Governments (1964–70). However, Heath's commitment to the market was never convincing and merely preceded a pragmatic but nonetheless total conversion to interventionism in 1972 as unemployment approached one million. Heath was essentially technocratic and pragmatic – 'a man of no fixed ideology' (Jenkins 1989 p60) – and saw little point in pursuing policies which demonstrably were not working. By the end of the decade, however, Heath's U-turn was to assume a notoriety which could not have been predicted at the time given the members of his Cabinet who were party to it. One such member was Mrs Thatcher.

Thatcher was determined not to reverse policy in the way of Heath. She was also determined not to pursue the type of policy in which both Conservative and Labour Governments had acquiesced since 1972 and which was labelled 'corporatism'. In a UK context this meant a tripartite form of government whereby the TUC (Trades Union Congress) and CBI (Confederation of British Industry) were involved in the national decision-making process. To Thatcher, this was a derogation of governmental authority which strengthened extra-parliamentary organisations, particularly trade unions. A combination of weak government, powerful unions and excessive public sector activity subverted parliamentary democracy, undermined individual freedom and resulted in economic sclerosis.

The intellectual attack on these developments was mainly rooted in the work of Friedrich von Hayek and Milton Friedman and espoused in the UK primarily by Sir Keith Joseph (see Kavanagh 1990 pp63–122). The result was an intellectual rationalisation and legitimation of Thatcher's convictions. The essence of the new right philosophy was the rejection of Keynesian collectivism and governmental interventionism. Power had to be restored to government but its economic role had to be reduced. Similarly, entrepreneurialism and individual incentives to work had to be increased by, *inter alia*, reducing union power, promoting the private sector and reducing state activity thereby facilitating reductions in public expenditure and direct taxation.

Unlike Heath, Thatcher's policies were ideologically-reinforced. She was not influenced, again unlike Heath, by increases in unemployment. However, it could be argued that she committed a U-turn every bit as fundamental as Heath's when she abandoned, in 1987, initially implicitly rather than explicitly, the economic philosophy on which policy had been supposedly based, *ie* monetarism. Its explicit abandonment came with the UK entry into the Exchange Rate Mechanism (Oct 1990). She also changed objectives with respect to public expenditure (for a discussion of macroeconomic policy under Thatcher see Vane 1992).

However, fundamentally her views on the public sector and public expenditure remained the same insofar as she believed the scale of each should be reduced relative to the private sector. The private sector was seen to be intrinsically superior to the public sector. The latter had to be energised and coerced into efficiency whereas the former contained an internal dynamic in the form of competition which guaranteed efficiency and innovation. In this respect, Major is perhaps Thatcher's natural heir.

Political environment: the present
Major's approach to the public services has been a continuation of the policies he inherited. This is clearly reflected in the 1992 Conservative election manifesto (*The Best Future For Britain*). The policies include an extension of privatisation and compulsory competitive tendering (see Chapter Five). The onus will be on public services 'to prove they can give the right quality at the right cost' (Conservative Party 1992 p29). A common theme is that of improved performance through competition and accountability. This involves the setting of standards and monitoring of performance, including the use of comparative statistics.

Education policy (Conservative Party 1992 pp35–39) includes the extension of the Grant Maintained (GM) scheme. Small schools will be allowed to group together when applying for GM status. GM schools will also be allowed to attract private technology sponsorship. From April 1993 further education and sixth form colleges will be independent of local authority control. A clear statement of education policy was made in the White Paper published in July 1992 (Dept for

Education 1992) whereby education is, in effect, to be nationalised. This has profound implications not only for pupils, parents and, ultimately, the economy but also for the future role of local authorities.

Health policy (Conservative Party 1992 pp57–61) includes a commitment to increase annually the level of real resources devoted to the NHS. These resources will be supplemented by ploughing-back efficiency savings. The Trust scheme and general practitioner fund-holding will also be developed and extended. There are also to be goals for female employment within the NHS and targets established for in- and out-patient waiting times (see Chapter Ten).

Housing (Conservative Party 1992 pp69–72) will be addressed by continuing the sale of council houses (Right to Buy) and introducing a national 'rents-to-mortgages' scheme. The management of council housing stock will be subject to compulsory competitive tendering. The policy of Large Scale Voluntary Transfer of council properties to housing associations will be continued.

Local government (Conservative Party 1992 pp78–84) in England is to be the subject of a commission into its existing structure. The aim is to improve accountability and efficiency. Local taxation will be based on a Council Tax. Local spending will continue to be 'capped' where necessary (see Chapter Nine).

Policies are also identified for the police (Conservative Party 1992 pp47–49), penal system (p51), voluntary sector (pp66–67), transport (pp72–73), and roads (pp75–76). The above programme represents a development of Major's key initiative, the *Citizen's Charter* (Command 1599 1991). According to the Conservative manifesto (1992 p27) 'The *Citizen's Charter* is the most far-reaching programme ever devised to improve quality in public services. It addresses the needs of those who use public services, extends people's rights, requires services to set clear standards – and to tell the public how far those standards are met. . . . The Charter will be at the centre of government's decision-making throughout the 1990s.'

The *Charter* was published in July 1991. In the foreword, Major states that achieving higher quality and more responsive public services 'have been ambitions of mine ever since I was a local councillor in Lambeth over 20 years ago'. During those two decades, however, there have been considerable changes to the public sector. The increased resource-constraints within which it has operated, particularly local government, can perhaps be traced to the policies of the Labour Government from 1976 onwards. Strict control of public expenditure, facilitated by the introduction of cash limits and monetary targets, was a condition of the loan obtained from the International Monetary Fund. These policies were pursued with determination by the Conservatives from 1979 onwards despite the fact that one of Thatcher's first acts was to honour the recommendations of the Clegg Commission for public sector pay rises and, secondly, the Conservatives were actually committed to increasing resources for some programmes (*viz* defence, law and order).

However, despite the rhetoric, the first two Thatcher administrations did not fundamentally alter the core state services. The scale of privatisation, including, in particular, the sale of council houses, represented a decisive break with previous policy but education, health, social services and social security were, for the vast majority of people, state-funded and state-provided. This, however, was to change in 1988 and 1989. According to Le Grand (1991 p1256) these are 'years that in retrospect will be seen as critical in the history of British social policy. For it was then that the Conservative Government began to apply a programme of market-oriented change to the welfare state'.

Le Grand identifies the main features of this programme as being the 1988 Education Reform Act which introduced local management of schools and colleges and the opportunity to opt out of local authority control (see Mann & Kogan 1989; Ransom 1992); a different funding system for universities and polytechnics; proposal to introduce student loans; publication of the White Paper *Working for Patients* (1989) which contained radical proposals for the reorganisation of the NHS; publication of the White Paper *Caring for People: Community Care in the next Decade and Beyond* (1989) which reflected the recommendations of the Griffiths Report on personal social services; Housing Act 1988, which introduced 'Tenant's Choice' and Housing Action Trusts (see Terry and Queen 1992; Mallinson 1990), and Local Government and Housing Act 1989 which was concerned, *inter alia*, with housing finance (see Mallinson 1990).

This programme, combined with increased resource constraints, has necessitated changes in working practices reinforced by changes in the structure of the public sector. The emphasis has been on privatisation (see Chapter Five) and exposing public sector services to private sector competition. Structurally, the policy has been to decentralise and, in so doing, devolve managerial and financial responsibility. Examples of this include the granting of budgets and recruitment decisions to individual schools and hospitals. There has also been the hiving-off of civil servants from Whitehall into *quasi*-autonomous agencies under the Next Steps initiative. The Conservative election victory will result in many Hospital Trusts, GM schools and agencies being established. This decentralisation has led to a fragmentation of procedures for pay determination, increased use of performance-related pay and flexible working practices. Adonis (1991) in commenting upon the *Charter* correctly observes: 'Choice, standards and quality are the catchwords; flexibility, performance and local management the tools; the private sector the model'.

The *Charter* has spawned numerous service-specific charters. This *corpus* of charters supposedly reflect Major's commitment to individual empowerment. The monolithic public sector can no longer ignore the people it serves; the economic principle of consumer sovereignty is to apply to public service delivery.

The application of economic principles to welfare services is problematic and this has led to the introduction not of markets but *quasi*-markets (Le Grand 1991; Glennerster 1991; Maynard 1991). They are markets in that state monopolies have been broken and competition introduced but they are *quasi* because they differ from conventional markets. On the supply side, the competing organisations (whether schools, universities, hospitals, private landlords *etc*) are not necessarily seeking profit maximisation nor will they necessarily be privately-owned. 'Precisely what such enterprises will maximise, or can be expected to maximise, is unclear as is their ownership structure' (Le Grand 1991 p1260). On the demand side, the consumer may be represented in the market place rather than exercising choice directly. For instance, the choice of which treatment to purchase is not made by the consumer (the patient) but by the consumer's representative (the GP). The rationale underpinning the introduction of *quasi* markets is that they will improve efficiency (X-efficiency *ie* increased output relative to units of input) and would compel the services to be more responsive to consumer preferences (*ie* improve allocative efficiency). The belief was that the welfare services were bureaucratic, monopolistic and excessively administered all of which resulted in wasteful use of resources and indifference to customer needs and preferences. This was compounded by an inherent inequity in the way resources were distributed. The pattern of distribution tended to reflect the preferences of those people able to articulate them and capable of exerting pressure through an ability and willingness to organise *ie* the middle classes rather than the poor.

The validity of these criticisms is debatable but *quasi* markets are now a reality. However, the case for them is far from unanswerable. There are problems concerning efficiency (X- and allocative-efficiency) and equity (Le Grand 1991) but as yet it is too early to reach any meaningful conclusions concerning the practical merits and demerits of Conservative policy.

Nonetheless, Major envisages the state to be the purchaser of services and not the provider. The contrast with the system which has prevailed since the creation of the welfare state at the end of the Second World War is clearly outlined by Le Grand (1991 pp1257–1258):

'If these reforms are carried through to their conclusion, the welfare state in the 1990s will be a very different animal from the welfare state of the previous 45 years. Under the "old" system of welfare local governments owned, operated and directly financed nursery, primary and secondary schools; they funded and operated local colleges and polytechnics; they owned and operated large stocks of public housing, letting them out to tenants at subsidised rents; they owned and operated residential homes and other facilities for the care of children, elderly people and people with physical or mental handicaps. Similarly, the central government owned and operated hospitals and other medical facilities; it funded and provided a General Practitioner service and it financed and allocated student numbers to universities.

'In the 1990s central government and/or local authorities will still be financing most of these activities. But . . . they will not be providing the services concerned. . . . Instead, welfare services will be provided by a variety of independent agencies. Opted-out and other schools will be competing for state-financed pupils; independent colleges, polytechnics and universities will be competing for students, more and more of whom will be privately financed. Independent hospitals . . . will be competing with directly-managed hospitals for patients; private and voluntary homes will be catering for the clients of local authority social services; housing associations, or even private landlords, will be managing erstwhile council estates.

'These changes thus represent a major break with the past'.

This is absolutely true but they are all changes which were in place prior to Thatcher's resignation. Major has simply supplemented these radical proposals with the *Citizen's Charter*, an idea about which there is nothing new. Willman (1991) points out that most of the work in developing citizen's charters had been going on in Labour local authorities such as York and Milton Keynes which had established customer contracts for services such as refuse collection, street cleaning and removal of graffiti. The Conservatives themselves had introduced two charters in the 1980s. The first (1980) dealt with tenants' rights against their landlord; the second (1986) was a taxpayer's charter offering improved practices in the Inland Revenue's dealings with taxpayers. In addition, both the Labour Party and the Liberal Democrats had developed policies throughout the 1980s to give rights to the consumers of public services (*eg* Labour Party 1989). Finally, the *Charter* includes restatements of existing entitlements.

More fundamentally, however, the problem with the *Charter* is one of funding. Improved services will almost certainly need increased resources. The Conservatives' commitment to improving services can be legitimately questioned given their explicitly stated policy to reduce public expenditure as a percentage of Gross Domestic Product and their aim to reduce direct taxation.

These points may be addressed in the future by the Conservatives but so far the conclusion of Willman, Smith and Tomkins (1992) seems valid: '. . . it is hard to see much which could not have been achieved without a charter. It certainly does not yet amount to a revolution in the public services which puts the consumer in the driving seat'.

Despite this, Le Grand's description of the public service environment throughout the 1990s, summarised above, accurately reflects the fundamental nature of the measures to be pursued. The division between purchaser and provider is understood in local and health authorities but is to be extended to professional services and to central government. This was made clear by William Waldegrave, public services minister and head of the Office of Public Services and Science, in a speech to the Institute of Directors on 20 July 1992. Waldegrave implied that the *Citizen's Charter* redefined the role of government. He said (see *Financial Times* 21 July 1992) 'We have had to restore the principle that the government's job is to govern, not to administer; to steer, not to row. There will continue to be areas where we must ask the question: is this really any business of government?'

It appears that the question posed by Waldegrave will be increasingly answered in the negative. This assertion is based not only on the general direction of domestic policy but also on the reality of UK involvement in the European Community (EC). The Major Government is operating within a restrictive international framework which is likely to result in considerable constraints on the scale and funding of public services. This is assuming that Major successfully pursues his policy towards the Maastricht agreement as outlined in his speech in the emergency debate to a recalled House of Commons, 24 Sept 1992.

The Maastricht agreement contains economic criteria which the member states have to meet if they are to participate in economic and monetary union (EMU). It is not certain, on political and economic grounds, that the UK will actually be such a participant but in the meantime it can be assumed that policy will be directed towards achieving the convergence criteria. This must eventually mean that the UK rejoins the ERM; it also means there can be no 'excessive deficit', defined as a general government budget deficit greater than 3% of Gross Domestic Product (GDP) or a ratio of gross public debt to GDP greater than 60% – unless this debt ratio is falling 'at a satisfactory pace'.

The Government must, therefore, seek to reduce public borrowing and this it is attempting to do by imposing stringent controls over public expenditure. Such a policy, however, may contribute to increasing unemployment and actually lead to an increase in unemployment-related expenditure in the short- and medium-term. The next few years may see a relaxation of the convergence criteria, particularly given the instability in the foreign exchange markets in Sept 1992 and, also, the concern at the level of unemployment throughout the EC. In the meantime, however, the Government's policy means that not only is there little scope for growth in the main public services (health, education, transport, housing *etc*) but also there may be demands for reductions in existing levels of service provision.

The debate concerning the EC budget also has implications for UK public services (Burkitt & Baimbridge 1992). The Lisbon summit, June 1992 failed to produce a compromise budget to succeed the 1988–92 finance package. The fundamental area of disagreement concerns the size of the EC budget. The European Commission wishes to see EC revenues increase by nearly a third *ie* from £47bn (Ecu66.6bn) in 1992–93 to £62bn (Ecu87.5bn) in 1997 at today's prices (Gardner 1992). Although the budget is very small when compared with the aggregated expenditure of member states, it has grown considerably and has been unequally funded, *ie* some countries are net contributors to EC funds and others are net beneficiaries. The UK is a net contributor (see Burkitt & Baimbridge 1992 p46 Table 3.1). Any enlargement of the EC budget, and the EC itself, is likely to worsen the UK position as a net contributor resulting in more resources being diverted to EC countries at the expense of domestic public expenditure programmes (see Burkitt & Baimbridge 1992 p48 Table 3.3, taken from Dilnot, A, *The Guardian*).

Political environment: the future
There is a paradox concerning public service provision in the UK. The political party which is perhaps least identified with the public services has won four consecutive general elections. Survey evidence, however, reveals little sympathy with their policies either towards the public services generally or their macroeconomic priorities.

The British Social Attitudes Survey (Jowell *et al* 1991) revealed that 90% of people questioned want more spent on health care even if taxes have to be raised to pay for it; 85% believed health care should be provided by the government. To improve primary education, the most important factors were seen to be smaller classes (mentioned by 28%), more resources for books and equipment (19%) and developing skills and interests (18%). In secondary education, the priorities were seen to be more preparation for training and jobs (21%) and stricter discipline (18%). In higher education, support for student loans has decreased from 38% in 1983 to 24% in 1990. On the economy, there was overwhelming support for the Keynesian policy of investment in construction projects to reduce unemployment (83%). Significantly, only 3% of people believed that taxation and public expenditure should be reduced (compared with 9% in 1983) whilst 54% believed both should be increased (32% in 1983).

The above statistics are obviously selective but they are not misleading. McKie (1991), commenting on the survey, points out: 'Its consistent conclusion is not how much of a mark, but how little, Mrs Thatcher's radicalism has left on British society. The people's devotion to state provision of welfare, especially the NHS, stays undiminished. The preference for maintaining public spending rather than cutting taxes has grown.'

Not all the above statistics are inconsistent with Conservative policy but, fundamentally, the survey reveals a difference between social attitudes and Conservative priorities. Perhaps this is not as paradoxical as it appears *prima facie*. A majority of those who voted in April 1992 did not vote Conservative (58%). The first-past-the-post electoral system enables majorities to be attained with a minority of the vote which means that the balance of the House of Commons is not representative of national opinion. Successive election victories and healthy parliamentary majorities can lead politicians to claim, and individuals to believe, that there is a groundswell of opinion in the country supporting individual pieces of legislation and the general thrust of policy when perhaps none such exists. However, it must also be remembered that the party perhaps most closely associated with the public services, the Labour Party, commanded only 35% of the vote. At its simplest level, this means that the anti-Labour majority is greater than the anti-Conservative majority even though on key issues the Labour Party appears to reflect popular opinion more than the Conservatives.

There are likely to be numerous reasons for individual voting behaviour. It is not the purpose of this chapter to explain the 1992 election result but it is important to point out that the public services constitute a crucial area of economic and social activity. They are of profound importance in the lives of millions of people. This importance, combined with the scale of the activity (see Chapter One), rightly ensures political debate about priorities, scale, funding and delivery.

The debate is continuous; policies change. The Labour Party has undergone considerable change as demonstrated in its 1992 election manifesto (*It's time to get Britain working again*). The policy review, following the 1987 election defeat, resulted in the jettisoning of certain policies and the relegation of others. Clause Four of the party constitution, which commits it to the social ownership of the means of production, distribution and exchange, remains but is now symbolic. There has been a *de facto* rejection of an article of faith which comes thirty years after a comparable, though in this case explicit, rejection by the German SPD in Bad Godesburg in 1959. Labour now stresses individual liberty and choice. Ownership is less important than the objective of economic efficiency. The role of the market within the mixed economy is championed but the necessity for the state to act is recognised. Labour emphasises 'supply-side socialism':

'To us the state is an instrument, no more, no less: a means not an end . . . private business can be the most efficient way of producing and distributing many goods and services – provided that government regulates commercial behaviour in the interests of the consumer, and restricts monopoly practice in the interests of competition. But the market, left to itself, does not invest adequately in the education and training, the science, technology and research and development which a modern economy needs . . . In our view, the economic role of modern government is to help make the market system work properly . . .'
(Labour Party 1989 p6)

This view underpins current Labour thinking and is unlikely to change in the foreseeable future. Labour has changed in response to the agenda established by Thatcher and in response to developments in eastern Europe. Perhaps Young (1991) is right in saying that 'the new model Labour party was one of her most important creations', though whether it is 'pseudo-socialist' as he goes on to claim is debatable. Its 1992 defeat and the election of a new leader will mean that policy will continue to be questioned and, perhaps, radical ideas put forward (Blackstone *et al* 1992; Meacher 1992; Coote 1992) but its fundamental commitment to redistributive justice and a high standard of public service provision is unlikely to alter given that this would question its basic *raison d'etre*.

The Liberal Democrats emphasise constitutional and electoral reform. On economic issues they 'know that the free market is the best guarantee of responsiveness to choice and change' but '. . . see the role of government as crucial in making the market work properly, by creating the conditions for success, promoting competition, breaking up monopolies and spreading information' (Liberal Democrats 1992 p6). It is unlikely that Liberal Democrat policy will change significantly between now and the end of the 1990s.

For the Conservatives, the party may eventually distance itself from the policies of the 1980s. Some (*eg* Willetts 1992) see Major as a Thatcherite with both Major and Thatcher representing traditional Conservatism (unlike Heath). Others believe this is wrong on two counts: first, Major is not a Thatcherite; second, Thatcherism was outside the mainstream tradition (more closely resembling nineteenth century liberalism with the emphasis on self-help).

Some evidence supporting this view was the publication in 1992 of a document by the One Nation group of Conservative MPs (founded in 1950 to promote the Disraelian concept of a united nation and not one divided by social class), *One Nation 2000*. The document contains implicit and explicit criticisms of social developments over the past decade and advocates a more positive role for government. According to the *Financial Times* (29 February 1992): 'The precise wording of the paper has been approved by Mr John Major's aides . . . Authorisation of the pamphlet's release so close to a general election will come as a further signal to the Thatcherite right that the party leadership supports a fundamental shift back towards more consensus politics.' This may be true. Major is less dogmatic about increases in public expenditure or public borrowing, though he was extremely dogmatic about the exchange rate. He has a more conciliatory style, claims to believe in a classless society and would never have said, as Thatcher did, that there is no such thing as society (October 31 1987 in a magazine interview) or that 'consensus is the absence of principle and the presence of expediency' (Thatcher 1992 p15). However, to repeat the contention of this chapter, the evidence indicates that the policies towards the public services will not be fundamentally altered from those pursued under Thatcher.

Conclusion
By the end of this decade it may be possible to say that Major did not simply continue the programme of his predecessor but in fact made a distinct imprint on UK socio-economic policy. However, that will depend initially on Major's survival as party leader and, thereafter, the result of the next general election and the policies on which it is fought. Major's personal survival is by no means certain. His authority and credibility have been greatly diminished by his handling of a diverse range of issues including economic policy, pit closures, Parliamentary votes on Maastricht, UK trade with Iraq and loyalty to Cabinet colleagues. He is also extremely unpopular with the electorate. A Harris poll for *The Observer*, 15 Nov 1992, showed that 73% of those questioned said they had 'not much' or 'no' confidence in him. Irrespective of Major's personal survival as Prime Minister, however, the policies designed for the next five years are contained within the manifesto and have been elaborated upon by Major in public statements.

However, UK economic policy remains unclear following the devaluation of the currency. The stated objectives still include the reduction of public expenditure as a percentage of GDP and a return to the ERM when this is considered appropriate; the commitment to zero inflation has now been abandoned and replaced by a target range for inflation of between one and four per cent initially. In addition, the emphasis within economic policy is now supposedly based on growth, with the emphasis on a relaxation of monetary policy, but it also embraces an incomes policy for the public sector (as announced by the Chancellor in the Autumn Statement Nov 1992). This actually represents an accumulation of economic U-turns which makes it increasingly difficult to predict future action. It may even be the case that the ever-increasing public sector borrowing requirement (£45bn in 1993–94 as per the Autumn Statement Nov 1992) may actually lead to the ultimate U-turn for the Conservatives – an increase in direct taxation. Whether or not this scenario materialises, the prospects for public expenditure and public services are very unfavourable.

Policy is also likely to include the continued marketisation of the NHS; centralisation and bureaucratisation of the education system; the restructuring of local government; little proven sympathy with the public services generally (particularly, perhaps, housing); continued privatisation; *etc.*

All the above could be said to be central to present and future Conservative policy towards the public services, at least under Major. The programme essentially constitutes a continuation of the past rather than a decisive break with it. Major played a central role in implementing past policy as Chief Secretary to the Treasury, briefly Foreign Secretary and then Chancellor of the Exchequer. Although Major has been forced to abandon the centrepiece of his economic policy – ERM – a mere five months after the election, the direction of policy towards the public services remains the same. Any U-turn in this respect would entail not simply distancing himself from the Thatcher past but from his own past also.

References

Adonis, A (1991) 'The leviathan limbers up', Financial Times, 26 July 1991

Blackstone T *et al* (1992) *Next Left: An agenda for the 1990s*, Institute for Public Policy Research

Britton, A (1991) *Macroeconomic Policy In Britain 1974–1987*, Cambridge/ National Institute of Economic and Social Research

Burkitt, B & Baimbridge, M (1992) 'European Community Developments', *Public Domain: the public services yearbook*, Terry F & Jackson P (Eds), Public Finance Foundation pp39–53

Conservative Party (1979) (1992) *The Conservative Manifesto*, Conservative Central Office

Command 1599 (1991) *The Citizen's Charter: Raising The Standard*, HMSO

Coote, A (1992) *The Welfare of Citizens* Institute for Public Policy Research

Department for Education (1992) *Choice and Diversity – a new framework for schools* HMSO

Gardner, D (1992) 'UK squares up for fight over finance' *Financial Times* 1 July 1992

Gilmour, I (1977) *Inside Right: A Study of Conservatism*, London

Glennerster, H (1991) 'Quasi-Markets For Education?', *The Economic Journal*, Vol 101 No 408 pp1268–1276

Jenkins, P (1989) *Mrs Thatcher's Revolution*, Pan Books

Jowell, R *et al* (1991) *British Social Attitudes: the 8th report*, Dartmouth

Kavanagh, D (1990) *Thatcherism and British politics: The End of Consensus?* Oxford University Press

Labour Party (1989) *Meet the challenge Make the change: A new agenda for Britain*, Labour Party

Leach, R (1991) *British Political Ideologies*, Philip Allan

Le Grand, J (1991) 'Quasi-Markets And Social Policy' *The Economic Journal*, Vol 101 No 408 p1256–1267

Liberal Democrats (1992) *The Liberal Democrat Manifesto 1992* Liberal Democrat Publications

McKie, D (1991) 'The smudgy marks of Thatcherism', *The Guardian*, 20 November 1991

Mallinson, H (1990) 'Housing', *Public Domain: The Public Services Yearbook*, Jackson P & Terry F (Eds) Public Finance Foundation pp135–151

Mann, J & Kogan M (1989) 'Education', *Public Domain: The Public Services Yearbook*, Jackson P & Terry F (Eds), Public Finance Foundation pp137-148)

Maynard, A (1991), 'Developing The Health Care Market' *The Economic Journal*, Vol 101 No 408 pp1277–1286

Meacher, M (1992) *Diffusing Power: The Key To Socialist Revival* Pluto Press

Ransom, E (1992) 'Education', *Public Domain: The Public Services Yearbook*, Jackson P & Terry F (Eds), Public Finance Foundation pp55–65

Smith, D (1987) *The Rise and Fall of Monetarism: The theory and politics of an economic experiment*, Pelican

Terry, R & Queen B (1992) 'Housing', *Public Domain: The Public Services Year-Book*, Terry F & Jackson P (Eds), Public Finance Foundation pp111–130

Thatcher, M (1992) 'Don't undo what I have done' *Newsweek* 27 April 1992 pp14–15

Vane, H (1992) 'The Thatcher Years: Macroeconomic Policy and Performance of the UK Economy, 1979–88' *National Westminster Bank Quarterly Review* May 1992 pp26–43

Willetts, D (1992) *Modern Conservatism* Penguin

Willman, J (1991) 'A big idea – but no panacea', *Financial Times* 19 June 1991

Willman J, Smith A & Tomkins R (1992) 'Still waiting for the revolution', *Financial Times*, 28 January 1992

Young, H (1991) 'Fighter to the bitter end', *The Guardian*, 23 November 1991

Young, H (1990) *One of Us*, Pan Books

CHAPTER THREE

CULTURE AND THE NEW MANAGERIALISM

Elisabeth Wilson

Introduction

This chapter looks briefly at concepts of organisational culture, and applies these to public services. The drivers and features of cultural change are discussed, before examining and evaluating the 'new managerialism', concluding with thoughts about the future of culture within public services.

There are many definitions of organisational culture (see Wilson and Rosenfeld 1990, pp 228–230), but a useful one is that given by Schein (1983):

> 'Organisational Culture is the pattern of basic assumptions that a given group has invented, discovered or developed in learning to cope with its problems of external adaptation and internal integration, and that have worked well enough to be considered valid, and, therefore, to be taught to new members as the correct way to perceive, think, and feel in relation to those problems.
>
> 'Culture is not the overt behaviour or visible artifacts that one might observe if one were to visit the company. It is not even the philosophy or value system which the founder may articulate or write down in various "charters". Rather it is the assumptions which lie behind the values and which determine the behaviour patterns and the visible artifacts such as architecture, office layout, dress codes and so on.'

Turning from definition to classification, cultures can be classified in different ways. First, one of the best known classifications is described by Handy (1985 pp 185–221), who identifies power, role, task, and person cultures within organisations. Handy points out that these are not necessarily mutually exclusive; any specific organisational culture can have elements of more than one culture, and organisations can have differing subcultures (a known phenomenon within public services). His description of a role culture applies to many public services today: set procedures and job descriptions, role more important than expertise, positional power, and coordination by a narrow band of officers at the top of the organisation. Second, using another classification, the main cultural shift perceived in the 1980s can be described as an administrative to a managerial culture (Thomson, 1992), a change which will be explored more fully later in this chapter, when the 'new managerialism' is discussed. This can be briefly defined as the importation of private sector concepts and techniques into the public sector.

Third, it is also contended that public services are moving towards a market, or profit orientated, culture (Lawton and Rose, 1991). Whilst this may be argued for those public service organisations which have been forced to enter a competitive market – *e.g.* internal markets in the NHS and Compulsory Competitive Tendering – this is still not the case for the greater part of the public services. Another argument has been put forward that there has been a move towards a client culture (Dawson, 1991), where the organisation sees its first concern as that of serving client interests and needs. A client culture may be seen as a variant of a market culture within public services: a market culture is financially orientated, and implies a choice between alternatives in the market by willing customers, whereas a client culture does not necessarily have financial goals, may offer no choice, and has some unwilling customers *e.g.* Environmental Health and Social Services Departments. A client culture is concerned with customer care where no market forces prevail. A client culture could itself be subdivided into a 'consumer' or an 'empowering' culture: the first embracing notions of customer care, but retaining decisions about policies and allocation of resources strictly within the power of the organisation; the second seeking to enable consumers who are also citizens to participate in some policy decisions. This distinction will be further explored as 'consumerism' and 'collectivism' (Hambleton and Hoggett 1987 pp 14–25) when discussing decentralisation later in the chapter.

Fourth, discussions about a male versus a female culture are apposite at the time of writing with the settlement of the Alison Halford case; the former Assistant Chief Constable of the Merseyside Police Force, who claimed systematic sex discrimination in promotion processes, and was herself made subject to disciplinary charges, alleged swearing, drinking and generally 'macho' behaviour as the dominant culture of the

Merseyside Force, a culture into which as a woman she could never enter fully. Male versus female cultures and styles of management have also been aired in the Social Services field (Eley, 1987, Lupton, 1992).

Lastly, one can point to both political and professional cultures within public services. For a fuller discussion of these, and their relationship to a managerial culture, domain theory offers an explanation. This postulates a series of co-existent domains, the policy domain consisting of the appointed or elected members, the management domain of managers, and the service domain of professionals. First hypothesised by Kouzes and Mico (1979) in relation to 'human service organizations', domain theory offers an explanation of some of the complexities of management in the public services. As can be seen in Table 3.1, the theory also fits neatly with Handy's classification: subsequent research by Kakabadse (1982) within Social Services Departments indicated the policy domain to have a power culture, the professional domain a role culture, and the managerial domain a task culture.

Table 3.1

Domain and Culture

Domain	Peopled by	Probable Culture
Policy	Appointed & Elected Members	Power
Professional	Professional Staff	Role
Management	Managers	Task

Public Service Culture pre 1975
The preceding chapters outlined the political and economic changes affecting public services in recent years. Later, this chapter addresses the advent of 'the new managerialism' (Pollitt 1990, Lupton 1992), and assesses to what extent this represents a culture change. It is helpful to look at the old order, to establish a bench mark for assessing change.

Taylor and Williams (1991) list several different facets of public administration, building on ideas from the Audit Commission. They describe the old order (which they date up to 1975) as one with a strategy of growth, a centralised structure, valuing professional and administrative skills, and with a bureaucratic, neutral, and risk avoiding style.

Clarke and Stewart (1990), writing specifically about local govern-ment, cite several assumptions currently under challenge: that authorities are self-sufficient and monopolistic or near-monopolistic in their discharge of functions and provision of services; control is by a traditional committee system; services are provided through bureau-cratically organised departments, each with a dominant professional culture; and accountability is based on detailed control. Stewart (1989) wrote about these organisational principles being embedded in culture.

Turning to the NHS, Burke and Goddard (1990 p 394) suggest that there was a culture within the NHS that 'held patient welfare above personal aims, *i.e.*, a high degree of goal congruence'. This contrasts with Harrison's (1988) view that managers prior to the 'Griffiths' report of 1983 had a role as diplomats, charged with facilitating the work of health care professionals, which fits more aptly with domain theory.

The first two accounts above describe role cultures in Handy's definition. The third is less clear. All three could be classed as administrative cultures.

Drivers of Change and their Tangible Manifestations

In considering the paradigmatic shift to the new managerialism from the former public service culture, five drivers of change are discussed: Post-Fordism; resource constraint; the excellence school; information technology; and the Thatcher Governments.

The conceptual model underpinning Fordism and *Post-Fordism* is that the socio-economic structures both shape and are supported by the institutions of the state. Stoker (1989) defines Fordism as the period from the 1930s to the 1970s when systems and techniques of mass production held sway, there was the rise of the large scale business corporation and the dominant private sector management culture was hierarchical and authoritarian. The mass consumption demanded by mass production relied for its success on the safety net of the welfare state, which was organised upon similar lines. Post-Fordism describes the move away from mass production to more flexible production systems and organisational forms, with greater fluidity in the labour market. This is paralleled in the public sector by the break up of state monopolies, and greater innovation in service delivery. Post-Fordism has been criticised both as an overstretched analogy, and as over deterministic (Cochrane, 1991). However, it offers some explanation of contemporaneous changes within both the private and public sectors.

Resource constraint has been with the public sector for a long time, but became a major concern for the Wilson/Callaghan government of 1974–9, and Mrs Thatcher's governments between 1979 and 1990 (Henkel 1991, Pollitt 1990). Amongst others, Taylor and Williams (1991) describe the changes from a strategy of growth to one of economy, efficiency and responsiveness, and from key systems concerned with the allocation of additional resources, to key systems concerned with strategic planning, customer service, and management information systems.

Many writers have attested to the widespread influence in the public sector of the '*excellence school*' of management literature (*e.g.* Hambleton and Hoggett 1987, Stoker 1989), propounded perhaps most effectively by Peters (Peters and Waterman 1981, Peters and Austen 1985, Peters 1987). Just as these concepts and ideas were disseminated in the private sector in the 1980s, so they spilled over into public sector organisations, which started to talk about 'mission statements', 'value-driven organisations', and being 'close to the customer'.

The fourth driver identified is *information technology* (IT). Taylor & Williams (1991) observing that public administration is by its nature labour intensive, describe four trends: a move from centralised facilities to networked systems; the computing facility no longer the sole province of finance departments; a general rise in computer expertise; and a rise in expenditure. They point out that IT can both permit greater decentralisation of decision making, and paradoxically, greater centralisation of control.

The last driver is the *Thatcher Governments* between 1979 and 1990. The importance of Mrs Thatcher's influence should however be put into a historical and international context. Observing the previous Wilson-Callaghan government, we can see elements of the new managerialism present. Comparing the UK with other traditional Western democratic countries with governments of various political hues, such as Australia, New Zealand (Hood, 1991) and Canada (Kersell *et al*, 1991–2), we see the new managerialism was espoused enthusiastically. The Thatcher government vigorously supported a movement which was already under way, and accelerated its progress (Metcalfe and Richards, 1990).

Turning now to the more tangible, surface changes in culture, the 'old' public service organisation used unexciting letter headings and a multiplicity of typefaces for internal and external communications.

Unusual in this respect was the University of East Anglia, which had a logo and corporate colours from its inception in the 1960s; corporate logos are now unexceptional. Those running public services are now aware of the importance of visual symbolism.

Dress was never a significant issue for the old public service organisation. Now smart suits and 'power dressing', copying the private sector, can be seen on those in, or aspiring to, the managerial ranks. Titles have become grander: sisters and charge nurses have become ward managers; Chief Officers have been reincarnated as Directors of their respective services. Taylor and Williams (1991 p 174) describe the 'pushing aside of the traditional language of public administration' as a challenge to the public service paradigm. Words and phrases like 'quality', 'performance indicators', and 'customer care', are now commonplace. Modes of address, formal in the past, have given way to extensive introductions on first name terms, extended on occasion to service recipients. Accommodation is still recognisably institutional in many public services, but two areas stand out as improved: reception areas and top managers' accommodation. Reception areas are improved to convey a message about customer care and corporate identity. A strong symbolic message in this respect is the foyer of 'Yorkshire Health' (the Yorkshire Regional Health Authority) at Harrogate.

Reward systems have changed in the public services. Status symbols and perks have crept in; the standardised pay systems in health and local authorities have been in many quarters replaced by performance related pay (Thomson 1992). Whilst timekeeping is more flexible for lower grade public sector employees with the introduction of flexitime, those at the top are expected to work extra, long, unremunerated hours. There is freer movement at top manager level between the private and the public sectors in both directions.

All the above changes appear to give a message about the nature of management in the public services: that it is clearer about projecting its identity, more businesslike, and offers rewards tied to performance for those at the top. The language used would indicate that private sector management techniques and attitudes have been adopted. Before examining the 'new managerialism' more closely, the deliberate, planned change of culture is considered.

Features of Planned Cultural Change
Burack (1991) and Thomas (1985) both point out the importance of

establishing carefully the features of the existing culture before attempting any change. Thomas also points out that awareness of culture does not always imply that a change of culture should be embarked upon; other strategies are possible, such as managing around the existing culture, or changing strategy to fit culture. Burack (p 89) states 'established cultures are not easily modified because their very reason for existence often rests on preserving stable relationships and behavioural patterns'. Frank (1987) suggests exploiting and systematically rewarding those subcultures which represent the desired culture; this might be difficult to achieve in the public sector where undesirable subcultures may exist which cannot be divested.

Turning to models of culture change described within the public sector, they appear to operate on three dimensions, described in the table below:

Table 3.2

Dimensions of change

coercion	– – – – –	persuasion
surface	– – – – –	depth
quick fix	– – – – –	time investment

Coercion – persuasion refers to the method used to make or encourage people to change. Overt coercion may not be present, but may use hostility as its means. Persuasion is more likely to use participatory methods and/or tools described by Richards (1989), such as language, management events, jokes and aphorisms, leadership behaviour and the promotion of heroes/heroines. *Surface – depth* refers to both the depth of understanding shown by the architects of change, and the superficiality or depth of the change they attempt. Pettigrew (1986) writes about it being easier to change the manifestations of culture than to change core beliefs and assumptions. *Quick fix – time investment* refers to the speed with which changemakers anticipate achieving their ends.

Change is more successful where persuasion, depth and investment of time in years are present together. Conversely where coercion, superficiality and speed of desired results are bedfellows, lasting success is less likely. Pettigrew *et al* (1992 p 31) writing about the NHS, state that a 'quick fix' is inappropriate in managing complex change. Some examples follow.

The Financial Management Initiative (FMI) was one of a number of successive drives intended to induce a culture of cost consciousness and resource management within the Civil Service (Henkel 1991). It says something about the relative strength of subcultures inside the Civil Service that the Treasury was able to insist that the management initiative was labelled 'financial' rather than being more holistically concerned with management (Gray *et al*, 1991).

Richards (1989 p 6) asserts that the trigger for change in the Civil Service was 'the combination of the intellectual and emotional hostility of the new government for its civil service'. She describes a model of change, based on initial work by Lewin (1952) and Schein (1973), in which the following steps are taken:

1. Unfreeze/destroy the old culture/bust the paradigm
2. Introduce new ideas about how things ought to be done/ construct a new paradigm
3. Systematically apply the new ideas
4. Re-freeze the new culture

Focusing on the change strategy of the first Thatcher government towards the Civil Service, Richards feels it fits well into the classic formula described above. Assuming a resistance to change in the *status quo*, Richards says that considerable toughness is required to achieve stage one. In relation to the Civil Service, she opines that expressions of hostility not only demonstrated the political energy that the Conservatives had available for change, but were actually functional for change. Accompanying these were tangible steps like job cuts to reinforce the message. Step two as described is to build the new paradigm, followed by the third step, the systematic implementation of the new model. Accountable management, through the FMI, provided the new cultural model, and is now established within the Civil Service. The last stage, refreezing the culture, Richards identifies as contemporaneous with Thatcher's second term. Looking at the three dimensions of change identified in Table 3.2, we can see that this change embodied elements of coercion, and was aimed at a long term, fundamental change.

An interesting application of this model occurred in Bradford, which is described in Illustration 3.1 at the end of the chapter. Indeed, Richards' article (1989) was used as a template for the management of change. There are parallels on both coercion and depth of change required. A major difference was the 'quick fix' approach, necessitated by the short time frame till the next local election. A gentler model of change implemented in the Grampian Health Board is described by Fullerton and Price (1991). This example indicates that persuasion and participatory methods were used, rather than coercion. An attempt was made to introduce depth change, but there was an underestimation of the time needed to accomplish this. There was an avowed intention to move from a bureaucratic culture, implicitly to a task culture.

Having observed some relatively successful examples of managing culture, some of the difficulties which can be encountered are described. Pettigrew (1986) writes about the factors which make corporate culture difficult to manage. These include: the fact that corporate culture exists at different levels; that it is not only deep but broad; that so much is taken for granted; that it has deep historical roots; that it is directly connected with power distribution within the organisation; that a variety of subcultures exist; and that it is interdependent on people, priorities, structure and systems. All of these would lead one to a 'depth' approach to culture change. Burack (1991) discusses the limited understanding of managers. He states that many have only vague or differing ideas about what corporate culture is in their organisation. This could be compounded in the public sector by limited understanding by councillors, NHS Trust non executive directors and others.

Even where the aspects of culture change are recognised, there may be underestimation of the difficulties of achieving change. Dixon (1989) states that after initial changes in Kent to devolve budgetary and managerial responsibilities – itself an intended cultural change – senior officers considered that there should have been more attention to culture, both in terms of identifying existing culture and the movement to the new. This is against a background of a Chief Executive, Paul Sabin, who started to change the organisation on appointment in 1986, and when interviewed in 1988, envisaged three further years as necessary (Fretwell, 1988). A less successful example of culture change is Solihull. Hicks (1991) describes how Solihull pulled together an existing package of initiatives under the name of a 'performance related culture'. Concentrating on seven target areas, it was hoped these would promote cultural change. Against an acknowledged background of strong individual departmental cultures, a subsequent survey of managers showed that only a small number of specific changes had ensued. Analysing this example, it appears that a surface, rather than a depth approach was initiated – there was, for instance, no attempt to explore culture and subcultures or seek staff views prior to change, and a short time scale was envisaged. In neither of these examples -Kent and Solihull – are the measures of persuasion or coercion known. However, both show an underrating of the complexities of cultural change and the length of time required. In terms of the model above, many organisations go for surface change and the quick fix; even those comprehending time and depth may fall short. One reason for the necessity of a 'quick fix' may be found in Duclos (1988/9); analysing the Canadian experience, he notes that less tolerance and time is allowed to the Chief Executive in the public services. Local elections supply a further imperative.

The 'New Managerialism'
The subject of this section is the new managerialism, described earlier as the importation of private sector concepts and techniques into the public sector. The new managerialism could be variously described as a culture change in its own right, as a particular style of management, or as an ideology . Whilst it has ideological features (Pollitt 1990), arguably, it is more than just ideology. Whether it is a culture change will be evaluated later in the chapter.

Writers describing the new managerialism observe overlapping features. These start from the assertion that management is superior to administration (Metcalfe and Richards, 1990); that management in the private sector is superior to that in the public sector; that good management is an efficacious solution for a variety of economic and social problems (Pollitt, 1990, Metcalfe and Richards, 1990); and that it consists of a discrete body of knowledge which is universally applicable and therefore portable (Hood, 1991). At times the tenets seem reducible to slogans: bureaucracy is inefficient; innovation is good.

Hood (1990) writes about 'New Public Management', identifying several doctrinal elements: hands-on professional management, explicit standards and measures of performance, greater emphasis on output controls, shifts to disaggregation of units in the public sector and greater competition, and stress on private sector styles of management practice, and on discipline and parsimony in resource use.

Identifying the new managerialism as 'neo-Taylorism', after Taylor, the father of 'scientific management' Pollitt (1990) points to the controlling, measuring and monitoring activities, such as tight cash limits and cash planning, staff appraisal and merit pay schemes, and planning systems emphasizing short term targets. A number of writers, (*e.g.* Henkel 1991) refer to the work of the Audit Commission's 'value for money' studies in local government. This refers to the 'three Es' of economy, efficiency and effectiveness, a phrase which quickly passed into common parlance. In Pollitt's terms economy and efficiency are aspects of neo-Taylorism, but effectiveness appears to go beyond this, as it raises questions about desired ends, not just means. Despite acknowledging differences, Pollitt (1990) offers too close an identification of the new managerialism with neo-Taylorism. Although he acknowledges the influence of the excellence school, he then criticises the lack of attention to human relations, distinguishing what he terms 'cultural approaches' as one alternative to neo-Taylorism. Arguably, there is more interplay and overlap between these two approaches than Pollitt allows.

Some writers acknowledge, but others fail to recognise, that the overlapping variants of the new managerialism give rise to inconsistencies and incoherence. At the same time as managers are urged to set targets, measure and monitor, they are enjoined to pay attention to the organisational and departmental culture (Pollitt 1990). The need for changes in culture, often referring specifically for a change from role to task, are seen as a necessary prerequisite of more innovative and entrepreneurial behaviour; attempts to change or manage culture may be made (see Illustration 3.1). Part of the 'culture approach' may be recognition of the need to treat employees as a valuable resource, to be nurtured and developed. As is shown by the examples of attempted culture change discussed previously, awareness of culture is an aspect of the new managerialism for some groups within the public services.

Having looked at some essential tenets of the new managerialism, implementation is now considered.

It is not possible to examine closely all the private sector ideas imported into the public sector (see *e.g.* Pollitt 1990, Metcalfe and Richards, 1990). In this section four are analysed: the concept of the flexible organisation, which is linked closely to ideas of task cultures and changes in employment patterns; cost centres, one of the most consistently introduced concepts; performance indicators, vital to assessment of the 'three Es'; and decentralisation, a structural and managerial change seen in both private and public sectors.

The concept of the *flexible organisation* is described by Atkinson (1985) as a move towards new organisational arrangements which enable functional, numerical, and financial flexibility; employees will be divided into core and periphery. The former will be permanent, well rewarded,and expected to display commensurate skills, retraining when necessary. The latter group will perform lesser skilled jobs, and be less well rewarded; they are unlikely to have a standard permanent contract of employment. Beyond the periphery are those not employed but providing a service to the organisation, including subcontractors. Comparing Atkinson's model to public services, one can see the moves towards this division into core and periphery. Many NHS hospitals have increasing numbers of staff on various types of contract. They use 'nurse banks', for instance, for temporary staff; natural wastage and short term contracts ensure numerical flexibility among less skilled staff such as porters and clerical staff; even managers may be on three year renewable contracts. Beyond the periphery of the organisation are contracted out support services, block contracts with nursing homes, and self employed management consultants. Atkinson suggests that the management style with the core will be participatory, whereas that with the periphery will be directive. This poses a question about the development of common organisational values. Whilst such an organisation has the advantage of flexibility and cost control, it raises questions about a diminishing skill pool, the training of the next generation of workers, and a tendency to 'short-termism'.

With *cost centres* a manager is held responsible for the costs accruing to a particular unit under his or her control. In the private sector, they form part of a hierarchy: cost centres entail responsibility for costs, profit centres for profit, and investment centres for investment (Drury 1985). The new managerialism demands an alignment of managerial and budgetary responsibilities, well described in 'Better Financial Management' (Audit Commission, 1989). The Financial Management Initiative (FMI) in the Civil Service predated this paper, as did developments in Kent County Council (Fretwell, 1988). Applied to public services, cost centres are becoming more common, and profit centres are mandatory in Direct Labour or Direct Service Organisations; investment centres are seen in their true form only within the trading part of the public sector. Some prefer the concept of responsibility centres instead of cost centres to describe the wider accountabilities of managers in public services. A cost centre is characteristic of changes made to encourage the development of a managerial culture.

Performance indicators are the necessary concomitant of cost and responsibility centres; when a manager is held responsible, there must be some way of judging successful performance. There are several difficulties in applying the concept of performance indicators to public services. First, financial and other quantitative measures cannot fully indicate the success of a service. The public service therefore needs to formulate qualitative indicators, which may be difficult; for example, a dignified and pain free death is a possible indicator for terminally ill patients. Second, by definition a performance indicator is *indicative*, that is, it may reveal where a service appears to be succeeding or failing, or where to look for further evidence, but it cannot necessarily provide a definitive judgement. Third, as Metcalfe and Richards (1990) point out, much of managing in the public services is about managing interdependencies, so shortfalls in another service may have a deleterious effect on the performance of the service under scrutiny; for instance, precipitous discharge from hospital may put great strain on community health and social services. Fourth, indicators often focus on inputs and outputs rather than outcomes, that is, economy and efficiency to the detriment of effectiveness; for example, counting the cost of Meals on Wheels, or the number of meals delivered, rather than their effect on the health status and quality of life of elderly recipients. Fifth, the question of who decides what is to be measured is more problematical. Some writers advocate the involvement of consumers in choosing performance indicators (Pollitt 1988); others point out that the choice of indicators is tied up with managerial and political perceptions about service priorities (Lupton, 1992). None of this is to say that performance indicators are not important; rather the obstacles in formulation, implementation and interpretation in public services should be noted and understood.

Decentralisation is a concept topical within the private sector. It is a term used somewhat loosely in relation to the private sector to describe both geographical dispersion and the devolution of decision making within an organisation. As it is applied to the local government sector of public services, however, decentralisation is differentiated in its application in that the application of the concept differs in quality and complexity from its application in the private sector. Hambleton (1992), building on earlier work (Hambleton and Hoggett 1987, Hambleton 1988) identifies five main strategies for achieving change: localisation, integration of services, delegation of management authority, democratisation of local government, and changing the organisational culture. The particular choice depends on the purpose being pursued; Hambleton identifies several possible political objectives pointing out that decentralisation is a means not an end in itself. Earlier Hambleton and Hoggett (1987) distinguished between the devolution of decision making as a 'collectivist' approach which focuses on the needs of the community/ electorate, and the 'consumerist' approach which focuses on the individual as customer (developed later in John Major's *Citizen's Charter*, (Command 1599 1991)). There is no equivalent to collectivism in the private sector. It could be argued that consumerism is a component of the new managerialism, whereas collectivism challenges it. Paradoxically decentralisation of budgetary responsibility can lead to greater centralisation of control, underpinned by new management information systems (Hoggett, 1991, Taylor and Williams, 1991). Hambleton and Hoggett (1987) write about the need for a new, more open organisational culture to replace 'bureaucratic paternalism'. Hambleton (1992) links decentralisation with attempted changes in organisational culture, citing councils which are trying to encourage risk taking and innovation alongside a commitment to service. In summary, in relation to decentralisation one can observe that the public sector reality is considerably more complex in its possible variations than its private sector counterpart. As with performance indicators, it is influenced and shaped by the public service context.

Evaluation of the New Managerialism

The new managerialism therefore represents a central core of resource accountability, monitoring and measuring; added to this are optional extras of mission statements, customer care, decentralisation, quality, innovation, entrepreneurialism and the 'culture' approach. Criticisms of the new managerialism can be grouped in the following areas: intellectual criticisms, values, and practicalities.

To start with the *intellectual* criticisms. First, the claims to universality (Willcocks and Harrow, 1992) and portability (Hood 1991) create an intellectual straightjacket, in that the new managerialism is prescriptive in its advocacy of techniques, not analytic. Willcocks and Harrow (1992) point out that the manager is cast as problem solver not problem poser. Second, the new managerialism has been criticised for its lack of coherence when applied to the public sector, for instance, in urging innovation and entrepreneurial behaviour (Harrow and Willcocks, 1992). The former is possible, within public services, but scope for the latter is limited if organisations are to avoid risks with vulnerable people, and are also to remain within the bounds of probity. An unfortunate example was the investment by a number of councils of funds in the Bank of Credit and Commerce International; the Western Isles suffered a loss of £23m in 1991.

The new managerialism presents itself as *value* free at the same time as ignoring the traditional values of the public service (Pollitt, 1990, Chapter One), particularly equity in service delivery, redistribution, and the rights of citizens as a collective. Empowerment, whereby individuals and groups are enabled to take more control over their lives, is an alien concept; thus the new managerialism preserves existing power relationships between officers and users. Moreover, because it is presented as value free, those who question it are seen as antagonistic to the welfare and progress of the organisation. It follows, therefore, that it is also portrayed as politically neutral (Hood, 1991), which clearly it is not if it ignores the traditional public service values referred to above. Whilst some writers – notably Pollitt (1990) – have identified it closely with Thatcher's Conservatism, it should be noted that politicians on the left have embraced techniques such as target setting and monitoring as means of ensuring the delivery of policy, for instance, Equal Opportunities or green policies. There is a sense in which the new managerialism is 'masculine'. Because of its denial of values it is gender blind (Pollitt, 1990), and ignores research on the different ways men and women manage. Despite Equal Opportunities, reorganisation in line with the new managerialism has favoured male incumbents, even in departments like Social Services, which are traditionally staffed by a majority of women (Lupton 1991). The emphasis on measuring and monitoring – analytic rather than intuitive qualities – reinforces this.

Turning to *practicalities*, reference was made earlier to the use of management language. From personal experience as a local authority officer at a time of change, it appeared that managerial concepts and techniques were sometimes shallowly understood, *e.g.* that managers talked glibly about 'marketing' when merely meaning advertising. Second, in a general sense, managerialism can be seen as socially divisive. Criticisms have been made that it serves a self interested elite (Hood, 1991). Third, managerialism is tested by the particular context of public services, where services cannot be expanded or divested as easily as in the private sector. The application of some concepts and techniques is less straightforward, as shown in the examination above of decentralisation and performance indicators. Many services are dependent on others for their successful execution. 'Customers' are multiple; a social worker may be concerned with a service user, relatives and informal carers, all to some extent customers for a respite care service, for instance.

In summary, the new managerialism can be seen as lacking intellectual coherence, denying yet promulgating values, and tested by the particular context of public services.

Conclusion

Earlier the question was posed as to whether the new managerialism is a culture change in its own right, or a managerial style. Returning to Schein's definition, the pattern of basic assumptions of the new managerialism has been alluded to several times – that the importation of private sector concepts and techniques will enable better delivery of public services. Schein refers to a given group; two such groups within the public services, the policy makers and, to a lesser extent, the managers, have discovered the nexus of new managerialist assumptions. The impetus for change has been principally to cope with the problems of external adaptation, the drivers of change discussed earlier in the chapter, and to a lesser extent with the problems of internal integration. The problem at this point is that the argument may appear tautological: if the assumptions of the new managerialism have been internalised by a group in the manner described by Schein, then the new managerialism is a culture change. If merely the outer manifestations – procedures and behaviour patterns, for instance – have changed then the change is one of style rather than culture. There seems sufficient of the former in evidence in the public services to describe the new managerialism as a culture change. (It was noted earlier that the new managerialism lacked internal coherence. It is quite possible for adherents to have a set of beliefs which are not internally consistent, particularly when assumptions are not necessarily articulated.)

The public services are not however uniform. Whereas some groups (services or departments) have internally embraced the new managerialism, others may have made a pragmatic adjustment to external reality, acting out the requirements, but internally discordant. It is helpful to think in terms of a continuum of engagement, from the enthusiastic groups, who have accepted and effected a total culture change, and internalised a new set of assumptions; through the pragmatic accepters, who feel coerced by external pressures; to the rejecters. Both the pragmatic accepters and the rejecters may be aware of conflict about values and assumptions. Where different subgroups are acting on the basis of different assumptions, there will be dominant and subordinate cultures, rival subcultures as described by domain theory, or a culture where conflict is endemic. To establish the given culture for any group or organisation and discover whether an apparent change is real and permanent, or superficial and ephemeral, organisational development techniques to 'surface' culture *e.g.* Lundberg (1990), may be employed. Without conducting such a study organisation by organisation, the answer necessitates an element of personal judgement.

Reviewing now the awareness of culture within the new managerialism, as discussed previously, familiarity with the concept of culture is an aspect of the new managerialism, attaining greater or lesser importance according to the group's web of assumptions; for some enthusiasts and pragmatic accepters it is integral, for others a peripheral or mysterious entity. Rejecters, whilst aware of a conflict of values, may have little familiarity with the concept. Understanding of the concept, as opposed to superficial acquaintance, is more problematical. As evidenced by the examples previously discussed, comprehension can range from the superficial 'quick fix' approach (Solihull) to a realistic acknowledgment of its complexities (Grampian).

As to the future of culture in the public services, they will be influenced firstly by their size, scope and structure, in turn determined by political considerations; at the time of writing the Government is contemplating a review of local authority boundaries and functions, and the slimming down of Regional Health Authorities. In public services of all political colours, however, it appears the new managerialism is here to stay and will continue to encourage the push from an administrative to managerial culture. As stated earlier, the new managerialism is not associated solely with recent Conservatism. If it suits them, the left will use their tools for their own ends; so some of the political debate in the future may be, for instance, about the formulation and content of performance indicators, rather than about whether they should be used.

At the beginning of the chapter Schein's definition described the root of organisational culture as '. . . the assumptions which lie behind the values and which determine the behaviour patterns and visible artifacts'. From observation of the rise and fall of particular clusters of values extant in the public services in the 1980s and the early 1990s, the assumptions which may underlie them can be suggested. In the new managerialism is displayed a strong belief in the principles and practices of the private sector; in the future, awareness of Equal Opportunities, green issues, and humanistic values may assume greater importance. As such shifts in values and their underlying assumptions are easier to identify with hindsight, there may, well be unperceived changes under way which will shape and form organisational culture in public services in the future.

Illustration 3.1:

Proposals for Cultural Change in Bradford Council

In August 1988, the Conservative Party gained a crucial by-election, and control of Bradford City Council by virtue of the Mayor's casting vote. Immediately a new political and managerial style became evident.

Expressions of hostility by leading councillors towards Council officers were evident at an early stage, including comments about the rudeness of officers towards the public. Posts such as race trainers and press officers were axed; small cuts financially, but large symbolically. The Conservative administration made it clear that it intended to engender rapid cultural change in the organisation.

A working paper commissioned by Conservatives outline change issues and likely resistance (Bradford 1988a). 'Getting close to the customer' was advocated, with devolution of control to service Directorates. The building blocks for change included:
- strong leadership, and a market/service orientation
- new systems for policy planning, and performance review
- financial and personnel responsibilities delegated to line managers
- central support departments to be supportive not controlling
- pilot devolved management units
- management information systems

A later document, 'Bradford into the 1990s' (Bradford 1988b), commonly known as 'the Blueprint', set out the Conservatives' agenda for city government: it criticised the council as a bureaucratic system lacking proper mechanisms of accountability, and for using growth as a measure of success, with scant regard for efficiency and effectiveness. There is reference to the need to move to a structure which stresses innovation, devolution, and customer care, led by new style managers: 'leaders, strategists, and initiators'. The subsequent Strategic Plan specifically advocated a move from a role to a task culture.

In comparing the organisation they inherited with the organisation they desired, the Conservatives identified a clear performance gap.

References

Atkinson, J (1985) 'Manpower strategies for flexible organisations', *Personnel Management* Vol 28 no 31 August pp 28–31

Audit Commission (1989) *Better Financial Management.* Management Papers No. 3, HMSO, 1989

Bradford City Council (1988a) *Improving Management Arrangements in Bradford: Getting Finance and Personnel into Shape,* Bradford City Council

Bradford City Council (1988b): *Bradford into the 1990s,* Bradford City Council

Burack, E H (1991) 'Changing the Company Culture – the Role of Human Resource Development', *Long Range Planning* Vol 24 no 1 pp 88 – 95.

Burke and Goddard (1990) 'Internal Markets – The Road to Inefficiency' *Public Administration* Vol 68 Autumn pp 389–396

Clarke M and Stewart J (1990) 'The Future for Local Government: Issues for Discussion' *Public Administration* Vol 68 Summer pp 249–258

Command 1599: (1991) *The Citizens Charter – Raising the Standard* HMSO

Cochrane, A (1991) 'The Changing State of Local Government: Restructuring for the 1990s' *Public Administration* Vol 69 Autumn pp 281–302

Dawson, A.G. (1991) *The Art of Practical Management* Allen Accountancy

Dixon, G (1989): personal communication

Drury, C (1985): *Management and Cost Accounting,* Van Nostrand Reinhold (UK)

Duclos, G (1988/89): 'The management of change: theory and practice'. *Optimum* 1988/1989 volume 19–1 pp 26–31

Eley, R (1990): 'Women at the Top' *Insight* Vol 2 no 12 pp 12–14

Frank, E (1987): 'Organisational 'Culture': Some implications for Managers and Trainers'. *JEIT* Volume 11–7 pp 29–32

Fretwell, L (1988): ' . . . Right Shape for the Future', *Local Government Chronicle,* 16 September p 20–21

Fullerton, L & Price, C (1991) 'Culture Change in the NHS'. *Personnel Management,* March pp 50–53

Gray, A, and Jenkins, B, with Flynn, A, and Rutherford, B (1991) 'The Management of Change within Whitehall: The Experience of the FMI'. *Public Administration* Vol 69 Spring pp 41–59

Hambleton R, & Hoggett P (1987): 'Beyond Bureaucratic Paternalism' in Hoggett P and Hambleton R: *Decentralisation and Democracy – Localising public services,* School of Advanced Urban Studies, University of Bristol pp 9-28

Hambleton, R (1988) 'Consumerism, Decentralization and Local Democracy', *Public Administration,* Vol 66 Summer pp 125–147

Hambleton R (1992) 'Decentralization and Democracy in UK Local

Government' *Public Money and Management* Vol 12 no 3 July-September pp 9–20

Handy, C (1985) *Understanding Organisations*, third edition Penguin

Harrison S (1988) *Managing the National Health Service – Shifting the Frontier* Chapman and Hall

Harrow, J and Willcocks, L (1992) 'Management Innovation and Organizational Learning' Willcocks, L, and Harrow, J *Rediscovering Public Services Management*, McGraw-Hill

Henkel, M (1991) 'The New Evaluative State'. *Public Administration* Vol 69 Spring 1991 pp 121–136

Hicks, C (1991) 'Strategy for Shared Success'. *Local Government Chronicle*, 8th March p 18

Hoggett P (1991) 'A New Management in the Public Sector?' *Policy and Politics* Vol 19 no 4 October pp 243–256

Hood, C (1991): 'A Public Management for all Seasons?' *Public Administration*, Vol 69 Spring, pp 3–19

Kakabadse, A. (1982) *Culture of the Social Services*, Gower

Kersell, J E, DeSimone, M E., Mulamootil, G G (1991–1992) 'Some PS 2000 Principles Have Been Tested', *Optimum* (Canada) Vol 22 no 3 pp 25–30

Kouzes, J M, & Mico, P R (1979) 'Domain Theory – an introduction to organizational behaviour in human services organisations', *Journal of Applied Behavioural Science* Vol 15 no 4 pp 449–69

Lawton, A & Rose, A (1991): *Organisation and Management in the Public Sector*, Pitman

Lewin, K (1952) *Field Theory in Social Science* Tavistock

Lundberg C (1991) 'Surfacing Organisational Culture' *Journal of Managerial Psychology* Vol 5 no 4 pp 19–26

Lupton, C (1992): 'Feminism, Managerialism, and Performance Measurement', in Mary Langan and Lesley Day: *Women, Oppression and Social Work*, Routledge

Metcalfe, L & Richards, S (1990) *Improving Management in Government*, second edition, Sage

Peters, T, & Waterman, R H (1981): *In Search of Excellence*, Harper & Row

Peters, T & Austen, N (1985): *A Passion for Excellence*, Random House

Peters, T (1987) *Thriving on Chaos*, Alfred A Knopf, USA

Pettigrew, A H (1986): *Is Corporate Culture Manageable?*. Keynote address given to the Sixth Annual Strategic Management Society Conference, Cultures and Competitive Strategies, Singapore, October 13–16 1986.

Pettigrew A H, Ferlie E, McKee L (1992) 'Shaping Strategic Change – The Case of the NHS in the 1980s' *Public Money and Management* Vol 12 no 3 July-September pp 27–31

Pollitt C (1988) 'Bringing Consumers into Performance Measurement: Concepts, Consequences and Constraints' *Policy and Politics* Vol 16 no 2 April pp 77–87

Pollitt C (1990) *Managerialism and the Public Services, The Anglo-American Experience*, Basil Blackwell

Richards, S (1989) *Managing Cultural Change*, paper presented at London Business School, 22 March

Schein E H (1973) 'Personal Change through Interpersonal Relationships' in W G Bennis, D E Berlow, E H Schein, & F L Steel: *Interpersonal Dynamics*, Dorsey pp 237–267

Schein E H (1983) 'The role of the founder in creating organisational culture' *Organisational Dynamics* Vol 12 no 1 Summer pp 13–28

Stewart, J (1989) 'The Changing Organisation and Management of Local Authorities' in John Stewart and Gerry Stoker *The Future of Local Government*, Macmillan pp 171–184

Stoker, G (1989) 'Creating a Local Government for a Post-Fordist Society: The Thatcherite Project' John Stewart and Gerry Stoker *The Future of Local Government*, Macmillan pp 141–170

Taylor, J A and Williams, H (1991) Public Administration and the Information Polity, in *Public Administration*, Vol 69 Summer pp 171–190

Thomas, M (1985) 'In Search of Culture: Holy Grail or Gravy Train?' *Personnel Management* September pp 24–27

Thomson P (1992) 'Public Sector Management in a Period of Radical Change: 1979–1992' *Public Money and Management* Vol 12 no 3 July-September

Willcocks, L, & Harrow, J (1992) *Rediscovering Public Services Management*, McGraw-Hill

Wilson, D C, and Rosenfeld, R H (1990) *Managing Organizations; Text, Readings and Cases* McGraw-Hill

CHAPTER FOUR

QUALITY

Peter Hinton

Introduction

The word 'Quality' has featured prominently in the vocabulary of public service organizations in the last three or four years. Quality Assurance, Quality Management, Total Quality Management (TQM), and other 'quality' phrases abound. 'Quality' is the latest catchword used by all the main political parties and it has not yet become debased or repudiated. As this chapter explains, recent statements by the Government now make it imperative that all Local Government and Health Service Authorities have a quality framework.

At the risk of over-simplification, there appear to be three main areas where public service organizations are developing quality policies. It is possible to see these areas in systems terms of input, process(ing) and output. The first concerns the quality rating of suppliers of products and services to the public sector. Select list of contractors are by no means a new phenomenon. Recently, however, there has been an increasing demand by the public sector that its suppliers, whether within or outside the public sector, should possess proof of being quality certified. Whereas the first area involves the quality of input, the second area deals with quality as it affects internal operations and processes. Here the arrangements for quality management and the processes of quality assurance are the subject of attention. The third area features output in measures of quality service, codes of conduct, customer charters and service agreements. This can be summarised under the heading of the delivery of quality services to customers, both within and outside a public sector organization. While there is overlap of the areas and it is less satisfactory to consider one area in isolation, this chapter is confined in the main to looking at process and structure – the internal operations of public service organizations and the arrangements they are making for quality management. It begins with examining what is meant by 'quality' and looks at the background, both private and public sector, which has given rise to recent, intense, interest in quality. The major part of the chapter is devoted to presenting research findings from a study by Davies and Hinton (1993). These are used to highlight the experience of quality management in some local and health authorities. Areas for further study are suggested, before conclusions are drawn about the prospects for sustaining quality initiatives in the rest of the 1990's.

Defining Quality
There are many definitions of quality, quality assurance and quality management. For quality, the typical descriptions are in terms of products or services meeting the user's needs, fitting the purpose intended, conforming to requirements, but with resource economy and efficiency for the supplier. Quality is not luxury and it is not just meeting in house standards, but meeting the standards which customers decide. BT (1988), for instance, defines quality as 'Meeting the customer's (agreed) requirements at lowest cost . . . First time, every time. Customer requirements would include: fitness for purpose required, representing value for money'. Perhaps the best description of quality comes from those International and British Standards which set specifications for minimum quality management systems. Quality is defined as 'the totality of features and characteristics of a product or service that bear on its ability to satisfy stated or implied needs' (BS4778, 4.1.1,1987). Organizations complying with the Quality Assurance Standard, BS5750, and its international equivalent ISO9001, are accredited as having quality policies which give rise to quality assurance. BS4778 (1987) defines quality assurance as, 'All those planned and systematic actions necessary to provide adequate confidence that a product or service will satisfy given requirements for quality'. Quality management is a broad term covering the arrangements an organization makes for establishing and operating quality systems and the management structure to implement quality policies. Total Quality Management, (TQM), can be defined as the involvement of everyone in an organization in controlling and continuously improving how work is done in order to meet customer expectations of quality.

The Background to Public Sector Quality
Quality management has a long history. Its origins are with American

and Japanese companies, some of which have had a concern for quality for over thirty five years. Quality management in private sector organizations has become almost common place, especially in manufacturing and process industries. Its aim has been to increase the relevance of a company's product or service to the customer, its 'fitness for purpose', and of maintaining competitive advantage. BS5750 has been in place since 1979 and by 1991 some 12500 British businesses had gained accredited certificates. In 1991, Girobank plc became the first service company to gain a British Quality Award, won for four years of demonstrable and quantifiable business improvement achieved through a commitment to total quality. Its total quality programme achieved cost savings of more than £8 million yet raised the level of customer service.

The gurus of the quality approaches, Crosby, Deming, Juran, Taguchi and Feigenbaum, amongst others, have provided theoretical frameworks and models which have been followed by major organizations, such as BT, Nissan and Rank Xerox. This chapter does not have space to describe these theories and approaches except in reporting later where health and local authorities have applied them. A good summary of the theoretical background is given in Dale, Lascelles and Plunkett (1990).

At first sight, it might appear that a private sector quality approach is not directly suited to public service organizations. Concern for a product's suitability for customer requirements, perfecting the technical process of production, minimising waste, 'right first time', pursuing cost reduction, are understandable objectives in production based industries. However, it is the efficiency savings and customer care aspects of a quality programme which are attractive to service organizations. Unit cost measurement may be inadequately precise and market research of customer requirements may be less developed, but this does not restrict the application of a quality approach to the public sector.

In many ways, a quality approach builds on prevailing concepts of Value for Money (VFM) in the public sector. The last two decades have seen a shift in emphasis from service provision which satisfies demand to service provision which is affordable and of value. This partly reflects the resource constraints of the last twenty years but also reveals an attitude change. The consumer expects public services to be well delivered and resources to be demonstrably well applied. The 3 E's of VFM, economy, efficiency and effectiveness, have dominated the

Table 4.1

Distinctions between Economy, Efficiency & Effectiveness

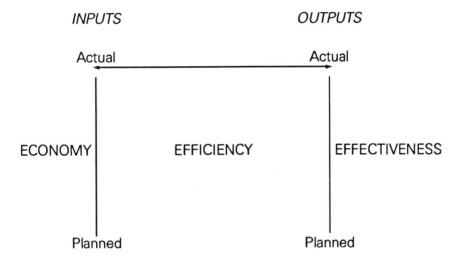

Source: Metcalfe, L. and Richards,S. 1990 p.29

language of the public service, to the point of becoming trite in their usage. In Table 4.1, Metcalfe and Richards (1990) show the relationship of the 3 E's diagrammatically in terms of inputs and outputs.

This is a useful analysis. While economy is about the acquisition of inputs on the best terms, with the least cost, efficiency is the input-output ratio and effectiveness is a measure of actual performance against planned performance. However, this description of effectiveness fails to convey the notions of impact or outcome. A broader definition of effectiveness might be a measure of the extent to which output contributes towards the achievement of objectives and how far meeting those objectives contributes to the health and welfare of the community. In this regard, a fourth 'E', equity, is used by Selim and Woodward (1992), amongst others, to describe the net effect that an organization or particular activities of an organization have upon society and the environment.

VFM uses the 3 E's despite conflicts between them and within them. For instance the most efficiently delivered service may not be effective if its 'output' fails to meet objectives. Within efficiency, technical efficiency, the process of transformation, conversion of inputs to outputs, may conflict with financial efficiency in that the best method may not be the cheapest.

Given the obvious merits the VFM E's have in presenting a framework for analysing the performance of public service organizations, it may seem peculiar that a quality approach is becoming increasingly fashionable. There are two possible explanations. First, VFM is arguably producer led rather than customer driven. It is concerned with supply not demand or user satisfaction. A similar argument applies in the private sector where cost reduction as a technique, in association with Zero Based budgeting, concentrates on the process of production not on whether the consequences of production are valued. Secondly, the advantage of a quality approach is that it provides a motivational stimulus to the staff of an organization and the possibility of a culture change, leading to a participative, adaptive and dynamic organization. It is this prospect of transforming style and outlook which has attracted major organizations, Rover for instance, to espouse the quality approach, as much as the commercial advantage in promoting cost reduction. For public sector organizations, faced with changes of structure, working practices and measures of success as managerialism and market testing take hold, quality provides a banner all staff can be encouraged to follow.

In some public service organizations, quality programmes, if not called by that name, have been under way for some time. In the Health Service, Duncan Nichol's letter to General Managers (Dept of Health 1989) gave initial areas for quality improvement and required General Managers to ensure that quality assurance activities became part of the total management process. The NHS Directorate in Wales (1990) produced a strategy for the development and quality of care within the National Health Service in Wales, recommending a total quality management approach (Table 4.2). *Competing for Quality* (Dept of the Environment 1991), in proposals extending compulsory competitive tendering, emphasises both the Government's concern that the public sector achieves best value for money and that consumers of services benefit from standards of service being set. *The Citizen's Charter* (HMSO 1991) sets out four main themes:-

Table 4.2
Total Quality Management
*Total
– A key element of overall policy objectives
– With clear leadership from the top
– Two-way communication involving all staff
– Supported by training to involve staff and fulfil their potential.

*Quality
– Meeting needs and expectations
– Customer centred
– Valuing people as individuals
– With agreed measurable standards of performance for all aspects
– Reinforced by robust and reliable processes
– So that standards are achieved consistently.

*Management
– An integral part of working practice
– Monitored, evaluated and reviewed regularly
– Continuously improving.
Source:– Welsh Office NHS Directorate, 1990.

Quality – A sustained new programme for improving the quality of public sector services.
Choice – Choice, wherever possible between competing providers, is the best spur to quality improvement.
Standards – The citizen must be told what service standards are and be able to act where service is unacceptable.
Value – The citizen is also a taxpayer; public services must give value for money within a tax bill the nation can afford.

Against this background of private sector interest in quality and the Government's statements, it is clear that public service organizations need to have an awareness of quality and begin to manage quality programmes. This chapter now considers the experience of a sample of local and health authorities in managing quality policies and programmes.

The research project
A pilot research study by the Liverpool Business School (Davies and Hinton 1993) in Spring 1992 examined how far public service organizations had gone in providing a structure and establishing a

culture for quality initiatives. A range of local and health authorities within North West England and North Wales were contacted to assess the development of awareness of quality management philosophies and the extent of implementation of quality management schemes.

A representative subset of twelve organizations was then selected for more in depth interviews. This selection was based on the extent of development of quality management philosophies, as it was felt that the research should attempt to identify good practice and experience to date. Key quality management personnel were interviewed using a structured questionnaire. It was agreed that in reporting the findings of the research, there would be no mention of an organization by name since some of the staff interviewed wished confidentiality to be respected. The focus of the research was on central services rather than on production or direct service functions. Within central services, most of the research related to Finance Departments. The study looked at six main areas:–

- General awareness of quality approaches.
- Type of quality policies.
- Arrangements for managing quality.
- Training requirements.
- Methods and techniques.
- Budget arrangements for managing quality.

Findings of the research
The six areas given above provide the framework for reporting the findings of the Spring 1992 survey. The research revealed that there was generally a good awareness of quality management, total quality management(TQM) and quality assurance and in some cases excellent knowledge of the theoretical background. In those Health Service organizations examined, there was heavy reliance on the work of Donabedian (1980) for improving the quality of performance. Here the emphasis was on setting performance standards, transferring the quality care approach used in clinical areas to administrative processes. The quality care approach relies on a Structure → Process → Outcome model; structure refers to the resources to be available or to be used, in order to carry out any activities or process related to a task or function; process refers to the activity necessary to achieve defined outcomes or results; and outcome refers to the results of any activity or process. Setting standards for each of these was felt to give scope for

indicating where non compliance and nonconformity, nonfulfilment of specified requirements, occurred. In District Councils, the emphasis was on quality assurance, establishing quality systems, whilst in County Councils and Health Authorities there was a desire to embrace TQM.

Interest in quality was found to be mainly the outcome of officer led initiatives, though in some Health and Local Authorities senior members of the organization had encouraged development. Members were generally not prominent in considering the detail of quality programmes but were supportive of broad policy. There was variation in how far organizations had taken a central, corporate, approach to managing quality as against departments or sections acting on their own initiative.

Five organizations had launched their quality programmes in September or October 1991, not as a reaction to Government requirements but more as a logical next step in a train of developments including, for instance, performance appraisal, devolution, management by business objectives, competition, and customer care and service programmes.

Some organizations could identify the philosophy of quality management they were employing. There was evidence that where a Crosby approach (Crosby 1979) had first been used, the statistical process control approach of Deming (1982) was beginning to be established in its place. This was a recognition that the absolutes of quality presented by Crosby (1979, 1984), were good for raising awareness but of limited use thereafter. These absolutes – quality has to be defined as conformance to requirements, not as goodness; the system for causing quality is prevention, not appraisal; the performance standard must be zero defects, not 'that's close enough'; the measurement of quality is the price of nonconformance, not indexes – by their very nature, did not offer scope for continuing improvement over time. The benefit of the Deming approach was felt to be its reliance on measuring deviations from quality standards and its extension of control processes already in operation.

The majority of organizations surveyed were relying on external consultants for advice about introducing a quality management approach. Firms of accountants, management advisers from computer firms, associates from specialist companies and private operators were employed. Typically, the consultancy fees were moderate, since the pilot nature of much of the work in the public sector was recognised and the consultants were keen to establish reputations. There was no definite allegiance shown by the consultants to any particular philosophy of quality. Material for training courses and presentations was from a collection of sources rather than drawn from a single approach such as Crosby's 14 steps or Deming's 14 principles.

In respect of the third of the six areas studied, arrangements for managing quality, it was found that most of the organizations surveyed had made structural changes. There are typical elements for managing quality which include the following:–

Quality Council usually comprising senior management, which decides strategic policies and receives feedback on quality initiatives.

Quality Task Groups which deal with particular inter-departmental or sectional problems. The Quality Task Group has a representative membership often selected by the Quality Council which nominates a leader and identifies a Champion (see below) for the project. The Task Group will disband once solutions to a problem have been found and implemented.

Quality Improvement Teams, by contrast, are permanent with objectives to set specifications for quality operation, to monitor performance and to demonstrate improved customer care and resource savings. They report to the Quality Council.

Quality Circles, informal or semi-formal teams, are encouraged to operate. These are voluntary meetings of staff who are keen to improve the quality of the service they provide. In one organization researched, a District Health Authority, restructuring and new senior personnel led to major changes in the direction of the quality programme. However, staff lower down the organization, despite the turbulence of the environment, continued their support for quality improvement in their informal Quality Circles.

Quality Co-ordinators are senior personnel knowledgeable in quality concepts. They are appointed to assist Senior Managers in the development of quality policies and to act as facilitators for groups and teams, usually through arranging training sessions and giving advice on procedures.

Quality Champions are senior staff who volunteer or are volunteered to keep task groups and teams well motivated and effective.

Quality Facilitators may be another name for Quality Co-ordinators. They are staff specifically charged with helping groups to meet and make progress on the identification, analysis and solution of problems.

Quality News is a regular bulletin communicating the quality message and progress.

Quality Awards are cash sums awarded to staff who the organization decides have made a significant contribution to improving customer care and achieving resource efficiency.

It would be wrong to suggest, however, that these elements were universally adopted by the organizations surveyed. One organization had made considerable progress in establishing groups for customer care and improving service provision, without explicit mention of quality management. 'Common sense' arrangements were stated to prevail without the need for fashionable terminology. Subsequent to the research, the organization formally adopted some of the elements of quality management, making use of consultants from a firm of accountants for advice. This was in response to the emphasis placed by the Government on quality in *The Citizen's Charter*. Where a very considered, methodical, approach to quality management was in place at the outset and being introduced top down, there was more use of

Table 4.3

Quality Management Structure in a Local Authority Finance Department

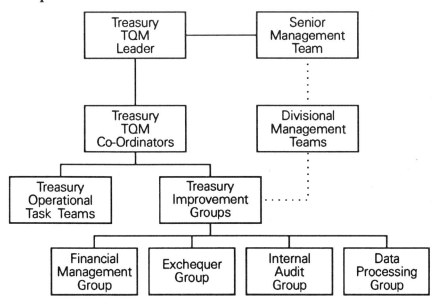

quality terms. The structure of quality management in one local authority's Finance Department is shown in Table 4.3.

Training requirements was the next area studied. In organizations where there was a systematic approach to quality management, it was found that there was an emphasis on formal training. Typically this began with senior managers attending a two day residential quality awareness course led by external consultants. Seminars were then held for section heads and unit managers to disseminate the organization's policies. Training for quality improvement teams and quality task groups took the form of courses of two or three days' duration, sometimes residential. In one Health Service organization, quality co-ordinators were given formal training in quality assurance on a two year part time course.

The methods and techniques for quality improvement and quality management were found to be those associated with the problem solving process and team building. The training courses for task group and team members referred to above were often led by consultants. They either presented sessions, or provided the material for sessions, aimed at developing effective groups and providing them with a 'toolbox' of the tools and techniques to apply in the problem solving process. An illustrative list of tools and techniques, drawn from

Table 4.4

Typical tools and techniques applicable for the problem solving process.

Brainstorming
Evaluation Grids
5-Way Problem Definition
Force Field Analysis
Cause and Effect (Fishbone) Diagrams
Action Plans
Effective Data Display
Flowcharts
Cost/Benefit Analysis
Critical Path Analysis
Tree Diagram
Performance Monitors
The Pareto Principle

operations' management and decision making approaches, is given in Table 4.4.

The final area of study was to look at the budget arrangements for managing quality. It was found that no organization had created a totally separate budget for its quality programme. Some local authorities had specific allocations for organization wide quality co-ordination, external consultants and quality assurance accreditation fees, but not for internal costs of training, newsletters and staff time. There had been no attempt to relate costs of the quality programme to the savings produced, although this was recognised as being a yardstick of performance and a Crosby absolute. Instead, organizations had been variously using their training budgets, surpluses from operating below staffing establishments or special funding from Health Service pilot programmes. How to fund the monitoring required to establish that service quality was improving was recognised as being a difficulty. The view was strongly expressed by some Health Authorities that the Government had not thought through the resource consequences of its drive on quality. The cost of quality assurance might be considerable in the first few years, until savings began to materialise.

Research conclusions

The pilot study resulted in Davies and Hinton making preliminary conclusions about the nature and extent of quality management in public service organizations. Some of these conclusions support the views of theorists. The first conclusion listed, for instance, may seem a truism, but those interviewed in the twelve organizations researched recognised its fundamental importance.

* The success of quality initiatives critically depends upon the commitment of senior managers, who must be, and must be seen to be, involved. Leadership from the top is vital and the head of the organization must be seen to be fully directing and supporting the initiatives. Assigning responsibility to one of the senior managers has the potential weakness of sidelining quality.
* The commitment to quality management, once made, is binding unless an organization is prepared to see its reputation suffer and staff morale decline. Given the cultural change aspect and the enthusiasm generated by sessions in quality awareness, there is an incentive and obligation on management to sustain momentum.
* Commitment implies considerable resourcing in the short term.

The costs of training, facilitation, staff time and monitoring performance are considerable before the benefits arising from Quality are achieved. After awareness has been created, it is important to make resources available for staff development in the use of the techniques and tools and in the processes of quality improvement.

* External consultants assist in raising quality awareness, introducing training programmes and facilitating group working. The process of changing the culture of the organization benefits from the objectivity and stimulus of external consultants.

* There is a science to quality management built upon problem solving techniques, operational research and business decision making approaches. Common sense approaches have their place, but formal training using a 'toolbox' adds to staff enthusiasm for the quality initiative, demonstrates management's continuing commitment to quality and leads to more analytical appraisal and better evaluated recommendations.

* A quality approach is top down through line management in a Quality Council and Quality Task Groups and bottom up through Quality Circles. Quality Circles are insufficient in themselves to provide a sustained programme of quality improvement. Top down initiatives are unlikely to be successful without the culture of the organization being conducive to quality programmes. Where organizations are going through radical restructuring and a clear purpose and mission are lacking, quality is often restricted to Quality Circles and without a line of access to a decision making forum for recommendations to be considered.

* Communication of the successes of quality programmes and of progress is vital. Finding ways to disseminate information and to obtain feedback is a high priority. Organizations renew their interest in providing and ensuring the effectiveness of channels of communication.

* Even in the short time since public service organizations launched their quality programmes, widely different approaches and practices have been followed. There is a need for experience to be exchanged about managing quality.

* Accreditation under BS5750 is not essential unless there are strong market pressures influencing an organization to gain competitive advantage. Where this is not the case, seeking accreditation may be a costly distraction from implementing an effective quality

programme because of the procedural demands imposed. Compulsory competitive tendering is encouraging organizations to set service standards and seek BS5750 in order to win contracts in-house.
* Staff are excited and enthusiastic about undertaking a Quality Programme. Cynicism can be overcome. There must be continuing effort to retain enthusiasm.

Areas for Further Research
The pilot study in 1992 has suggested several areas for further research. Resource consequences of the drive for quality, formulation of separate budgets, ways to disseminate information and obtain feedback, and the impact of organizational change on a quality programme, are worthy of continuing study.

In addition, five new research areas have been identified. First, much work is needed on setting specifications for activities and processes so that measures are available for judging quality improvement. The Health Authorities researched were beginning to develop a systematic methodology of producing standards for activities within clinical specialties. For administrative activities, however, little development work has occurred.

Secondly, the role of both Internal and External Audit in quality assurance and in assuring that quality assurance is sound needs defining. Further research should assess how far concern for Value for Money overlaps with concern for quality assurance. The Audit Commission has been active in providing an information exchange for local authorities on quality and has been given the role of watchdog of relative performance in the NHS and Local Government, arising from proposals in the Government's *Competing for Quality* White Paper. As reported in *Public Finance and Accountancy*, 25 September 1992, the Commission published a report in September 1992 entitled 'Minding the quality: a consultation document on the role of the Audit Commission in quality assurance in healthcare'.

Thirdly, key performance indicators by which quality can be assessed may require the application of risk analysis. It would be interesting to see if risk analysis techniques could determine the areas of an organization most at risk through a lack of quality and therefore most suitable for measurement of quality improvement.

Fourthly, the links between performance measures for quality and performance appraisal could be examined. There are separate monitoring arrangements, apparently, for quality programmes from those for staff performance appraisal and for audit requirements. It would be helpful to research how far a single set of performance indicators could be developed so reducing the workload of monitoring. The work of the Audit Commission is pertinent here and September 1992 saw the publication of 'The Citizen's Charter performance indicators' which proposed 152 local government indicators (reported in *Public Finance and Accountancy*, 18 September).

Finally, the democratic aspect of quality initiatives could be investigated by researching how far Quality Circles take on the task of appraising the effectiveness of senior staff in implementing their proposals. Staff assessment of managers, upward feedback or-appraisal, is beginning to occur in some companies. Quality initiatives challenge senior staff to demonstrate that they have a role to play in an organization where everyone is committed to quality improvement.

In conclusion, further research is clearly necessary as it is premature to dismiss quality management as transient or to hail it as a resounding success in giving public service organizations the processes for achieving quality improvement. Liverpool Business School intends to continue its research through its Accontancy and Financial Management Unit. A more detailed study of quality management is now being undertaken. This is investigating how corporate initiatives on quality are being affected by devolution and how far the momentum for quality improvement is being sustained. Until the publication of findings from this research, it is only conjectural that there has been a promising start to quality management.

Prospects for sustaining quality programmes
Since the pilot study was undertaken in the Spring of 1992, many of the organizations researched have completed the inauguration of their quality programmes and carried out awareness and 'toolbox' training. One organization has received the first recommendations of two task groups. These looked at dealing with customers and promoting the finance department, common areas for first exercises in quality along with examining internal communications and post systems. This is a useful start as there is considerable publicity value and acceptance of the merits of the approach when recommendations are adopted and acted upon by management to solve problems, however minor, which have been long standing and the cause of much frustration. Most organizations have appreciated, though, that the work of quality

improvement extends well beyond problem solving and needs a continuing effort. This is a major factor in the prospects for success.

It is worthwhile assessing how far the experience of quality initiatives to date, admittedly from the partial evidence of limited research findings, suggests that quality will be more than a current fad. Crosby (1984,pp.53–54) has identified companies that do not do well with quality because they are just not determined enough. Amongst the common characteristics he lists, three are pertinent for analysis in this context.

First, *'The effort is called a program rather than a process . . .* A "program" lets people know that if they wait and go through the motions, it will soon be replaced by something else. Governments call everything programs. A "process" is never finished and requires constant attention.'

As this chapter has recorded, it is often quality *programmes* rather than quality improvement *processes* which are referred to by the organizations investigated. Indeed, the White Paper of *The Citizen's Charter* refers to quality as a sustained new programme. This suggests a limited time scale for an initiative rather than real cultural and attitudinal change. Moreover, there is scepticism about the value of quality approaches in the private sector, as reported, for instance by The Economist (1992,pp.85–86), casting doubt upon the long term ability to sustain quality initiatives. In the public sector, there is the danger that quality will become a term empty of meaning, perhaps even conveying a pejorative connotation much as efficiency savings now is synonymous with cuts. The emphasis on the permanence of pursuing quality is apparently missing. Maintaining momentum is important and as Wood (1992) and Clark (1992) have identified, the process of accreditation for BS5750 is not enough. A total quality approach which is about continuous improvement is needed.

Secondly, *'All effort is aimed at the lower level of the organization.* It is easy to identify this situation. Just try to find something that senior management has to do differently: all the schooling is for someone else. The Productivity (with a capital P) efforts all are for low levels. Quality circles never begin in the boardroom. Statistical quality control is not applied in white-collar areas'.

Evidence from the experience of the organizations researched reveals the truth of this statement. After introducing awareness training of senior management, organizations have neglected to consider how the work of senior managers, particularly their decision making function, might be improved. Furthermore, the democratic emphasis on every-one having a share in bringing about quality improvements appears illusory if senior managers imply that the exercise is for staff down the line and not themselves as well. This may be an unjustified criticism at this stage, since much will depend upon the way Quality Councils function and senior managers respond to proposals to improve quality.

Thirdly, Crosby (1984,p 54) identifies as a characteristic weakness that, *'Management is impatient for results.* As soon as it learns about the cost of quality, management notifies everyone that it expects an immediate reduction. . . . Impatience also leads to centralization of the program. This means that the individual managers lay back and wait for the word to come down. That brings everything to a slowdown since it increases the hassle.'

In one of the organizations surveyed, there was keenness to publicise the first results of investigations by quality improvement teams. However, when management realised that there would be difficulties making further progress and that the costs of the proposals and the further training of quality teams would be significant outlays, interest declined in continuing the quality programme. Additionally, the prospects for success of quality initiatives do depend upon the stability of the environment in which they are introduced. Some of the Health authorities examined had gone through major structural change, setting back developments in improvements to quality of service. With further change due in Local Government, through the proposals to create unitary authorities and to extend contracting out of services, in the National Health Service with further waves of Trust Hospitals, and in Central Government building on Next Steps, the stability required for sustaining a programme of quality improvement, let alone introducing the processes, seems scarcely obtainable.

Furthermore, it is doubtful whether there are the resources to support the monitoring and measurement of quality. Brockman (1992) expresses the view that a system for monitoring the development of quality management initiatives in government departments and agencies is needed. He compares the experience of the United States and the United Kingdom and agrees that the latter faces important difficulties in implementing quality management namely:–

* The UK's limited experience of implementing quality strategies in government, and consequent absence of a cadre of senior civil servants with the appropriate background, from which a body like the FQI could be staffed.

* The limited number of British quality consultants with service sector experience.
* The high engineering content of the Institute of Quality Assurance's professional qualifications (compulsory subjects include calibration systems, metrology and materials testing), which are not relevant to service-sector quality management. . .
* The British Standard BS 5750, Part 8 (1991), tends to reflect the needs of services with a high product content, such as after-sales servicing of consumer durables, rather than personal services of low product content, with which the government is usually involved; local authority circles are expressing dissatisfaction with this Standard.
* Britain's lack of so-called quality gurus, influential in the FQI's thinking, of the stature of the Americans Joseph Juran, Philip Crosby, and especially J. Edwards Deming, who today is regarded as a national hero in Japan for his contribution to Japanese quality during the post-war reconstruction period.'

Much will depend upon the success of the Audit Commission, or a future quality commission, in influencing public service organizations to provide performance measures in a resource efficient way.

Conclusion
The prospects for quality programmes and quality management are uncertain. If the concept of *The Citizen's Charter* continues to have broad political acceptance, quality will remain high on the political agenda. However, economic and European issues may well dominate and as the public sector reduces in size through further cutbacks and privatisation, quality may become an issue of concern primarily to the individual consumer, rather than the public at large or the public service provider.

References

Brockman, J. (1992) 'Total Quality Management: the USA and UK compared'. *Public Money & Management*. Vol 12, Number 4,pp.6–9.
BS 4778 (1987), *Quality vocabulary. Part 1 International terms*. British Standards Institution, London.
BS 5750 (1987), *Quality Systems*. British Standards Institution, London.

BT (1988), *ISO9001 (BS5750) Management for Quality*. British Telecom, London.

Clark, F. (1992) 'Quality and service in the public sector.' *Public Finance and Accountancy*. 23 October, pp.23–25.

Crosby, P.B. (1979), *Quality is Free: The Art of Making Quality Certain*. McGraw-Hill, New York.

Crosby, P.B. (1984), *Quality Without Tears*. McGraw-Hill, New York.

Dale, B.G., Lascelles, D.M. and Plunkett, J.J.(1990), 'The Process of Total Management'. In *Managing Quality*, edited by B.G. Dale and J.J. Plunkett. Philip Allan, London.

Davies, K. and Hinton, P.G. (1993), 'Managing Quality in Local Government and the Health Service'. *Public Money & Management*. Vol.13, Number 1, pp.51–54

Deming, W.E. (1982), *Quality, Productivity and Competitive Position*. MIT, Centre for Advanced Engineering Study, Cambridge, USA.

Department of the Environment (1991), *Competing for Quality. Competition in the Provision of Local Services: a Consultation Paper*. Department of the Environment, London.

Department of Health (1989), *Quality (EL(89)/MB/117)*. NHS Management Executive, London.

Donabedian, A. (1980), *The Definition of Quality and Approaches to its Assessment. Explorations in Quality Assessment and Monitoring, Vol.1*. Health Administration Press, Ann Arbor, USA.

Economist, The (1992), *The cracks in quality*. Business article,pp85 and 86, April 18, London.

HMSO (1991), *The Citizen's Charter. Cm 1599*. HMSO, London.

Metcalfe, L. and Richards, S. (1990), *Improving Public Management* (2nd edn). Sage, London.

NHS Directorate in Wales (1990), *A Quality Health Service For Wales*. Welsh Office, Cardiff.

Selim, G.M. and Woodward, S.A. (1992), 'The manager monitored'. In *Rediscovering public services management*, edited by L.Willcocks and J.Harrow. McGraw-Hill, London.

Wood, P. (1992) 'Total Quality Management: in search of the Holy Grail'. *Public Finance and Accountancy*. 28 August,pp.19–20.

Acknowledgement
The author wishes to thank Dr Ken Davies for his comments on an earlier version of this chapter.

CHAPTER FIVE

PRIVATISATION

John Wilson

Introduction

A fundamental belief upon which Conservative policy has been based
since 1979 is that the extent of governmental involvement in the UK
economy is excessive. Conservatives support the principle of public
sector provision but nonetheless believe that its magnitude in the UK is
both politically unacceptable and economically damaging. This can be
illustrated by Mrs Thatcher's foreword to the 1979 Conservative
manifesto in which she wrote:

> 'No one who has lived in this country during the last five years can fail to
> be aware of how the balance of our society has been increasingly tilted in
> favour of the state at the expense of individual freedom. This election
> may be the last chance we have to reverse the process, to restore the
> balance of power in favour of the people. It is therefore the most crucial
> election since the war.' (Conservative Party 1979 p5).

This image of inexorable state expansion imperilling individual liberty
provided an ideological basis for attempting to reduce significantly the
scale of state activity and thereby create the conditions in which private
enterprise could flourish. Political and economic 'liberation' from the
deadweight of state bureaucracy were seen to be inextricably related.

The main objective of Conservative policy was, therefore, clear but
the means by which it was to be achieved were not explicit. However,
with hindsight it can be seen that a primary role was assigned to the
policy of 'privatisation' (for a discussion of the background to
privatisation see Swann 1988 pp222-238).

Privatisation: definition
The neologism 'privatisation' quickly became an accepted part of the
political lexicon throughout the 1980s but the word itself is definition-

ally imprecise. It is an umbrella term but, for the purposes of this chapter, included within its meaning are policies designed to enhance private enterprise and ownership. In this respect, it is possible to identify two broad types of policy: denationalisation and liberalisation (more detailed descriptions have been provided, *eg* see Heald 1984; Pirie 1985). These policies may be seen to be distinct (*eg* Rees 1986), but, interpreted broadly, encompass the main features of the privatisation programme (including the sale of council houses but this will not be considered in this chapter).

Denationalisation entails a total or partial transfer of ownership from the public to the private sector (for simplicity, this includes the sale of governmental shares in companies which were not actually nationalised *eg* Rolls Royce). Liberalisation embraces various measures intended to introduce or increase competition in the provision of services.

The liberalisation policies essentially involve deregulation and competitive tendering. By deregulation is meant the dismantling of legal and operational barriers to more competitive, efficient and effective service provision (bus deregulation, for example); by competitive tendering is meant the introduction of competition into the provision of publicly-provided goods and services in an attempt to improve efficiency and value for money.

Deregulation is considered in more detail later (Chapter Six). The focus here is on denationalisation – for which the word privatisation will be used as a synonym – and competitive tendering. Both policies are considered in separate sections and conclusions are drawn in the final part of the chapter.

Nature of Privatisation

The emphasis given to privatisation could not have been predicted in 1979. The word did not appear in the Conservative manifesto, which simply referred to the 'offer to sell back to private ownership the recently nationalised aerospace and shipbuilding concerns' and the 'aim to sell shares in the National Freight Corporation' (Conservative Party 1979 p15).

However, by 1983 the policy had acquired momentum. The manifesto of that year contained a commitment, *inter alia*, to ensure that 'British Telecom. . . . Rolls Royce, British Airways and substantial parts of British Steel, of British Shipbuilders and of British Leyland,

and as many as possible of Britain's airports' become private sector companies (Conservative Party 1983 p16).

The 1987 manifesto added water and electricity to the list (see Conservative Party, 1987 p10) and the 1992 manifesto states that the Conservatives 'have returned to private enterprise two-thirds of the companies once owned by the state: 46 businesses employing about 900,000 people' (Conservative Party 1992 p19) and commits the Party, *inter alia*, to privatising British Coal, ending British Rail's monopoly and privatising Northern Ireland's electricity, water and sewage services (see Conservative Party 1992 p20). The extent of privatisation is illustrated in Table 5.1.

It can be seen that the policy has grown enormously in the last thirteen years (for discussions of the privatisation programme see: Kay & Silberston 1984; Vickers & Yarrow 1985; Heald & Thomas 1986; Kay et al 1986; Yarrow 1986; Kay & Thompson 1987; and Veljanovski 1987; given the extensive literature on the subject it is also useful to refer to Marsh 1991). The scale of the transfer from public to private sector has been immense. 'The state sector of industry, predominantly nationalised industries, accounted for 11 per cent of GDP in 1979. Forty six major (and dozens of smaller) companies have been privatised since then. By the middle of 1990 the nationalised industries' share of GDP had fallen to just over 3 per cent, down from just under 9 per cent in 1979; over the same period the numbers employed in nationalised industries has more than halved to 660,000 and more than 920,000 jobs have been transferred to the private sector.' (Treasury HM 1992 p104).

Privatisations include twelve Regional Electricity Companies and ten Water Companies in England and Wales, British Steel, Rover Group, British Airports Authority, Rolls Royce, Royal Ordnance, British Airways, British Gas, BT, Jaguar, British Aerospace, Enterprise Oil, Scottish Power, Scottish Hydro-Electric, Royal Ordnance, Associated British Ports, Britoil, National Freight Consortium, Amersham International and Cable and Wireless.

Net proceeds from privatisation total £41.7bn since 1979–80 plus an additional £1.1bn relating to sales of subsidiaries (*eg* sale of Jaguar by BL, £297m; Sealink by British Rail, £40m; Girobank by Post Office, £112m; see Treasury HM 1992 Table 8.4).

However, the scale of the policy – and its undoubted domestic and international popularity (see Jones 1989; Treasury HM 1986) – does not mean that its economic merits should be regarded as axiomatic.

Table 5.1

Privatisation proceeds 1979–80 – 1991–92 (outturn)

Financial Year	£million
1979–80	377
1980–81	210
1981–82	493
1982–83	455
1983–84	1139
1984–85	2050
1985–86	2706
1986–87	4458
1987–88	5140
1988–89	7069
1989–90	4219
1990–91	5345
1991–92 (1)	8000
Total	41661

Note: 1 Estimated outturn

Source: *Public Expenditure Analyses to 1994–95: Statistical Supplement to the 1991 Autumn Statement*, HM Treasury 1992, Table 2.4

Conflicting claims are made concerning its inherent validity. For instance, Cable (1986 p225) stated that 'the privatisation programme is going forward on a general belief in the superiority of competition and private ownership *per se*, rather than as a result of research into the likely consequences in particular circumstances. In fact, it has become clear as the programme advances that the government's objective has less to do with enhanced competition and efficiency than with simply augmenting government revenue. Six years later, however, Moore (1992 p36) believes that privatisation has had significant political as well as economic benefits, claiming that privatisation 'is a tool whose (*sic*) utility is not in doubt. In Britain it helped rescue an economy heading for disaster and so made more secure the world's oldest parliamentary democracy.'

Given such differences of opinion over the policy it is necessary to consider the assumed merits of privatisation and evaluate them on the basis of UK policy objectives.

Objectives of Privatisation
The objectives of privatisation as summarised by Vickers and Yarrow (1988 p157) are to:

(i) improve efficiency;
(ii) reduce the public sector borrowing requirement;
(iii) reduce government involvement in enterprise decision-making;
(iv) ease problems of public sector pay determination;
(v) widen share ownership;
(vi) encourage employee share ownership;
(vii) gain political advantage.

To this list can be added the objectives of improving profits through diversification and allowing the opportunity for changes in fiscal policy (*eg* cuts in taxation or, perhaps, increases in public expenditure).

With the exception of the final objective identified by Vickers & Yarrow – political advantage – those listed above would be agreed by Conservatives (see Moore 1992 pp6–13). The list involves macroeconomic and microeconomic considerations but essentially the main alleged advantage of privatisation concerns improved efficiency.

The belief is that the greater the degree of competition in the market place the greater is the incentive for firms to maximise efficiency in order to minimise the charge to the consumer thereby discouraging a switch to competitor suppliers.

Competition therefore encourages productive efficiency (X-efficiency – Liebenstein 1976), *ie* improvements in productivity resulting, firstly, in more output relative to units of input and, secondly, minimisation of cost. It also encourages allocative efficiency, *ie* the production and distribution of goods and services is consistent with consumer preferences and priced to reflect the costs of production. Additionally, there is an incentive to maintain market position and profitability through technological innovation. Competition, therefore, brings positive benefits to the consumer (increased choice, lower prices and greater conformity between goods supplied and demanded) and stimulates economic growth.

Reducing governmental involvement in decision-making reflects the problems with which former and current nationalised industries have had to contend. Investment and pricing decisions, for instance, have had to be consistent with the requirements of the White Papers of 1967, 1976 and 1978 (mainly concerning marginal cost pricing and achieving a given rate of return on new investment) and the criterion of political acceptability considered along with commercial viability.

Easing the problem of public sector pay is also considered a significant advantage. The Conservatives, in particular, claim that governments should not be involved directly or indirectly in pay negotiations. Wage rates should be determined by market forces and this is facilitated by privatisation.

The related aims of widening share ownership and employee share ownership (objectives *v* and *vi*) encompass both economic and political objectives. Economically, they provide an incentive for employees to work efficiently in order to improve the value of their shares and to be the recipients of well-earned dividends. It is a means of inseparably uniting organisational performance and individual self-interest. This should have benefits at both macro and micro levels in that the economy grows with improved industrial performance. The political dimension to this – the share-owning democracy – is perhaps to encourage people to appreciate and defend the merits of a particular political and economic system ('popular capitalism'). In so doing they would also logically support the political party which had made it all possible - the Conservative Party (political advantage as identified by Vickers & Yarrow).

The point concerning improved profits through diversification is that when faced with contracting markets a private firm would seek ways of diversifying in an attempt to find new markets. However, nationalised industries are not only statutorily debarred from diversifying but also, it is argued, they have no incentive to do so because, unlike firms in the private sector, persistently poor performance leads to increased governmental subsidies rather than liquidation. Moore (1992 p9) states the case simply: '. . . a nationalised industry does not have to succeed to survive, and everyone in it knows it.'

The remaining objectives (*ie* objective *ii* plus the point concerning fiscal policy) must be seen within the context of Conservative policies concerning taxation and public expenditure. Whether one agrees with the objectives (*eg* reducing direct taxation) is not at issue here but it is important to appreciate that the policy of privatisation facilitated governmental attempts to achieve related economic objectives.

Critique of Privatisation

The objectives identified have varying degrees of validity. The microeconomic arguments concerning the merits of competition are theoretically sound but there are several caveats. Firstly, nationalised industries and those in which the state had a substantial shareholding were not, in fact, totally free from competition. In some cases – *eg* cars, shipbuilding, steel, international airlines – there was quite intense competition domestically, internationally or both. Secondly, in the case of commodities such as gas, electricity and telecommunications, single-supplier industries may make economic sense given the type of network upon which production depends and from which economies of scale can be experienced. Because of the nature of the market for these commodities privatisation may not have resulted in any real increase in competition but rather the substitution of a private for a public monopoly.

The microeconomic merits of privatisation should also have led to improved performance. Several points can be made here. Firstly, although the Labour Party was ideologically-committed to public ownership (particularly after the Second World War), there was also an economic argument put forward in its favour, *ie* the failure to achieve allocative efficiency. This failure was due to two factors: the monopolistic character of certain industries and the existence, in certain cases, of non-commercial objectives (*eg* social benefits) which meant that some outputs should be produced even though the associated costs were not recovered. The opportunity cost of achieving allocative efficiency may have been a loss of productive efficiency but there is no inherent reason why a privately-owned monopoly has a greater incentive to achieve productive efficiency than a publicly-owned one.

Secondly, there is no unambiguous evidence that privately-owned companies always perform better in a competitive market than publicly-owned ones. The evidence is mixed. Vickers and Yarrow (1988 pp41–42) refer to a study of two Canadian railroad companies (published in 1980) – one privately- and the other publicly-owned. The study concludes 'public ownership is not inherently less-efficient than private ownership' and that the 'oft noted inefficiency of government enterprises stems from the isolation from effective competition rather than public ownership *per se*'. However, Vickers and Yarrow refer to other work which indicates that private companies perform better in competitive environments than public ones. On the basis of US and more limited UK studies Vickers and Yarrow (1988 p43) conclude that 'evidence suggests that private enterprise is generally to be preferred on both internal efficiency . . . and social welfare grounds . . . [but] . . . this does not mean that, in competitive markets, we believe that public enterprise is always and everywhere the less efficient type of owner-ship.' In assessing the research, Kay and Thompson (1987 p269) conclude that 'no simple generalization about superiority of private sector performance can be sustained. But there is support for the view that the efficiency of all firms – public or private – is improved by a competitive environment.'

This leads to a more specific point concerning the performance of the industries which have been privatised. Again, definitive conclusions cannot be reached but any identified differences in performance pre- and post-privatisation could not, in the main, be attributable to market forces. It may be argued that the Conservatives have been more concerned with changing ownership than with increasing competition. This reflects the nature of the industries concerned – effectively giving a choice between public ownership or regulated private ownership – and this should be recognised. Rees (1986 p25) concludes: 'Privatisation ι . . is associated with continued restrictions on the possibility of competition and the avoidance of the kinds of structural change which might increase the pressures of market forces.' Seven years on, this conclusion may still be regarded as valid.

Insofar as performance has improved it is necessary to identify the measures indicating this but also to remember the reasons why industries were nationalised originally and the circumstances within which they have operated (notably relevant here is the issue of political interference). In assessing the relevant statistics, Johnson (1991 p167) concludes that 'the performance of the privatised sector improved, but so did that of the private sector and the remaining public corporation sector . . . Much of the improvement due to privatisation might have been secured in its absence, and there could have been an even greater improvement in all types of companies' performance had competition had more of a cutting edge' (see also Kay & Thompson 1987 pp270-277).

Consistent with the arguments in favour of privatisation, it might also be contended that the depoliticisation of decision-making has been a contributory factor to any improvement in performance. However, transfer of ownership does not eliminate political involvement or result in *laissez-faire* given the regulatory agencies which have to be estab-lished and the shares which the state retains. In fact, Fine and Poletti

(1992 p318) in a radical assessment of privatisation argue that the result is the worst possible outcome with extensive intervention – varying with the industry under consideration – combined with weakened political control. They state that 'Regulation is . . . industrial policy by other means – but limited in scope, power and accountability. This "half-way" reform has at once precluded the realisation of a coherent institutional system for the direction of industry.' The short- and long-term implications of this are debatable but the underlying point about the existence and extent of governmental intervention is valid.

The argument concerning profit-improvement through diversification and risk of bankruptcy is also somewhat flawed. Firstly, it is not an argument against nationalised industries *per se* because the law could easily be changed to allow them to diversify. Secondly, it is not really credible to argue that the threat of bankruptcy forces privatised industries to be efficient. It is inconceivable, for instance, that British Gas or British Telecom would ever be allowed to go bankrupt assuming they ever found themselves in such an unlikely hypothetical situation.

The belief that privatisation eases the problem of public sector pay determination is a valid one. Even though pay negotiations were meant to be confined to the boards of nationalised industries and the relevant unions, in reality government was always involved.

The view that wider share-ownership is politically desirable is subjective; whether it is economically beneficial is debatable. It raises questions concerning the level of shareownership – is there a level above which economic benefits will be evident? Is there an optimum level? In the UK the number of shareholders rose from just over 2 million in 1979 to 10.6 million in 1990.

However, the percentage of total shares held by the personal sector actually fell over the period from 54% to 20% (see *The Observer* 21 October 1990 reporting on a CBI Task Force document '*A Nation of Shareholders*', 1990). In other words, privatisation has increased the number of shareholders but the proportion of total holdings held by individuals has fallen dramatically. Additionally, of the 10.6 million shareholders more than half – 6.5 million – owned just one share and as little as 300,000 owned portfolios containing more than 10 shares. These findings prompted the chairman of the CBI Task Force, Sir Peter Thompson, to say:

'Like many others, I suspect, I thought that the 1980s was the decade when popular capitalism really took root in the UK. Driven by the privatisation programme the number of shareholders had increased threefold. The seeds had apparently been planted and all that was required was to sit back and wait for the harvest. The reality is very different. Millions of the new investors have never traded a share, nor do they know how. They only own one or two shares bought in the generously priced and heavily marketed privatisation issue. They tend to see share ownership rather as a sophisticated gamble than as a long-term investment in the wealth-creating process.' (Quoted in *The Observer*, 21 Oct 1990).

This view is an echo of a finding three years earlier by Buckland (1987 p255) whose evidence supports the view that 'privatization will make little long-term impact upon personal share ownership in the UK. It illustrates that the personal sector applicants have not gained significantly from the programme; indeed it is the institutional applicant which increasingly dominates and profits from the sale arrangements.'

The macroeconomic merits of privatisation also largely depend upon the desirability of the objectives they supposedly further. The revenue can be used in several ways – invested, used to finance public sector asset creation or reductions in taxation, debt repayment, reductions in public borrowing or whatever. However, it is economically sensible to take a long-term view; revenue should not be treated as a lucrative windfall but invested in a way which yields future streams of income thereby compensating for the profits foregone of formerly nationalised industries.

There are other important considerations – the cost of privatisation including underwriting, marketing, professional advice, discounts on shares, and writing-off public corporation debt. Johnson (1991 pp162–163) estimates these at approximately £20bn in total. The need for continued regulation also has a cost.

All these points need to be considered when assessing – the merits of privatisation but, before doing this, it is necessary to consider the second policy relevant to this chapter – competitive tendering.

Competitive tendering – definition

Competitive tendering is the process by which private contractors have traditionally competed with each other in an attempt to be awarded a particular contract. Recently, however, services normally provided by public sector organisations have also been subject to competitive tendering. This has involved an in-house team competing against private contractors for a service it previously provided.

The term 'competitive tendering' is sometimes used interchangeably with the term 'contracting-out'. This, however, may refer to a political decision to transfer a service to a private contractor irrespective of the cost *vis-a-vis* in-house provision. Competitive tendering implies the existence of an in-house tender.

Background to Competitive Tendering
There is nothing new about competitive tendering; it can, in fact, be seen within the context of public procurement policy *ie* public sector purchases of goods and services from the private sector. There is a long tradition of the National Health Service (NHS) purchasing pharmaceutical products and hi-tech medical equipment from private companies. Similarly, the Ministry of Defence purchases a vast range of equipment and services from the private sector. However, the process became increasingly politicised after the election of the Conservatives in 1979.

Prior to this, competitive tendering measures were essentially pragmatic, ad hoc responses to identified needs but the 1980s witnessed systematic attempts by central government to impose compulsory competitive tendering (CCT) particularly upon local government and the NHS because of its assumed inherent merits. The relevant legislation for local authorities is the 1980 Local Government Planning and Land Act, the 1988 Local Government Act and the 1992 Local Government Act. For the NHS, CCT was introduced in 1983 and has since been gradually expanded by means of circular rather than legislation. In addition the Government published two consultation documents in 1991, to accompany the Local Government Bill which was enacted in 1992, *ie Competing for Quality: Competition in the Provision of Local Services; Competing for Quality: Buying Better Public Services* and *The Citizen's Charter: Raising The Standard.*

The 1980 Local Government Planning and Land Act required local authority Direct Labour Organisations (DLOs) to compete with private contractors for certain building and works contracts. To win a contract the DLO had to submit the lowest tender, thereafter a financial rate of return (specified by the Secretary of State) had to be achieved. Throughout the 1980s the application of the Act was extended, as evidenced by the 1988 Local Government Act. The Act lists 'defined activities' including refuse collection, cleaning of buildings, street cleaning, schools and welfare catering, grounds maintenance, vehicle repair and maintenance, which must be put out to tender if estimated gross annual expenditure exceeds a specified minimum level. In addition, the Secretary of State has the power to add activities to the list (*eg* the management of sport and leisure facilities was added in Dec 1989). The main services affected in the NHS have been the 'hotel' ones *ie* cleaning, catering and laundry.

The Local Government Act 1992 and the preceding consultation documents aim, *inter alia*, to increase competition by extending the principle of CCT to a range of services in both local government (Cmnd 1730 pp22–26) and the NHS (Cmnd 1730 pp14–22) including direct public services (*eg* libraries, theatre management), construction-related professional services (*eg* architecture, engineering, property management), and internal services (*eg* finance, legal, personnel, information technology).

There is also an important European dimension. EC (European Community) directives on contracting for supplies and works have been in force since the 1970s and have important implications for public bodies in that they lay-down procedural rules which must be followed. It is anticipated that a new public service Directive will come into effect in 1993 (see Terry 1992; Digings 1992).

The extension of CCT application reflects the Conservative belief that it is desirable in principle and has proved to be so in practice. It is necessary to consider whether this is the case.

Objectives of Competitive Tendering
The merits of CCT overlap with those identified earlier in assessing privatisation (*viz* microeconomic). The central objective is to achieve 'value for money' and it is assumed that the *sine qua non* is competition. The Conservatives believe that competition exposes waste and in-efficiency in the public sector and leads to new standards being set. Related economic benefits include:

(i)   competitive tendering may lead to contracting out and it may be assumed that commercial organisations provide a better and more economical service as they compete with each other;

(ii)   even where services are retained in-house, the process of CCT compels public authorities critically to consider the cost and level of existing service provision and forces public managers to become more commercially-oriented (INLOGOV 1990);

(iii) contracting out leads to the replacement of direct labour by private companies thereby reducing the size of public sector manpower and placing pressure on the workforce to adopt flexible working practices and accept sensible pay awards;

(iv) it leads to lowering of wage expectations facilitating control of inflation;

(v) control of public expenditure, particularly local authority expenditure, is also helped as money is saved by putting contracts out to tender.

These economic benefits are reinforced by the political attractiveness of the policy to the Conservatives. It can be seen as a way of reducing public sector manpower and weakening the power of trades unions – whether operating in the public sector (loss of members and therefore inability to protect take-home pay) or the private sector (fragmentation of members across numerous firms reducing bargaining strength or, perhaps, leading to non-recognition). It is debatable whether the policy was primarily based on the purported economic advantages which coincided with ideologically-desirable political benefits or vice versa (see Ascher 1987 pp47–49). The arguments against competitive tendering include the costs involved in-house in preparing the specification and evaluating the tenders, combined with the adverse impact on the morale of the workforce in the interim. In addition, there is the risk of loss-leader activity whereby a private contractor may submit an uneconomic bid in order to undercut the in-house tender so as to establish a foothold. In so doing the public authority may in the future become dependent upon a private sector monopoly which can then raise prices (loss of a contract may be irreversible for a public authority given the laying-off or transfer of staff and the disposal of equipment which is likely to ensue).

Private contractors may also achieve savings by offering lower wages, worsening working conditions and cutting jobs. Public authorities begin the tendering process at a disadvantage given the labour-intensive nature of many services and their commitment to nationally-determined wage levels. In other words, savings to the local taxpayer, for instance, may be at the expense of poorly-paid members of society. This raises fundamental economic questions of equity and income distribution though these issues can be addressed by central government by other means (*eg* fiscal transfers).

Insofar as competitive tendering results in lower wages and, perhaps, unemployment, the cost in terms of public finances and economic activity also needs to be quantified *eg* transfer payments (unemployment and related benefits), reduced tax revenues (direct and indirect), impact upon private sector activity *etc*. Such calculations may reveal a 'loss' to the economy exceeding the 'gains' to the public authority resulting from competitive tendering. However, where unemployment has resulted, the economic justification is that in the long-term the unemployed should secure employment at a wage and in industries where demand for their labour exists.

Finally, there may be serious reservations about the reliability and quality of certain private contractors. Doubts may be eliminated, or at least alleviated, by careful vetting of contractors – perhaps inviting only certain ones to tender – but statutory requirements may circumscribe public authority freedom in this respect.

There are, therefore, several points which can be made for and against CCT (see Parker and Hartley 1990) but it is important to focus on economic issues rather than political. Instinctive support or opposition on the basis of right- or left-wing views largely misses the point. Competitive tendering in both central and local government and the health service was well-established prior to the Conservative's election victory of 1979. This does not mean that policy since 1979 has been devoid of ideological content or universally acceptable. The compulsory nature of competitive tendering has antagonised local and health authorities. However, it does mean that the origins of competitive tendering can not be traced to a national political event fourteen years ago. It is also relevant to note that the Government could have chosen mandatory contracting-out as opposed to CCT had it been motivated exclusively by dogma.

Critique of Competitive Tendering
The Government remains 'convinced that the widest possible application of competition will benefit the local taxpayer and consumer of services alike' (Cmnd 1599 1991 p34) and there is some empirical evidence to support this view. Domberger, Meadowcroft and Thompson (1986) estimated that CCT by local authorities had reduced the cost of refuse collection services by an average of 20% irrespective of whether contracts are awarded in- house or to private contractors. Subsequent research by Cubbin, Domberger and Meadowcroft (1987) revealed that these savings were efficiency gains stemming largely from greater productivity of inputs. Domberger,

Meadowcroft and Thompson (1987) conclude that achievable cost reductions in respect of hospital domestic services are likely to be approximately 20%. Hartley and Huby (1985) revealed yearly savings to local authorities and health authorities averaging 26%. Thompson (1990) estimates savings to local authorities of 20%.

Other economists, however, have reservations about the impact of CCT. Ganley and Grahl (1988) challenge the conclusions of Domberger, Meadowcroft and Thompson (1986) by querying the 'source' of the cost reductions *eg* losers among the workforce, loss-leading and reductions in the level of service. Similarly, Hartley (1987 p160) when considering the size of cost savings from contracting-out states that 'much of the existing evidence fails to compare like with like; it is politically-biased, based on casual empiricism and often reflects American experience.' He proceeds to point out that savings are often the result of lower employment, reduced pay and fringe benefits and greater use of part-time staff. However, he also refers to the contribution of better organisation and more modern equipment. This illustrates the point that the economic research should encompass all costs and benefits to the community resulting from CCT. This, in turn, raises all the problems of cost-benefit analysis – not least the identification and valuation of all costs and benefits – but too narrow an approach reduces the validity of any findings.

CCT may have resulted in savings to local and health authorities but it has not effected a substantial shift of service provision from the public to the private sector. On the contrary, research by the Joint NHS Privatisation Unit (1990) has revealed that health authorities have won approximately 77% of all contracts put out to tender since 1983. Similarly, as can be seen from Table 5.2, the Local Government Management Board (1991) has shown that local authority DSOs (Direct Service Organisations) have won 69.7% of a survey of 2558 contracts – equivalent to 84.3% of contract value – in the first four rounds of CCT. Further evidence of the effect of CCT has been provided by the Institute of Public Finance (1992). The findings are largely consistent with those of the Local Government Management Board:

Table 5.2

Local Authority Compulsory Competitive Tendering

Activity	Direct Labour % of contracts	Organisation Success % of contract value
Building cleaning	59.8	85.9
Refuse collection	72.8	78.7
Other cleaning	75.2	81.0
Vehicle maintenance	76.9	85.7
Catering (education and welfare)	98.5	99.4
Catering (other)	75.4	78.9
Ground maintenance	68.6	82.2
Overall	69.7	84.3

Source: Local Government Management Board, *Compulsory Competitive Tendering Survey* as reported in Financial Times, 13 May 1991

It must be pointed out, however, that any shift from the public to the private sector may be said to be of importance and certainly a shift of 30.3% as revealed above could be said to be significant. This point is reinforced by the assumed efficiency gains which result from the process even if the contract remains in-house.

It is also interesting to note that the Local Government Management Board revealed significant variations between activities in terms of competition. For instance, catering (education and welfare) was the least competitive, averaging 1.2 tenders per contract with the DSOs winning 72.8% of contracts without competition. In contrast, refuse collection was the most competitive averaging 3.4 tenders per contract with only 10% being won by the DSOs without competition. There were also marked regional variations which actually corresponded to councils' political control. For instance, in Labour-dominated Wales and also Yorkshire and Humberside the DSOs won 100% of refuse collection contracts. This contrasts with less than two-thirds success in Conservative-inclined East Anglia and the south-east. More detailed information is given in Table 5.3.

Despite this in-house success, note that the main economic objective of CCT was to improve efficiency rather than transfer contracts to the private sector. Though it is not possible to say that this has been achieved, the Government wishes to extend CCT on the basis of alleged savings and also, for local government, because it is consistent with the type of authority which it intends to create ie 'enabling authority'. Such an authority acts as purchaser of services rather than a direct provider.

Table 5.3

Refuse Collection Contracts

Area	Direct Labour % of contracts	Organisation Success no. of contracts
Northern	78.3	18
Yorks and Humberside	100.0	14
North-west	73.1	19
East Midlands	68.6	24
West Midlands	82.8	24
East Anglia	65.0	13
South-east	64.4	47
South-west	71.1	27
Wales	100.0	21
London	57.7	15

Source: as Table 5.2

Unsurprisingly, this meets with the opposition of local authorities which do not accept the justification for such a role and, along with health authorities, emphasise the inadequacies of private contractors.

Privatisation: conclusion

Privatisation in terms of transfer of ownership and sale of share-holdings has been popular with the public and beneficial politically. The policy is obviously associated with the Conservatives and has provided the opportunity to finance reductions in taxation through proceeds generated (this is not to state a causal relationship but merely to highlight the opportunities created by the magnitude of the revenue involved). The inherent economic benefits, however, require closer examination, especially in the cases of large monopolistic public utilities which may not be subject to real competition, unlike other companies which have been privatised (Jaguar, Britoil, Amersham for example).

There may often be a significant difference between hypothesised merits and their practical realisation but perhaps this particularly applies in the case of privatisation given the overlap with political ideology. There is some validity in the statement of Rees (1986 p19): 'Prior political beliefs lead to acceptance or rejection of these hypotheses in spite of the absence of evidence . . .'

The lack of evidence also applies to compulsory competitive tendering. More research is required which considers not only the impact on the cost-effectiveness of the local or health authority concerned but also the wider economic issues *viz* external costs and benefits.

The direction of Governmental policy over the next five years is, however, clear in the light of the general election. Denationalisation will continue and compulsory competitive tendering will be extended, particularly to central government and to professional services. Both main opposition parties will have to respond to these developments in local and by-elections between now and the next general election in 1996 or 1997. On the basis of 1992, the Labour Party had no plans for nationalisation other than returning the National Grid and Water to 'public control' (Labour Party 1992 p13 & p21) and rejected Conservative plans for privatising British Rail and British Coal. Labour also rejected compulsory competitive tendering for hospital support services and local authorities (Labour Party 1992 p16 & p20) but proposed the establishment of a Quality Commission which would have had the power, *inter alia*, to force authorities to subject a service to tender where this was considered necessary on the basis of inadequate local provision. The Liberal Democrats sought to strengthen a reformed local government and assign to it greater responsibilities 'to ensure the delivery of services in ways they think best' (Liberal Democrats 1992 p49). They also sought to 'break-up the monopoly providers of services such as British Telecom and British Gas . . . permit access by private operators to the British Rail track network . . . liberalise the coal industry [by] issuing licences to operate pits to other groups, as well as British Coal' (Liberal Democrats 1992 p21). Both Labour and the Liberal Democrats were committed to encouraging employee share ownership.

The opposition manifestos of 1992, particularly Labour's, are significant as much for what they exclude as for what they include. Labour, for instance, no longer attaches doctrinal importance to nationalisation, reflecting a shift in political priorities. The scale and popularity of privatisation has been important in this respect. Although it is not possible to predict the nature of the policies on which Labour or Liberal Democrats will fight the next election, they will nonetheless be formulated in response to further privatisations and changes to the structure of the NHS and the role and functions of local authorities. Whichever party is in power at the end of the 1990s, privatisation is an issue on which there is likely to be a degree of consensus. This could not have been predicted in the early 1980's. However, despite this decadal shift in opinion, perhaps no aspect of privatisation should be regarded as politically irreversible.

References

Ascher, K (1987) *The Politics of Privatisation: Contracting out Public Services*, Macmillan

Buckland, R (1987) 'The Costs And Returns Of The Privatization Of Nationalized Industries', *Public Administration* Vol 65 No 3 pp241–257.

Cable, J R (1986), 'Industry', *The UK Economy: A Manual of Applied Economics*, 11th edition, Artis M J (Ed), Weidenfeld and Nicolson

Command 1730 (1991) *Competing for Quality: Buying Better Public Services*, HMSO

Command 1599 (1991) *The Citizen's Charter: Raising The Standard*, HMSO

Conservative Party (1979) (1983) (1987) (1992), *The Conservative Manifesto*, Conservative Central Office

Cubbin J, Domberger S & Meadowcroft S (1987) 'Competitive Tendering and Refuse Collection: Identifying the Sources of Efficiency Gains' *Fiscal Studies* Vol 8 No 3 pp49–58.

Digings, L (1992) 'Tendering the European Way' *Public Finance and Accountancy* 29 May 1992 pp53–54

Domberger S, Meadowcroft S & Thompson D (1987) 'The Impact of Competitive Tendering on the Costs of Hospital Domestic Services' *Fiscal Studies* Vol 8 No 4 pp39–54

Domberger S, Meadowcroft S & Thompson D (1986) 'Competitive Tendering and Efficiency: the Case of Refuse Collection' *Fiscal Studies* Vol 7 No 4 pp69–87

Efficiency Gains' *Fiscal Studies* Vol 8 No 3 pp49–58

Fine, B & Poletti, C (1992) 'Industrial Prospects in the Light of Privatisation' in *The Economic Legacy 1979–1992*, Michie, J (Ed) Academic Press: Harcourt Brace Jovanovich pp315–330

Ganley, J & Grahl, J (1988) 'Competition and Efficiency in Refuse Collection: A Critical Comment' *Fiscal Studies* Vol 9 No 1 pp80–85

Hartley, K (1987) 'Competitive Tendering', *Public Domain: A yearbook for the public sector*, Jackson P & Terry F (Eds) Public Finance Foundation pp 156–166

Hartley, K & Huby, M (1985) 'Contracting-Out in Health and Local Authorities: prospects, progress and pitfalls', *Public Money* September 1985 pp23–26, Public Finance Foundation pp 23–26

Heald, D & Thomas, D (1986) 'Privatization as Theology' *Public Policy and Administration* Vol 1 No 2 1986 pp49–66

Heald, D (1984) 'Privatisation: analysing its appeals and limitations', *Fiscal Studies* Vol 5 No 1 pp36–46

INLOGOV (Institute of Local Government Studies) (1990), *Competition for local government services: a summary report of initial research findings*, Dept of Environment

Institute of Public Finance (1992) *The Competitive Edge: Early Trends in CCT*, Chartered Institute of Public Finance and Accountancy

Johnson, C (1991) *The Economy Under Mrs Thatcher 1979–1990*, Penguin

Joint NHS Privatisation Unit (1990) *The NHS privatisation experience*, as reported in *Public Finance and Accountancy* 27 April 1990

Jones C (Ed) (1989) 'Privatisation', *Review* Vol 10 No 2, Indiana University

Kay, J & Thompson, D (1987) 'Privatization: a Policy in Search of a Rationale' in *Politics and Economic Policy*, Gillie A, Levacic R & Thompson G (Eds), Hodder and Stoughton pp261–279

Kay, J A et al (1986) *Privatisation and Regulation: The UK Experience*, Oxford: Oxford University Press

Kay, J A & Silberston, Z A (1984) 'The New Industrial Policy – Privatisation and Competition' *Midland Bank Review*, Spring pp8–16

Labour Party (1992) *Labour's election manifesto*, The Labour Party

Libenstein, H (1976) *Beyond Economic Man*, Cambridge Mass.: Harvard University Press

Liberal Democrats (1992) *The Liberal Democrat Manifesto*, Liberal Democrat Publications

Local Government Management Board (1991) *Compulsory Competitive Tendering Survey 3*, as reported in *Financial Times* 13 May 1991

Marsh, D (1991) 'Privatisation Under Mrs Thatcher: A Review Of

The Literature' *Public Administration* Vol 69 No 4 pp459–480

Moore, J (1992) *Privatisation Everywhere: the world's adoption of the British experience*, Centre for Policy Studies

Parker D & Hartley K (1990) 'Competitive Tendering: Issues and Evidence' *Public Money & Management*, Public Finance Foundation Vol 10 No 3 pp9–16

Pirie, M (1985) *Privatization*, Adam Smith Institute

Rees, R (1986) 'Is There an Economic Case for Privatisation?' *Public Money*, March 1986 pp19–26

Swann, D (1988) *The Retreat Of The State: Deregulation And Privatisation In The UK And US*, Harvester Wheatsheaf

Terry, F (1992) 'The Single Market and Public Services' *Public Domain: The Public Services Yearbook* Terry F and Jackson P (Eds) Public Finance Foundation pp189–207

Thompson, D (1990) *The Tender Traps*, Adam Smith Institute

Treasury HM (1986) 'Privatisation overseas' *Economic Progress Report* No 183 March-April

Treasury HM (1992) *Public Expenditure Analyses to 1994–95: Statistical Supplement to the 1991 Autumn Statement*, HMSO

Veljanovski, C (1987) *Selling the State: Privatisation in Britain*, Weidenfeld & Nicolson

Vickers, J & Yarrow, G (1985) *Privatization and the Natural Monopolies*, London

Vickers, J & Yarrow, G (1988) *Privatization: An Economic Analysis*, Cambridge, Massachusetts Institute of Technology

Yarrow, G (1986) 'Privatization in Theory and Practice' *Economic Policy* Vol 2 pp324–377

Acknowledgement

The author wishes to thank Dr John Thompson of The Liverpool Business School for his comments on an earlier draft of this chapter.

CHAPTER SIX

REGULATION

David Gardner

Introduction

Regulation describes the imposition of controls, restraints, and rules in a way which directs or curtails the freedom of action of bodies or individuals in the private and/or public sectors (Swann, 1988). Its use, primarily by the state, but also by supranational bodies like the European Commission, has ebbed and flowed over the course of the twentieth century as state concern over the risk of abuse of power by corporate and public agencies has varied. This has meant that regulation has increased in some areas of the economy such as in the broadcasting industry, whilst simultaneously receding in others such as in passenger transport. The United Kingdom in the 1980s exemplifies this phenomenon. The government from 1979 saw great merit in enhancing competition by reducing state regulation, yet recognised the need to protect the consumer, particularly in the case of the newly privatised public utilities, such as telecommunications after 1983.

Justification for Intervention in a Market Economy

Regulation is one of two practical responses (the other being public ownership) to the fact that, in a market economy, whilst the provision of goods and services by a monopolistic concern is open to an abuse of power, to the detriment of the consumer, extreme forms of competitive provision (near perfect competition) may fail to provide a satisfactory alternative.

Microeconomic theory argues for production to be organised according to the economists' ideal of perfect competition, in that it maximises productive efficiency by minimising the cost of resource inputs used to produce a given output, and ensures the optimal match between goods produced and sold, and people's wants, thereby maximising societies' sense of well being when all production is organised in this way.

However, monopolistic organisations in the economy fall well short of this ideal. The monopolist has power to restrict his output or increase his prices in order to maximise his 'monopoly' profits, those above profits normally earned by perfectly competitive firms over time. The resulting accumulation of wealth in the hands of a small number of monopolists is hardly equitable, and may result in an unhealthy concentration of economic and political power. Restricted output ensures that consumers' wants are not fully met, resulting in a loss of social welfare. The absence of competitive pressures means that a restraint on cost levels is absent and costs may tend to rise over time, (a phenomenon described as 'X-inefficiency' in Liebenstein,1966), whilst the absence of competition eliminates choice for the consumer. All in all, the ideal of perfect competition and rivalry is much preferred to monopoly. Where monopoly unavoidably arises, it is argued that the state is justified in intervening to prevent or minimise its abuses.

Perfect competition is not, however, observed in the real world. The very restrictive assumptions made by economists in order to provide a workable analytical model are not realised together, (see Sloman, 1991 pp190–201). There are instances where competitive market provision of goods and services may fail to achieve the beneficial consequences of perfect competition in a serious way. In short, even without monopoly, markets fail in a number of ways, the four major ones being summarised below.

First, externalities can arise. They are the effects on other people's well-being arising incidentally out of the production or consumption of a commodity. They can be beneficial or disbeneficial. Beneficial externalities may well lead to underproduction. An example of this is where a doctor provides and sells innoculations against a contagious disease. In addition to the benefit to the direct recipient, society as a whole benefits through the reduced risk of contracting the disease. An example of a disbeneficial externality is where producers have to be productively efficient, and use the lowest cost technology. Failure to do so may lead to extinction in a competitive market. Minimum private/internal costs, however, may lead to other costs, such as pollution costs, imposed on third parties. When the costs of these externalities are added to private costs, they make up the social costs of an activity. They are not taken into account in the determination of market prices and hence misallocations of the commodities can arise. Proposals for eliminating the effects of the externality through taxes, subsidies or the bestowing of property rights, whilst attractive in theory, are potentially cumbersome and costly administratively.

Secondly, there are certain goods and services the consumption of which is non-excludable and non-rival, and which are non-depletable, not lending themselves to competitive provision. These are 'Public Goods' which, when supplied to one individual or group, must be supplied to others or all, including those who may not want them, or do not benefit from them. Examples are defence goods, street lighting and public parks. People realise that they can obtain the goods whilst denying that they wish to consume, becoming 'free riders'. The activity becomes underfunded and undersupplied. Government cannot allow this to occur in the case of activities providing goods and services deemed to be essential. The market has clearly failed to provide these goods effectively. Thirdly, for other goods, imperfect knowledge, in particular consumer ignorance, prevents effective provision of an activity in a competitive market. A good may be so technically complex that the average consumer is unable to relate benefits from consumption with the price he or she has to pay, undermining the efficient working of the market which depends on consumers revealing their preferences at the market price. Health care is an example of this; not everyone has a degree in medicine. For some goods, for instance health care provided to individuals who pay through insurance arrangements, there is a separation in time between payment and consumption, which again inhibits the consumer's ability to judge the worth of the good. For others, for example primary and secondary education, under market provision, the consumer of the service (the child) is not the same person as the customer who pays for the service (the parent). This clearly presents a limitation to the payer's ability to evaluate the service in quality and quantity terms.

Finally, in some industries, economies of scale are so great that it would be uneconomic and unreasonable to force competition on them. These are the so-called 'natural monopolies' which, given that many occur in essential public service activities, like gas supply, despite an element of indirect competition from other energy sources, cannot be left to exploit the consumer, who is unlikely to agree that monopoly profits represent no loss to society. There needs to be a mechanism to push this monopolist towards productive (X-) efficiency and technical progress, and to control price structures.

All these instances and others demonstrate that, even in the absence of monopoly in markets, there are sufficient imperfections to prevent the idealised advantages of market provision from being realised. In the more serious instances of market failure, and under monopoly, the state is justified in intervening to protect the public interest.

Is Public Ownership the answer?

There are two principal, realistic ways in which the state might intervene. They are where the state takes and exercises regulatory powers over such activities, or where it assumes ownership over them. The case for public ownership is very well documented (for example, see Swann, 1988, pp75–85). It is seen as a solution for natural monopoly industries. It is compatible with political philosophies that encompass the state's coordination of the activities of large productive entities, and very large scale capital investment. It is a convenient approach when the government is an industry's largest customer, and provides a means of protecting national security when 'sensitive' industries are involved, for example in manufacturing defence goods.

However, there are strong arguments against the use of public ownership, not the least of which is the view that it perpetuates monopoly, which can be abused as easily under public ownership as it can under private control. It artificially protects the industry from the threat of corporate takeover and bankruptcy, which would otherwise serve to sharpen up the performance of management. Public ownership exposes an industry to the risk of ministerial meddling for political ends (Swann, 1988, pp200–201), and leaves government exposed to trade union power and the political consequences of confrontation and pay settlement precedents. The trading performance of industries operating under these conditions can hardly be expected to be good. In the United Kingdom, over the post-1945 period, industries under public ownership have been characterised by trading losses, over-manning, low levels of internal investment, reliance on state subsidies, and poor industrial relations (Pryke,1981). Government frustration at its inability to eliminate these features contributed significantly to the privatisation developments of the 1980s (Swann, 1988, pp199–200. See also Chapter Five).

Since privatisation, over the late 1980's, 'the financial performance of the regulated (privatised) industries has, in general, exceeded prospectus forecasts' (Vass, 1992, p211). Their turnover and profitability have been very good, with outstanding rates of return in many cases, reaching 22.4% in 1990/91 in the case of British Telecom, though this may suggest an inadequacy in the regulatory machinery in combating the use of monopoly power. Nevertheless, regulated privately owned productive industry appears to be an attractive proposition, when viewed against the failings of public ownership, and it is not surprising that in the UK and elsewhere in recent years there has been a major tendency for the state to withdraw from involvement in industrial ownership, preferring to rely on regulation.

Approaches to Regulation – Some Misconceptions
It is not unreasonable for people to see regulation in terms of the state regulating private productive industrial concerns. However, there are numerous instances where private concerns establish arrangements to regulate themselves (Baggott, 1989). It must be said, though, that many cases of self regulation are 'encouraged' by government under implied threat of direct regulatory action by the state, for instance in the case of the professions, such as accountancy in the 1970s and 1980s, and in the case of the travel business and ABTA. Self regulation can occur where private firms recognise a marketing benefit from being seen to comply with safety, conduct, or food content rules, or with environmental standards devised by themselves. An example occurred in the 1980s when B.P. advertised the reinstatement of pipeline sites to their natural state. It can occur when competition law is incomplete in its coverage, and associations of firms step in to regulate pricing or market participation in their own industries. Examples here include the regulation of airline ticket prices and routes by the International Air Transport Authority (IATA), and, until the mid 1980s, stock jobbing and dealing by the Stock Exchange Council.

Another public misconception is that regulation is carried out by the state on private firms and individuals only. There are a number of public bodies which are, constitutionally in an 'arm's length' relationship with central government, yet are large enough to have an impact on the economy. Amongst these are Public Corporations, the agencies of the National Health Service, and Local Authorities. Clearly, it is imperative that the public interest is served by ensuring the maintenance of service standards by preventing the abuse of monopoly power, national or local, and by ensuring that the best use is made of public money, in terms of rates of return, efficiency and effectiveness, and value for money. Hence, extensive regulatory mechanisms exist in these areas. Amongst them are Standard Spending Assessments, capital spending controls and Charge Capping for local government, resource allocation formulae and performance indicators for health authorities, Required Rates of Return, and Financial Targets for public corporations, though the principal reasons for their use extends well beyond the prevention of monopoly abuse towards macroeconomic management and the achievement of 'political' leverage.

With the above exceptions, regulation does involve state agencies regulating private bodies or individuals. (Within this is included regulation by the super state, the European Community, the E.C.). It can take the form (Swann, 1988,pp27–28) of Anti-Trust regulation to counter the abuse of monopoly power, through the work of bodies like the Monopolies and Mergers Commission (dating from 1948), and the Office of Fair Trading (established in 1973). Secondly, it can take the form of social regulation to protect the individual against the physical consequences of market failure, through environmental, public safety, anti-discrimination, or customer protection regulation. Thirdly, it can take the form of economic regulation, aimed at rectifying, or at least offsetting, the economic consequences of market failure, though some American economists argue that in practice it has had the opposite effect by worsening the consequences of market failure (Benston 1982, Llewellyn 1986).Measures include price controls, devices to increase competition or curb excessive competition, plus measures to maintain market stability in areas such as banking, essential to the smooth operation of the economy, and the agricultural sector, producing essentials for life, and to ease the process of economic adjustment and its effects on individuals.

The Economic Case for Regulation
There is a significant body of economic research (see Utton, 1986, Ch2) which has sought to analyse the origins of regulatory activity and to consider the strengths and weaknesses of regulation, especially the economic regulation of monopolistic industries, though it is inadequate in addressing other examples of market failure. This has led to the so-called 'Public Interest Theories'. They arise out of the need to prevent natural monopolies from exploiting their markets freely. They accept the inevitability of natural monopoly in certain circumstances, where there are significant economies of scale, and unit costs fall over normal output ranges. Two or more smaller entities could share the market, but it would be economically unstable, undesirable, and would run the risk of collusion to maintain prices at an artificially high level. Without collusion, competition would lead to price cutting, attempts to increase sales, and cost cutting, until other firms are driven out of the market,

and a single firm – a natural monopoly – remains, capable of exploiting the market to the full. Regulation is deemed essential on public interest grounds because monopoly profits, generated by high prices, are unacceptable for equity reasons, concentrating wealth in the hands of the few; losses in social well-being would arise through output restriction; and productive inefficiency would occur through the absence of competing firms to encourage management to curb costs. Regulation is therefore needed to restrain price, though this, as will be seen later, is not without its own problems.

Another thread of Public Interest Theory stems from the monopolist's ability, in certain circumstances, to engage in price discrimination, the charging of different prices to different parts of a market, where the separateness of those parts can be maintained (no trading between parts), and the parts are characterised by differing levels of responsiveness of demand to price changes. An Italian example is found in the Rome area where a public concern runs two rail routes on either side of the River Tiber from Rome to the coast. The river effectively separates the two. One takes locals to a coastal resort/dormitary town, the other takes tourists and business people, presumably with money to spare, to and from the international airport at a fare four times that on the other route, a very lucrative operation.

This phenomenon enables the monopolist to make even higher monopoly profits, and the arguments against monopoly are thus amplified. However, there are certain activities which would not be undertaken if price discrimination were not allowed, where costs are relatively high so that only by price discrimination can the monopolist hope to generate revenue sufficient to cover total cost. If this activity were an essential community service, it would be hard to justify its abolition, though its careful monitoring and regulation would be essential. Swann (1988, p68) quotes the example of a rural medical practice in this context.

Other instances where the public interest might be served by regulation include the following. In some activities, the natural characteristics of the market restrict the volume of competition. In broadcasting, the limited size of the radio and television wavebands has this effect. To prevent abuse by near-monopolistic concerns, regulation is needed. In other areas, there is a risk of excessive competition, undermining the stability of a sector upon which the whole economy depends, where a rush of business failures would seriously damage many other businesses and the health of the whole economy. Whilst this sector might not consist of a monopoly, there is a clear need to regulate the few participants to avoid the social cost of widespread business failure. The banking sector in the UK is an example of this. So are certain aspects of public transport, which have very heavy specialised fixed investment, and relatively low operating costs, such as the railways (Peterson, 1985), which are prone to price cutting in a recession, or where overcapacity exists. Finally, activities which are fundamental to life and yet are prone to severe instability are also suitable cases for regulation. The agricultural sector, with extreme supply fluctuations, is a good example. In other activities, the structure of the industry is unable to respond sufficiently quickly to changing demand conditions, without serious social and economic consequences. The coal and iron/steel industries have hence justified regulation in the recent past.

Towards a Case Against?
An alternative view is put forward in a number of 'Private Interest Group Theories'. Posner (1971, 1976) argued that there is much evidence to show that regulation is not strongly correlated with the incidence of monopoly and externalities. The alternative to regulation in the public interest is where it is supplied in response to demands by specific interest groups, who stand to gain from the outcome of regulatory law and decisions. Stigler (1975, p114) showed that 'as a rule, regulation is acquired by the industry and is designed and operated primarily for its benefit'. That benefit derives from the state's ability to extract money from some individuals to subsidise others, to restrict entry to the industry, to fix prices and to affect supply and demand for interdependent commodities. Stigler argued that regulation is the result of forces of supply and demand. Interest groups demand it to add to their wealth; politicians, keen to be re-elected, supply it in return for political votes, or party contributions. Peltzman (1976) reinforced this view. Clearly, this argument undermines a number of the benefits of regulation identified in the public interest theories.

A further private interest view is the 'Capture Theory'. Although regulators start out as guardians of the public interest, they may quickly succumb to the power and influence of the industry they are supposed to regulate, and finish up protecting it rather than the public (Utton 1986). This does not necessarily suggest that regulators are corrupt, rather that they come to identify with the concerns of the industry, and to depend on it for information, on which to judge its performance against regulatory criteria. This is never more apparent than in the run up to a review of regulatory criteria, for example, in the case of British Telecom in 1989. Russell and Shelton (1974) argue that regulators try to maximise their personal well-being, which may be a function of their survival needs – to curry favour to retain office, their need to assure their future after retirement, their need to preserve their reputations among peers and associates, and the need for them to maintain their integrity by not doing anything to offend their notion of the public interest. Bernstein (1955) argues that regulators ultimately become the tools of those they are supposed to regulate. Utton (1986, p22) identifies a 'mature regulated industry', where the regime is well established and 'regulation will be seen to work in favour of the members rather than correct a market failure and improve resource allocation. At this stage the outcome of both (private interest group) hypotheses will be the same'.

There are a number of other arguments either against the use of regulation, or which suggest that it is unnecessary, or could be avoided. The Chicago School of Friedman, Hayek, Stigler, and Posner criticised regulation as an attack on economic and political freedom (Swann, 1988, pp135–136); an insidious form of government intervention, for which, in many cases, there were market based alternatives, such as the use of franchising (Demsetz 1968), or the creation of private property rights (Coase 1960). The Contestable Markets Theory of Baumol (1982) argues that a competitive outcome is possible, even with only one firm in the industry, if that firm faces potential in addition to actual competition. This depends on the threat that firms can freely enter or leave the industry. For this to be so, sunk costs (heavy fixed equipment costs) need to be hived off, for example, in the case of the airline industry, the costs of terminal facilities, baggage handling, etc. The result is more flexibility in the industry, with competitors capable of 'hit and run' operations, whereby, if the principal airline were to raise prices, the result would be the immediate entry of new firms which could withdraw if prices were reduced. Under these circumstances, no price regulation would be necessary. Further, where economic regulation has existed for some time, consumer groups, who might expect to benefit, have been very critical of its use. In the USA, Ralph Nader, in the 1970s (Green, 1973) argued that regulation of the energy industry failed to discourage excessive consumption, and failed to deter pollution. However, his campaign pressed for more measures aimed at consumer protection. Others point to instances where deregulation has occurred without the serious economic consequences of mass instability or bankruptcies, that one might expect. In the UK, the road passenger transport industry and the Stock Exchange are sound examples (Swann, 1988, pp273–283). The economic environment in which regulation is imposed is dynamic, and there are frequent occasions where developments take place, which markedly increase competition potential, and render obsolete existing regulatory regimes. Developments in telecommunications concerning satellite and cable television have resulted in significant UK deregulation (Swann, 1988, pp283–289).

Despite the varied arguments against regulation, the political attractiveness of it in the public interest will serve to try to ensure that economic regulation will continue to play an important part in making the conduct of productive activity in modern economies acceptable.

Mechanisms for Regulation

An institutional framework must be established for any form of regulation to operate. Statutory measures are normally necessary to define what is to be regulated, and to set up the agencies to undertake the regulatory activity. Areas to be regulated, defined in this way, may include, firstly, activities that impose external costs on society. Laws can be passed to prohibit or restrict these and can apply to firms and individuals. They may seek to control pollution, to establish workplace safety standards or building controls in rural areas, or to impose bans on smoking in public places or drink-driving, for example. They are, in general, simple and clear to understand and administer; the police can do spot checks, though harsh penalties and frequent rigorous inspections may be needed. Statutory controls are a safer approach where dangers are very great, preferred to, say, deterrent taxes where, for example, nuclear waste dumping necessitates a total ban, and they represent an easier approach where a rapid response or emergency measure is needed, for example, as happened with banning cars from Athens to counter a sudden smog.

However, they are a blunt instrument. Where, for example, a company is required to cut effluent discharges to 1000 gallons per day, no incentive is provided to cut any further, and a scaled tax would clearly be more effective in eradicating the problem. Furthermore, enforcement measures are required in terms of an inspectorate, a scheme of penalties, and an administrative bureaucracy, which may represent a sizable cost.

Other laws may seek to prevent or curb monopolies and oligopolies by restricting structures, making illegal certain mergers or takeovers achieving market concentrations exceeding defined levels, or by affecting behaviour by banning collusion or cartel arrangements aimed at price or market fixing, or refusing sales to non-compliant retailers. Finally, other statutory measures may seek to prevent firms exploiting public ignorance by banning false claims about products, poor quality products and the sale of dangerous goods. This type of measure, however, is only effective in dealing with regular, continuing traders. It is almost wholly ineffective in handling 'fly by night', elusive operators who can move or shut down quickly or temporarily to avoid prosecution. Expensive surveillance measures and legal support activities are needed to stand any chance of combating 'cowboy' storm damage repairers, and these in turn depend on a vigilant public, willing to take action.

In many instances it is necessary to set up dedicated regulatory bodies, such as Oftel, the Monopolies and Mergers Commission or the Audit Commission. Their functions are largely those of policing activities defined by statute to ensure compliance with statutory requirements and/or licence terms. They can be set up to regulate either public or private sector bodies. In the UK they are used extensively to effect anti-trust, economic and social regulation. To carry out their roles, they must seek out cases for scrutiny, such as instances of monopoly abuse or pollution. They must then conduct an investigation to determine whether statutory criteria have been exceeded and then determine whether the activity should be permitted, reduced, modified, or banned. Finally, they must either take direct enforcement measures where so empowered or report to a higher authority, such as government, as does the MMC, and monitor compliance with subsequent requirements. This regulatory activity is costly and time consuming and may only be able to examine a few cases. Even then, offending firms may give undertakings about future behaviour and duly ignore them. Follow up activity is vital if the deterrent value of such bodies is to be effective.

Statutory conditions and the obligation for an activity to be subjected to scrutiny by a regulatory body may be contained in a licence issued by the state to participants in prescribed activities. These have been used widely in the context of the UK's newly privatised public utilities, such as telecommunications, water, gas, and electricity supply. They contain the terms of operation for firms in such industries specifying qualitative conditions, perhaps relating to their output, technical competence, or financial standing, as in the water industry. Quantitative conditions may be included, specifying output levels or, perhaps, a restriction for the firm to operate in certain markets only, as in air transport. They may contain requirements for the firm to serve the public interest in some way, for example, providing telephone services to remote areas, to provide information to a regulatory body, and the public, to accept oversight and inspection by that body and to comply with operational conditions, often expressed as performance requirements.

Performance requirements are what is generally meant by the term 'methods of regulation'. They are designed to protect the public against exploitation, particularly by the monopolist. They fall into two principal types. The first to be developed was 'Rate of Return' or 'Rate Base' regulation, used extensively in the USA. Profits are limited to an amount required to provide a predetermined fair rate on the firm's net assets, or rate base. A major flaw in this approach is that it tends to encourage firms needlessly to expand their asset base to permit more profit. Averch and Johnson (1962) identified this 'Overcapitalisation Effect', sometimes named after them, by which firms adopted too capital intensive production techniques.

Furthermore, according to Demsetz (1968) and Bailey (1973), there is a serious risk of regulatory capture (see 'Towards a case against' earlier in this chapter, plus Utton, 1986, pp19–24), as regulatory bodies, set up to enforce performance conditions, and protect the consumer, come to form a 'symbiotic relationship' (Kay et al, 1986, p23) with the regulated firm, promoting the interests of the firm as well as, or instead of the customer. A feature which makes this more likely is the fact that, in many instances, regulatory bodies are almost wholly dependent on the firms themselves for information on profits, costs, assets, etc, and their work could hence be subverted by the unscrupulous firm.

A further difficulty is the so-called 'Regulatory Lag'. This occurs where performance criteria are reviewed at regular, say five yearly, intervals. Firms will attempt to demonstrate difficulty in compliance towards the end of the period by using reserves built up in the early part of the period to absorb the consequences of poorer performances. The effect may be to generate regular fluctuations in investment and trading performance patterns.

These defects are widely recognised, and, faced with the need to develop effective regulation for the privatised utilities in the UK, Littlechild (1983) developed a form of price regulation, specifically for the Telecommunications industry, but since adapted widely to other applications. This is the 'RPI-X%' formula, whereby the firm is allowed to increase its prices, for a defined bundle of goods or services, each year, by X% below the Retail Price Index. The X% is determined in such a way as to encourage efficiency savings and cost reduction. Littlechild emphasised the simplicity of the scheme, the lack of discretion for regulators and the fact that it avoided overcapitalisation. However, by targeting an incomplete range of goods and services, this method provides an incentive for the firm to overprice other items. Over time, the range has therefore had to be broadened so that in 1992, 'controlled services now account for 70% of BT's group turnover' (Vass 1992 p221). It does not, however, address the problems of capture and regulatory lag. Littlechild (1986) observed that it is now evident that rate of return considerations are necessarily implicit in setting and resetting X. Vass (1992 p227) states that the RPI-X formulation may become 'indistinguishable from rate of return regulation' with all of its faults. In the case of British Telecom, despite upward revisions of 'X', from 3% in 1984 to 6.25% in 1992 for the main basket of services, huge profits continue to be made. This suggests regulation of doubtful effectiveness despite the obvious activity of the regulator. However, similar revisions to the price cap formula have been forced by the regulator on British Gas in 1991, followed in 1992 by reluctantly agreed tarrif reductions for its domestic customers in the face of government pressure, together with a series of measures to reduce its monopoly of supply to industrial and domestic customers. These steps indicate a firming up of the Government's position over regulation with little evidence of capture.

It was Littlechild himself (1983, p1) who observed that 'competition is by far the most effective protection against monopoly; regulation is merely a stop gap until sufficient competition develops'. There is therefore an option of promoting competition wherever possible, even in industries viewed in the past as natural monopolies. Several of these involve distribution or transport networks, such as electricity or the railways. These networks are sustainable monopolies, given their heavily capital intensive nature. Competition here is improbable. However, some parts of these industries are capable of supporting competition, if hived off from the rest, such as generating in the electricity industry (Yarrow 1985, in Kay et al, 1986) and train operations (Starkie 1984 in Kay et al, 1986). In the case of British Rail, the monopolistic track and signalling activity could be retained by the state and regulated, whilst the right to run privately owned trains could be auctioned or franchised. In 1992, the Government put forward firm proposals for a partial privatisation of British Rail following this pattern. Similar features are apparent in the electricity supply industry, where a three-way competitive model, widely held to be an insufficient split, was developed for England and Wales, involving National Power PLC, PowerGen PLC, and the state owned Nuclear Electric PLC, with a jointly owned National Grid PLC running the main distribution network.

Franchising may be viewed as a further answer to the difficulties of enforcing performance conditions. Chadwick (1859) proposed arranging for 'competition for the monopoly market, rather than competition in the market'. The state could either auction the rights to the monopoly, giving the contract to the highest bidder and contribute useful revenues to the state (Domberger 1985 in Kay et al, 1986), or it could award the contract to the bidder who offers to provide the service at least cost to the consumer (Chadwick 1859, Demsetz 1968). Variations of these are used in the UK for regulating the use of terrestrial television wavebands, the allocation of North Sea oil exploration rights, and airport support services. The major difficulty is akin to the regulatory lag problem. When the franchise falls due for reletting, if the activity is capital intensive, with high sunk costs, is there likely to be serious competition, the second time around, from firms who would have to provide these expensive capital assets in an instant, in order to compete with the incumbent firm? Perhaps there is a case for creating a contestable market here (Baumol 1982).

Regulatory Case Studies in the UK
It is now useful to consider two illustrative examples of developing regulatory practice in the UK. Some preliminary general observations must first be made about the trend in government policy towards regulation in the 1970s and 1980s. In common with the USA especially, and others (Swann 1988, pp42–44), the UK government embarked on a process of significant deregulation based on an emerging belief in the value of competitive forces, and the view that excessive regulation blunted the edge of management, and limited the wealth creating

capacity of industry. Whilst this deregulation began in the 1970s, it gathered pace under the Thatcher governments in the 1980s.

At the same time, a political philosophy (see Chapters Two and Five) favouring the privatisation of public utilities/corporations, with similar liberating aims, was developing, to be implemented in the 1980s. This did not represent a rejection of the arguments that monopolists can exploit consumers. In parallel with privatisation, the UK witnessed a major extension in the use of regulatory devices, and not just in the newly privatised utilities. Protective measures were evolved in other changing sectors. The 1980s saw a simultaneous development of regulation to protect consumers, and deregulation to further the pursuit of the benefits of competition.

The Financial Services Sector is discussed below as it provides a good example of this apparently schizophrenic approach. The Stock Exchange has traditionally been an illustration of self-regulation, by its Council representing its members. Since 1908, those able to trade in the market were restricted in number by the so-called 'single capacity system', and since 1912 a fixed scale of commission for brokers has been enforced. The Stock Exchange members protected their monopoly in security trading by restricting entry and by fixing their prices to the detriment of the public.

All this ended following the reference of the Stock Exchange Rule Book to the Restrictive Practices Court in 1979, exposing 150 alleged restrictive practices. The Secretary of State for Trade and Industry stepped in and 'negotiated' a settlement with the Stock Exchange. From 1983, the single capacity system was abandoned, as was demarcation between jobbers and dealers. In the face of intense international competition, brokerage commission has been negotiable since 1986, and new firms admitted to the Stock Exchange – in short a case of massive deregulation, the so-called 'Big Bang' (see Swann, 1988, pp279–283). Other financial institutions, up to the 1980s, were regulated in a variety of ways. The banks were subject to regulation of their working environment through government monetary policy controls. There was strict statutory regulation, aimed at consumer protection, of the banks, building societies, and insurance companies, providing safeguards against insolvency. A licensing system applied to banks and building societies, whilst the Bank of England exercised control by 'moral suasion' over the banks, whereby the banks accepted supervision in return for the lender of last resort facility. Effective interest rate and business delineation cartels existed for the banks and building societies. All this began to change in 1971 with the 'Competition and Credit Control' declaration, by the Bank of England, which removed institutional ties between the banks' interest rates and the bank rate of the Bank of England, whilst freeing the banks to compete in the mortgage market, undermining the building societies' cartel. In 1986, the Building Societies Act allowed the societies to retaliate and compete directly for banking business, and to engage in insurance broking, pensions, property sales, and other related activities. This competition-orientated deregulation was accompanied by parallel reregulation, providing prudential control to protect the customer, with the Deposit Protection Scheme for the banks in 1982, and the Investment Protection Scheme for the building societies in 1986.

Other financial institutions, such as dealing firms, investment advisors, unit and investment trusts, insurance companies, and pension funds were regulated for the first time after the 1986 Financial Services Act, which set up the Securities and Investment Board (SIB), which now oversees a range of self-regulating bodies, established to cover each major finance market and to regulate the conduct of its participants in accordance with SIB rules, a combination of statutory and self regulation to protect the customer. The effectiveness of many of these has, however, recently been called into question by the scandals surrounding the Maxwell Pension Fund, BCCI, Barlow Clowes, and the Lloyds Insurance controversy (Hutton 1992).

The second example selected is the Water Industry, chosen because it is an example of a privatised utility industry where competition is limited, where there are several relevant regulatory bodies whose efforts do not appear to be showing significant results in terms of price restraint and quality improvements. It was privatised in 1989, with a regional structure of organisations for water supply, sewage disposal, and water management. Statute (Water Act 1989) defines the basis of regulation, reflecting concerns over potential for abuse by local monopolies, social, environmental, health and safety concerns, and the fact that water supply and other water services have externality characteristics. Licenses have to be obtained by suppliers, which lay down performance conditions, public obligations, information supply and inspection requirements, and acceptance of the role of the regulators. A regulatory body, the Office of Water Services (OFWAT) was established to monitor compliance, the National Rivers Authority regulates the water environment, whilst the Drinking Water Inspectorate monitors water purity. The European Commission has augmented statutory requirements with more stringent consumer protection measures of its own. The performance criterion applied to a basket of services is a variant of 'RPI-X%', namely 'RPI+K%'. 'K' represents trends in investment needs and efficiency improvements, and is determined individually for each water PLC, reflecting differences between the old industrial parts of England and Wales and the rest. Despite this apparently severe regime, large profits are being returned. Consumers are critical of price increases which are sizable, and there have been frequent charges in the press of poor water quality, environmental pollution and inadequate sewage disposal methods from sources as diverse as local authorities and the E.C. . The regulatory methods do not appear to be wholly effective and, despite the regional structure, there appears to be little scope for competition at a trading level in particular geographical areas.

The European Community and Regulation

Since 1973, the European Community (EC) has had a developing impact on regulation in the UK. Its foundations in the 1958 Treaty of Rome are laid on a belief that impediments to free trade within the EC, to free movement of people and capital between member states, and to competition, should gradually be removed. The result has been the elimination of inter-member tarrifs and quotas, measures to standardise company law and tax regimes, and steps to eliminate preferential treatment of firms by member governments. Vigorous anti-trust regulation has been pursued, aimed at limiting monopolistic mergers, takeovers, and cartels by the use of legal powers. Discriminatory subsidies are scrutinised and frequently banned. Standard product descriptions have been imposed and measures have been taken to remove barriers to the free movement of labour and capital, for example by removing exchange controls. Contracts for tender over a defined size must be advertised without prejudice throughout the EC. However, one regulatory activity could be said to run contrary to all this competitive philosophy, and that is the Common Agricultural Policy, which seeks to protect farm prices and incomes at the expense of the consumer. It appears to discriminate in favour of inefficient producers and to encourage gross overproduction. The strength of the agricultural political lobby in countries other than the UK has served to perpetuate this very large and wasteful anomaly. Other EC regulation has been aimed at public protection, including environmental protection, whereby the Commission can require an environmental audit of any major capital scheme and whereby legal enforcement of water purity standards is being applied. It also serves to provide regulation of social standards, especially working conditions and pensions, together with monetary and fiscal controls, such as through the Exchange Rate Mechanism.

The Future
Whichever political party is in government in the UK in the 1990s, moves towards closer European integration are likely to lead to a reinforcement of these measures and an increase in the extent to which EC measures override those of member countries. A further development in the 1990s, which is likely to lead to a revival of regulation, is the use to be made of Charter documents to establish, police and enforce performance standards in public and private services. The *Citizens' Charter* (Cabinet Office and Central Office of Information, 1991) of the Conservative Government under John Major, together with various service specific spin-offs, appeared to usher in significant moves in the direction of improving service quality, with greater emphasis on public services than appeared to be the case in the 1980s. The *Social Charter* of the Labour Party (1991) pursues a similar theme. The Social Chapter of the EC broadens this theme into employee protection measures, union law, and women's rights, and although not yet endorsed by the UK government, it appears likely to be an influence on the course of regulatory development over the next decade. The return of a Conservative government in April 1992 has ensured that new regulatory controls will be established to prevent monopoly abuse once the remaining public corporations have been privatised. This is instanced by the proposal for a Rail Regulator (Conservative Party, 1992, p35). The manifesto expresses concerns over blanket regulation coverage and the need to ensure that existing regulations are scrutinised and perhaps removed when shown to be too wide in their application (p10). However, its emphasis is much less forceful in opposing regulation than its predecessors.

A further general election must take place by 1997. Whilst it is reasonable to assume that Conservative thinking will continue along present lines, the views of the two main opposition parties can best be gauged from their 1992 manifestos (The Labour Party, 1992, and The Liberal Democrat Party, 1992). Labour propose, *inter alia*, a deregulation of the finance of rail transport (p13), the ratification of the EC Social Chapter (p13), the establishment of an Education Standards

Commission (p18), a 'Quality Commission' (p20) to oversee the quality of local services, and a Consumer Protection Commission (p21); on balance, a move towards reregulation. The Liberal Democrats propose liberalisation of the rail and coal industries (p21), more consumer protection powers, an Animal Protection Commission (p24), an Environmental Protection Agency (p25), a Food and Drugs Commission (p29), and a Charter of (local) Services (p49); again, a net increase in regulation.

It appears therefore, that the trend towards net deregulation in the 1980s has stalled and looks like being modestly reversed in the 1990s, regardless of the party in power.

References

Averch H. and Johnson L. (1962), 'Behaviour of the Firm Under Regulatory Constraint', *American Economic Review*, 52, pp1052–69.

Baggott E.E. (1989), 'Regulatory Reform in Britain: the Changing Face of Self Regulation', *Public Administration*, 64, pp435–454

Bailey E.E. (1973), *'Economic Theory of Regulatory Constraint'*, (Lexington, Mass)., D.C. Heath & Co.

Baumol W.M. (1982), 'Contestable Markets: An Uprising in the Theory of Industry's Structure', *American Economic Review*, 72/1, pp1–15.

Benston G.J. (1982), 'Why did Congress Pass New Financial Services Laws in the 1930's ?', *Federal Bank of Atlanta Economic Review* 67/4 pp7–10.

Bernstein M. (1955), *'Regulating Business by Independent Commission'*, Princeton University Press, Princeton, New Jersey.

Cabinet Office and Central Office of Information (1991) *'The Citizens' Charter'*, HMSO.

Chadwick H. (1859) 'Results of Different Principles of Legislation and Administration in Europe: of Competition for the Field, as compared with Competition within the Field of Service', *Journal of the Royal Statistical Society*, 22, pp381–420.

Coase R.H. (1960), 'The Problem of Social Cost' *Journal of Law and Economics*, 3, pp1–44.

The Conservative Party (1992), *'The Best Future for Britain – The Conservative Manifesto 1992'*

Demsetz H. (1968), 'Why Regulate Utilities?', *Journal of Law and Economics*, 11, pp55–65.

Domberger S. (1985) 'Economic Regulation through Franchise Contracts', in *'Privatisation and Regulation – the UK Experience'*, Kay J.et al, Ed, Ch14, (1985)

Green M.J. (Ed). (1973) *'The Monopoly Makers'*, Grossman, New York.

Hutton W.(1992) 'Shake Up or Shake Down' *The Guardian*, March 13

Kay J., Mayer C., & Thompson D., (Eds) (1986), *'Privatisation & Regulation – The UK. Experience'*, Clarendon Press, Oxford.

Labour Party (1991) *'The Social Charter'*, Labour Party.

Labour Party (1992), *'It's time to get Britain working again – Labour's election manifesto, 1992'*, Labour Party.

The Liberal Democrat Party (1992), *'Changing Britain for Good – The Liberal Democrat Manifesto*, Liberal Democrat Publications..

Liebenstein H. (1966), 'Allocative Efficiency vs X-Efficiency', *American Economic Review*, 56, pp392–415.

Littlechild S. (1983), *'Regulation of British Telecommunications' Profitability'*, Department of Industry, London.

Littlechild S. (1986), 'Report to the Department of the Environment on the Economic Regulation of the Privatised Water Authorities', cited in *C.A.A (CAP 599)*, November, 1991

Llewellyn D.T. (1986) *'The Regulation and Supervision of Financial Institutions'* Institute of Bankers, London, pp27–28.

Peltzman S. (1976) 'Toward a More General Theory of Regulation', *Journal of Law and Economics* 19, pp211–240.

Petersen H.C. (1985),*'Business and Government'* Harper and Row, New York, 183–184.

Posner R. (1971),'Theories of Economic Regulation', *Bell Journal of Economics and Management Science'*, 2, pp335–358.

Posner R. (1976), *'Anti Trust Law, An Economic Perspective'*, University of Chicago Press, Chicago, 1976, Ch 2.

Pryke R. (1981), *'The Nationalised Industries'* Martin Robertson, Oxford.

Russell M. and Shelton R.B. (1974),'A Model of Regulatory Behaviour', *Public Choice*, 20, pp47–62.

Sloman J. (1991), *'Economics'*, Harvester Wheatsheaf.

Starkie D. (1984), 'British Railways; Opportunities for a Contestable Market', *'Privatisation and Regulation – the UK Experience'*,Kay J.et al, Ed, Ch9, (Oxford,1986).

Stigler G.J. (1975) *'The Citizen and the State'*, Univ. of Chicago Press, 1975.

Swann D. (1988), *'The Retreat of the State – Regulation and Privatisation in the UK and USA.'* Harvester Wheatsheaf.

Utton M.A. (1986), *'The Economics of Regulating Industry'*, (Basil Blackwell).

Vass P. (1992), 'Regulated Public Service Industries', in *Public Domain*, Terry F.,and Jackson P. (Eds), Chapman & Hall, pp209–237.

Yarrow G. (1985), 'Regulation and Competition in the Electricity Supply Industry', *'Privatisation and Regulation – the UK Experience'*, Kay J.et al, Ed, Ch10, (Oxford,1986)

Acknowledgment

The author wishes to express his thanks to Dr. John Thompson, of the Liverpool Business School for his comments on an earlier draft of this chapter.

CHAPTER SEVEN

ACCOUNTABILITY

Peter Hinton and Elisabeth Wilson

Introduction

Accountability is a familiar concept within public service organizations and much has been written on its nature and significance. This chapter does not intend to describe all its features and meanings but concentrates on those aspects of accountability identifiable with a more market orientated, managerialist, public sector. Arguably, the 1980's began to see a shift from accountability encompassing probity, stewardship and the concept of ultra vires, to accountability focusing on positive action – managerial performance, the effective use of resources and professional and personal integrity.

After giving definitions of accountability, the chapter examines some of the various types observable within the public sector. The impact consumerism has had and the proposals of the Financial Management Initiative and Next Steps programme are described. Three areas are then considered in more detail, since it is felt that they are good illustrations of the changing nature of accountability in public service organizations in the 1990's. These are the use of a market approach for accountability; redefining the scope of professional accountability; and, integrity, personal accountability and the role of whistleblowing. Finally, issues which could lead to further changes in the nature of public sector accountability are discussed and conclusions drawn.

Definitions of Accountability

Accountability is a concept which is familiar yet intriguing in its complexity, history and implications. It connotes for instance, stewardship and audit; exercise of responsibility; reporting of performance; answering for behaviour, decisions and actions; being open to inspection and judgement; subject to sanctions and rewards. Day and Klein (1987) call accountability a chameleon word and a slippery and ambiguous term, while Lawton and Rose (1991,p.17) describe it as a complex phenomenon which operates in different ways in different circumstances.

It is helpful to consider accountability, as Gray suggests (1983,pp.29–31), in the context of a principal – agent relationship, using the senses of the terms found in the common law of contract. A contract exists, implicit or explicit, written or not, which determines the rights and duties of the parties. Agents will normally be bound by two distinguishable responsibilities, one for the actions they take, and the other for accounting for those actions to their principals. Gray notes that it is the second responsibility that we know as accountability, and states, ' In order to establish what constitutes the required account-ability in any particular situation it is necessary to determine:

(i)   the general form of the principal – agent relationship or contract;
(ii) the actions to which that contract relates;
(iii) the information relating to those actions which will satisfy the principals' (*sic*) needs of accountability; and
(iv) the channel(s) through which accountability will be dis-charged.'

This analysis gives precision to the meaning of accountability but also suggests why accountability can be complex or obscure. In the context of Local Management of Schools, a headteacher is agent of the governors for the management and running of the school, of parents for the education and care of their children, of the local authority for the resources used and of the Department for Education for delivering the National Curriculum. The relationships become entangled and accountability in a single, simple, manner is impossible. Furthermore, accountability is restricted in those situations where there is no clear agreement between principal and agent on one or more of Gray's four requirements.

Accountability can also be viewed in terms of authority, responsi-bility, power and delegation. In a hierarchical organisation, a manager delegates duties and tasks to a subordinate who will be given the authority to take action and make decisions. Authority legitimises the use of power in the area over which the subordinate has been given responsibility. Day and Klein (1987, p.5) then define accountability as acknowledging responsibility for one's actions, adding, 'Indeed accountability and responsibility are often held to be synonymous: a reminder that one cannot be accountable *to* anyone, unless one also has responsibility *for* doing something'.

In the context of the public sector, those with delegated authority are answerable for their actions to the people. Day and Klein (1987, p 229) refer to the notion of a mandate, implying that those with delegated authority possess an approved remit from the public. In their view, accountability, in its strict sense, is the revocability of a mandate. For members of nominated authorities, this would be the secretary of state or his agents revoking the mandate, and among the members of elected bodies, in theory it would be the voters. This definition of account-ability owes much to the concept of representative democracy. As Hambleton (1992,p.12) indicates, this assumes a community – based approach, protecting collective interests through appropriate political accountability. Services 'cannot be individualised, but relate to groups of consumers or society at large'. However, an alternative definition of accountability is based on the concept of consumerism. There is now a market model for the public sector whereby individual consumers are assumed to have power over the producers and providers of public goods and services. Public sector bodies are accountable to individual consumers for the quality of service. *The Citizen's Charter* (The Prime Minister, 1991) embodies the consumerist approach, emphasising the responsibilities of public sector bodies in six key areas – publication of standards and performance against set targets; customer consultation; clear information about services; courteous and efficient customer service; easy to use complaints procedures; and a commitment to value for money.

It is not possible, therefore, to give a single definition of account-ability which does justice to its several shades of meaning and connotations. A good summary of the difficulty in defining the concept is provided by Patton (1992, p.166). 'Sometimes the term implies only a literal accounting/reporting; at other times it also implies explanation or justification of the actions or other phenomena being reported. Some authors infer from the use of the term accountability the existence of a variety of sanctions/rewards; others do not. Sometimes the term implies a direct hierarchical relationship based on a contractual relationship between the accountor and the accountee for specific actions; at other times (especially in the case of "public" accountability and accountability to one's peers), the "who", the "what", and the "when" of the accountability relationship are not so obvious.'

Types of Accountability

Lawton and Rose (1991,p.23) give a useful list of the types of accountability to be found in public sector organizations:–
* political accountability;
* managerial accountability;
* legal accountability;
* consumer accountability;
* professional accountability.

However, it is important to note that the vagueness attaching to accountability as a concept also applies to the definition and scope of the types of accountability. Other types of accountability can be identified and the list above provides a framework for further analysis.

Political accountability, according to Day and Klein (1987), is about those with delegated authority being answerable for their actions to the people. It embraces the doctrine of Ministerial Responsibility, ministers being responsible to Parliament, and the collective responsibility of members of the Cabinet for Government decisions. Parliamentary accountability is a term sometimes used instead of political accountability, signifying this duty of ministers to be answerable to the people through Parliament for their ministerial areas and actions. Political accountability also covers constitutional issues, the sovereignty and subsidiarity of Britain within the European Community, as well as relationships between local authorities and agencies and Central Government.

The political accountability of members of public service organizations has been investigated by Day and Klein (1987, p 229). From their survey they found that members use a 'clutch of words' – accountability, answerability, and responsibility – to describe their sense of duty to the community being served, pursuing the public good according to their own criteria of what is right. Few appeared to use accountability in its strict sense, the revocability of a mandate.

Political accountability can also be linked to legal and administrative types of accountability. The concept of *ultra vires* – going beyond or outside the mandate – is central to legal accountability, in that the courts will deal with matters where ministers, state bodies and local agencies and authorities have exceeded their powers. Administrative accountability has a broad meaning as Peters (1984,pp.241–261) reveals, but it is concerned with the control of bureaucrats, namely non-political public service employees. Peters identifies the characteristics of the civil servant's job and role which makes administrative accountability important. These are security of tenure; unresponsiveness to the wishes of markets, politicians, or the public; and, insulation from political pressures because of the desire of Western societies and nations to separate administration from politics. Among the instruments of accountability devised to attempt to control the administration, is the ombudsman system which enables aggrieved citizens to seek support in the investigation of alleged cases of maladministration.

Managerial accountability embraces notions of stewardship, audit and performance assessment. Day and Klein (1987,p 27) indicate the links with Value for Money concepts, '. . . managerial accountability is about making those with delegated authority answerable for carrying out agreed tasks according to agreed criteria of performance . . . (It) has a number of dimensions. . . . *Fiscal/regularity accountability* is about making sure that money has been spent as agreed, according to the appropriate rules; legal accountability can be seen as a counterpart to this, in so far as it is concerned to make sure that the procedures and rules of decision making have been observed. *Process/ efficiency accountability* is about making sure that a given course of action has been carried out, and that value for money has been achieved in the use of resources. *Programme/ effectiveness accountability* is about making sure a given course of action or investment of resources has achieved its intended result.'

Managerial accountability has gained prominence in the public sector as the trend towards decentralization has continued. Metcalfe and Richards (1990) have reported on the progress and prospects of the Financial Management Initiative (FMI), launched by the Thatcher government in May 1982. This advocated accountable management in the Civil Service. FMI was the precursor of the Next Steps initiative which since 1988 has seen the establishment of executive agencies in central government, for instance, Land Registry and the Employment Service.

Accountable management in its FMI form, according to Metcalfe and Richards (1990,p.187), '. . . appears in a number of guises, including more systematic use of management accounting, creation of cost or responsibility centres to clarify managerial tasks by establishing links between resources and objectives, and subdividing departmental activities into separate accountable units or businesses instead of basing organization on management functions'. In their appraisal of the FMI, Gray and Jenkins (1991) state that it has been operationalized through three major elements; top management systems, which provide information for planning and control; decentralized budgetary control, with a hierarchy of cost centres; and, performance appraisal, with a range of indicators being used to indicate the efficiency and effectiveness of performance. With the Next Steps initiative, accountable management has meant the recognition of the title of Chief Executive for the manager of an agency, the setting of clear objectives and allocating sufficient resources to enable them to be achieved, the establishment of agreed performance targets, and the definition of the relationship of an agency's responsibilities to those of its government department through a Framework Document. Importantly, chief executives, though still accountable to their departmental ministers, can be questioned directly by select committees about the day-to-day running of their agencies. The concept of accountable management, therefore, embraces the notion of personal responsibility and has a link to political/ administrative accountability.

Consumer accountability is referred to by Lawton and Rose (1991,pp.21–22) mainly in the contexts of members of the public using the ombudsman procedures to pursue complaints of maladministration and seeking greater responsiveness from public service organizations. However, as can be seen from the definitions of accountability given above, the influence of consumerism suggests that there is almost a contractual obligation on the providers of public sector services and goods to meet customers' and clients' needs. This market aspect of accountability is considered more fully later. By contrast with managerial accountability, where the performance of the manager is the issue, consumer accountability is concerned with the performance of the deliverers of the service. The distinction is an important one because managers may shield themselves from complaints about the quality of service by not accepting that responsibility for how service deliverers perform arises from the contracts they as managers should devise and monitor. Further aspects of the relationship between the manager and consumer can be found in the analysis by Harrow and Shaw (1992).

In examining the concept of professional accountability, it is necessary first to look briefly at the characteristics of a profession. These include:

- ownership of a body of specialised knowledge, which is standardised
- restricted entry via training and certification
- the exercise of autonomy within the field of expertise

- implicit or explicit requirement to keep abreast of knowledge
- control of delivery of service
- standards of conduct often embodied in a code of ethics
- enforcement of competence and ethical behaviour, often by a self regulating body
- status, mystification, and power, the degree depending on the particular profession.

Whatever accountabilities the organisation may wish to prescribe for the professional employee, professional status creates a further accountability to the profession and/or professional body. Where the aims of the public service organization and of the professional are congruent, membership of a profession reinforces the delivery of organizational accountabilities. Where, however, there is disparity between these stated accountabilities, professionals may claim a prime accountability to their profession. This commitment is seen to transcend the accountability demanded by current employment. Metcalfe and Richards (1990, p 124) describe the very limited need for supervision or control among professionals where accountability is through standards generated within the professional peer group.

Finally, there is an important type of accountability which can be added to the Lawton and Rose list. This can be termed personal or individual accountability and relates to the integrity and morality of public service officials. Dobel (1990,p 356) has commented, 'Public office presumes that individuals will bound their judgments by authorized standards and procedures and will exercise power in a manner accountable to these authoritative criteria. . . . In a liberal democracy, the legitimacy of delegated powers to office stipulates several crucial conditions. First, public servants should act in accord with the basic principles which sustain the authority of constitutional government. Individuals in office are expected to see themselves and others as citizens possessing dignity and basic rights which are to be protected and ensured in the performance of duty. Such respect should bound and inform all their actions. Second, individuals agree to subordinate their personal judgments to the outcomes of legitimate processes and to frame judgments by the constitutional and legal directives in their areas of authority. Third, individuals agree to remain accountable for their actions to the relevant authorities and broader public. Fourth, individuals agree to try to be honest and accurate in their accounting for their actions. Fifth, individuals agree to try to act competently and effectively to achieve the purposes within the above constraints. Last, individuals agree to use public funds, especially those acquired by taxation, with care and efficiency for authorized public purposes, not their own gain or the private gain of others. Any serious delegation of power by democratic citizens concerned for human dignity specifies such conditions.'

To conclude this section, the types of accountability that have been analysed are in no way capable of definitive treatment. It will be apparent that one type of accountability can merge into another, for instance the requirements of accountable management necessitate the personal or individual accountability of a Chief Executive of a Next Step agency. The agency itself is a consequence of greater consumer accountability, possibly because of a lack of responsiveness by the politicians and/or by the professionals providing the service. In order to see how types of accountability are changing in the early 1990's, three areas are now considered by way of illustration.

Use of a Market Approach for Accountability
Metcalfe and Richards (1990,p.158) have described the Thatcher Government's market oriented approach to public management as being 'an attempt to raise efficiency by subjecting public organisations to market conditions, by relying more on businesses that are subject to market forces to provide public goods and services and by stimulating market conditions within government to ensure tighter discipline in those areas that cannot be opened up to direct market pressure.'

John Major's Government has given formal expression to this market approach through *The Citizen's Charter* (The Prime Minister 1991) and especially through the White Paper, *Competing for Quality* (HM Treasury 1991). The latter focuses on how managers are to be held accountable for their performance and it is worth quoting in full the Government's intentions:-

A More Business-Like Approach

Greater competition over the past decade has gone hand in hand with fundamental management reform of the public sector.

This means moving away from the traditional pyramid structure of public sector management. The defects of the old approach have been widely recognised: excessively long lines of management with blurred responsibility and accountability; lack of incentives to initiative and innovation; a culture that was more often concerned with procedures than performance. As a result, public services will increasingly move to a culture where relationships are contractual rather than bureaucratic.

The Government's programme of reform will continue into the 1990s with the aim of:

* making managers accountable for performance within a clear framework of objectives and resources;
* distinguishing the roles of policy formulation and service delivery;
* introducing, wherever feasible, contracts and service level agreements which define standards of performance and responsibility for meeting them.

All these changes enable managers to focus on buying the best standard of service achievable within a given budget.

In central government, the Next Steps programme, launched in 1988, is reorganising the business of government to take greater account of the needs of customers. Executive functions are being transferred to Agencies headed by Chief Executives who are set tough financial and quality targets and given the management and budgetary freedom to help them do their job more effectively. This is in itself akin to a contractual relationship: Ministers agree the terms on which the Agency Chief Executive will carry out a defined task within a defined budget. This gives Chief Executives a strong incentive to buy all the services they need from the most advantageous supplier, whether within or outside the public sector, so that they can meet both the quality and financial targets that Ministers have set.

The NHS reforms have given health authorities the strategic role of assessing the health needs of their population and purchasing care to meet them. The job of providing health care –whether in a directly managed unit or trust – is undertaken by the management of those units. Separation of the role of customer and provider, negotiating contracts for services, makes hospital managers accountable for performance against specified standards and allows health authority managers to achieve the best value for their resources.

'For local services, the Government's model of an enabling authority will promote more effective, business-like management, which pays more attention to customer requirements and value for money. The separation of service delivery from strategic responsibilities enables authorities to concentrate on the core responsibilities of setting priorities and standards and finding the best way of meeting them. We set out new approaches to achieve more business-like management methods in a consultation paper on the internal management of local authorities issued in July.'

(Source:– *Competing for Quality*. HM Treasury November 1991, p.2)

Particularly important in breaking the bureaucracy of the traditional pyramid structure has been the development of Service Level Agreements/Internal Service Agreements, SLA's or ISA's. Central support services, for instance legal, administrative, financial, computer, property, were traditionally a recharge to service providers/ deliverers. Managers of direct services to clients were unable to question either the amount of the charge or the quality of service provided. The recharge was seen by the service provider as a below the line budget item, ie. a non-controllable item yet clearly an element of the total cost of a service or process. For the support service manager, there was no incentive to keep costs down or recognise the needs of the internal customers of the organization for the support services provided. By encouraging an internal market through the provider and purchaser/internal customer split of responsibilities in a contractual relationship, managers of central support services are now accountable to managers of direct services, who in turn are accountable to their external customers and the public at large.

The elements for a Service Level agreement, drawn from CIPFA guidance, are as follows:-

SERVICE LEVEL AGREEMENTS

Definition

Service Level Agreements (SLA) are business contracts agreed between the providers of central support services and their clients aimed at specifying the service requirements of the client, the services to be provided to meet these requirements and the basis of charge for the provision of those services.

The agreement establishes the responsibilities of both parties and ensures as far as is possible that no surprises arise in the business relationship.

Implications of Service Level Agreements

SLAs will make central support service providers think more about their own business both in terms of the type and extent of services which they are able to offer and the costs of providing those services. It is not good business practice to be providing services which are not required or at prices which cannot be afforded.

Framing a SLA

The ground-rules in framing a Service Level Agreement are to ensure that the SLA:
- contains all the relevant information
- is nevertheless short and concise
- is unambiguous
- is sectionalised.

Main Sections of a Service Level Agreement

Introduction
- To establish the identity of the 'contractor' and the 'client'.
- To establish in general terms the type of services involved.

- To set out arrangements for communication and liaison between the parties.
- To establish the period of the agreement.
- To detail any statutory or other requirements in respect of the services provided.

Service Requirements
- To outline the services required by the client.
- To define any special requirements or conditions to be met in the provision of the service.

Level of Service
- To describe in some detail all the elements of the service to be provided.
- To give indicative operational details of the scale of the service to be provided in terms of, for example,
  - numbers
  - frequencies
  - volumes
  - timescales.

- To define the standard of service to be provided in terms of, for example,
  - availability
  - accuracy.
- To specify, if appropriate, the client's role in the provision of the required services – what must be done, and when.

Basis and Frequency of Charging
- To define the basis of charge in terms of, for example,
  - hourly/weekly
  - per person
  - per task
  - per unit
  - fixed charge
  - by results.

- To define the frequency of charge, which might depend upon, for example,
  - the complexity of the charging system

- the type of service being provided
- the basis of charge
- internal cash flow considerations.

Other Conditions
- To set deadlines for the flow of information, when required,
  - from client to contractor
  - from contractor to client
  - from contractor to a third party.
- To define a complaints procedure, including the appointment of an arbiter, to be invoked in the case of disagreements between client and contractor.
- To establish any penalty arrangements in respect of the non-delivery of the services by the contractor.

(Source:- Based on Chartered Institute of Public Finance and Accounting (CIPFA) material, 1990)

However, the benefits which can arise by adopting the more business-like approach of SLA's must be judged against the costs of their introduction and the implications for an organization. Service specifications will need to be drawn up with great care in setting out the precise nature of the service required. SLA's may not always be practicable for very small support services or where a support service has a large number of customers, each with very small requirements. Moreover, a critical analysis is needed to ensure that SLA's do not become an added layer of bureaucracy, requiring excessive extra administration and monitoring. For instance, there is a need to establish a negotiations/ disputes procedure on such issues as the quality of service, price changes, or need for the service. Furthermore, clients will become more aware of opportunities for the external provision of support services. This creates a tension within an organization in that a decentralised/devolved responsibility centre will seek to secure the most economic arrangement for obtaining a support service, yet the organization as a whole may benefit from the economies of scale of the in-house provider of the support service being engaged by all the client departments.

Nonetheless, SLA's have made a significant contribution in encouraging managers of central support services to reassess the quality of their provision. They have helped staff of these services to set objectives and to take pride in the part they play in meeting internal customers' needs. SLA's have also prepared the way for producing tenders in readiness for ' white collar' compulsory competitive tendering, CCT. Details of the extent of this for local authority professional services were announced in November 1992. CCT will apply, sometime after April 1994, to 90% of an authority's spending for construction-related services, 15% of corporate and administrative, 25% personnel, 33% legal and 80% computer, with credit being given for work already contracted out.

The use of the more business-like, market oriented and consumerist approach has added to the importance of accountable management. The next section looks at the impact this is having on professional accountability.

Redefining the Scope of Professional Accountability
A significant change has been taking place in the status and power of professional groups within the public sector. Consumerism has become so much the guiding philosophy that anything which restricts the operation of the market in the interests of the client is unacceptable to the government. The supposed self-interest of professional groups has therefore been a target of attack. The medical profession provides possibly the best example of how professionalism has been subdued by bureaucratic controls and the shift to managerialism.

Professional accountability for the doctor has largely been inter-preted in terms of providing the best possible service for the individual patient. 'Clinical freedom', for the doctor to take whatever action thought necessary, was argued as a logical extension to accountability to individual patients, regardless of resource implications. The provision and management of resources was seen by doctors as the responsibility of managers, and any attempts to ration or re-allocate were greeted with dire warnings and 'shroud waving', dramatising the likely deaths through no or inadequate treatment. Traditionally, doctors have continued to exercise clinical responsibilities as they accrue managerial responsibilities.

Conservative Governments have tried to tackle what they perceive as inadequate managerial accountability in the Health Service during the last decade; first by reforms arising from the 1983 Griffiths 'Report', which introduced general management within Health Authorities; by the Resource Management Initiative, which sought to involve consul-tants in comparing resources and procedures used against results – in managerial terms, comparing inputs and process against outcome;

and, since 1991, by indicative prescribing for General Practitioners (GPs), which sets an amount or budget for drugs expenditure. GP contracts were changed so that payments for vaccinations and other procedures were only triggered if certain percentage levels were reached; a way of inducing managerial accountability, by rewarding performance. The biggest onslaught on professional accountability came with the NHS and Community Care Act 1990, which sought to strengthen managerial as opposed to professional priorities.

The main changes from the Act for GPs have been analysed by Laughlin, Broadbent and Shearn (1992). Family Health Service Authorities (FHSAs) replaced the much less influential Family Practitioner Committees. The new 1990 GP contract makes clear that GPs now have responsibilities from the FHSAs and therefore accountability to them. FHSAs encourage the provision of good quality services from GP's and help to ensure that there is greater value for money in the general medical services. An annual report is required as a useful input into the medical audit arrangements. This contrasts with medical audit based on peer review.

Laughlin, Broadbent and Shearn (1992, p.137) conclude that, '. . . what the Government is trying to do is institute a 'hierarchical' . . . form of accountability with a new 'principal' (the FHSA) (who is in turn, an agent in a nesting of other principal/agent relationships (the Regional Health Authority and ultimately the Government)) of newly defined 'agents' (the GPs) who are being obliged to perform certain functions in return for definable rewards and is requiring accountability information on actions and activities undertaken. This is in marked contrast to the very different relationship which existed between FPCs and GPs prior to these changes . . . where the FPCs were seen by GPs as simply administrative servants (agents?) to serve the interests and concerns of the medical practitioners (principals?). Such a role reversal is clearly conflict ridden.'

Moving from the specific case of GPs and the medical profession in general, an illustration of how the Government is limiting the independence of professional groups is provided by the incentive to senior public sector professional staff to accept a performance related pay component of their remuneration. This can be seen as a way of emphasising the responsibility the professional has to achieving organizational objectives in preference to serving the interests of the professional body.

Integrity, Personal Accountability and the Role of Whistleblowing
The final area of change for specific attention concerns the growing
emphasis on individuals both being answerable for their performance
and almost being required to report on the performance of their
colleagues, to ensure the consumer of public sector services receives
quality.

Chief Executives of the Next Steps agencies and other responsibility
centres where clear targets are set and standards of performance
measured, are personally accountable, much more so than the civil
servants who create rather than execute policy. Where service performance is inadequate, Chief Executives may have to resign or may
not have their contracts renewed nor receive the performance related
pay element, in part or completely, of their salary package. In
November 1992, for instance, when the new £1.5 million control room
computer for the London Ambulance Service failed, the chief executive
felt responsible, and was seen to be responsible, and resigned. The
principle does not extend apparently to all parts of the public sector.
Officials involved in policy decisions on BCCI or other central
administration policy failures have not assumed responsibility for their
mistakes.

Whistleblowing is the term which has become fashionable to
describe reporting on the performance of colleagues. Specifically, it
refers to individuals taking actions to expose what they consider
wrongdoing in their own workplace, especially when that wrongdoing
is by their superiors. The fear of reprisal may test the conscience of the
whistleblower, and loss of employment or demotion because of being a
troublemaker is a strong possibility.

Draft guidance on whistleblowing was issued by the Department of
Health in October 1992. This stressed that NHS managers must draw
up procedures for staff to express their concerns right up the
management line. However it still left potential whistleblowers with the
threat of disciplinary action if they spoke to the press without
permission.

Further Changes in Accountability
There appears to be no questioning by the Conservative administration
of John Major of the prevailing assumption that the discipline of the
market provides the best test of the quality and value for money of
public sector services. Inevitably, therefore, the more market-oriented
approach recorded above will continue and intensify.

Ironically, improved accountability to the consumers of public sector services may in fact lead to less accountability to the public. This can be illustrated by two examples. First, in its bid to give greater responsibility to the governors of schools and more power to parents over the quality of education for their children, the Government is encouraging schools to opt out of local authority control and seek grant maintained status. The Funding Agency for Schools, FAS, which replaces Local Education Authorities, will no longer have any democratic accountability as its membership will be appointees of the Secretary of State for Education. Admittedly, there will be a Chief Executive and individual accountability will be expected, as in the Next Steps agencies, but there is a change in the arrangements for accountability.

The concept that education is a public good with collectivist benefits is less prominent when local, political/democratic, accountability is replaced. Although there will be political/democratic accountability at central government level, this will be very much for strategic decisions about the design and content of a national curriculum and the resources to be allocated to education. 'A Charter for Parents' in *The Citizen's Charter* (The Prime Minister, 1991, p.13) makes clear that the key notion now is accountability to parents. In this regard, the publication for the first time in November 1992 of secondary schools' GCSE results and the distribution in England of three million booklets detailing the results are designed to assist parents to judge the quality of service and to exercise choice for their children's education. There is the possibility that focusing so strongly on the consumer's experience, measured primarily in examination results, will detract from any assessment of and accountability for, the quality of education provided for society at large.

The second example concerns the Government's proposal, introduced in *Competing for Quality* (HM Treasury, 1991, pp.24–25) that local authorities should establish internal trading accounts, 'with separate commercial-style accounts for each service. This will expose the true cost of providing individual services and will help improve performance monitoring and cost control. The introduction of internal trading accounts will also form the necessary first step to introducing competition in corporate functions'. Internal trading accounts will formalise the approach used in Service Level Agreements. They should have a clearly defined charging mechanism, enabling the client to determine the level of service required. There should be standard unit costings, which include an element for a profit margin. Accounts should be maintained on the basis of accurately recorded time and should enable the contractor to exercise proper control over resources. They should provide the client with costings comparable with that of other potential service providers. The Government considers that the accounts should be part of the financial reporting by local authorities to the public.

However, many local authorities have no wish for the wider publication of the performance of their internal services, not because of embarrassment but because of genuine fears that their competitiveness will suffer if rivals have knowledge of how they are doing. Internal trading accounts are viewed as management accounting documents strictly for internal consumption. Rather than encouraging more openness and accountability, the effect of competition is to make local authorities more protective of the services they can provide. A perfect market is not present and it is only to be expected that public service organizations will guard with jealousy their interests if they are correct in their assumption that the public will benefit from their secrecy.

The extent of financial reporting and the appropriateness of information for monitoring performance are likely to be key issues for accountability in the rest of the 1990's. Mayston (1992,p.225) draws attention to the need for the more autonomous public sector bodies, such as Grant Maintained Schools, central government Agencies, and National Health Service Trusts, as well as now privately owned utilities, to be adequately monitored so that they are accountable to the public. According to him, ' One of the main reasons for the introduction of increased autonomy and greater devolution of decision-making in the provision of public services, as under the Local Management of Schools initiative, has been to increase the operational efficiency of the bodies concerned. However, greater autonomy and devolution also increase the extent of the formal *principal-agent* separation between the devolved agency and the principal,in the form of central (or local) government and its electorate.'

Conclusion

The first definition of accountability used the legal interpretation given by Gray (1983) of the principal – agent relationship. Clearly, this contractual basis for accountability is the one which pervades Government policy towards public sector services. The success of the contractual approach depends upon how far the Government can make the consumer the judge of the quality of public service provision, allow for consumer choice by the beneficiaries of services but not ignore the collectivist interests of the public at large. Too much attention by the Government to the market approach may bring the criticism that the welfare of the community is being neglected.

References

Day, P. and Klein, R. (1987), *Accountabilities: five public services*, Tavistock Publications, London.
Dobel, J. P. (1990), 'Integrity in the Public Service'. *Public Administration Review*. Volume 50, Number 3, May/June, pp 354–366.
Gray, A. and Jenkins, W. with Flynn, A. and Rutherford, B. (1991), 'The Management of Change in Whitehall: the Experience of the FMI'. *Public Administration*. Vol 69, Spring, pp 41–59.
Gray, R. (1983), 'Problems of Accountability'. *Public Finance and Accountancy*, November, pp.29–31.
Hambleton, R. (1992), 'Decentralization and Democracy in UK Local Government' *Public Money & Management* Volume 12, Number 3, July – September,pp.9–20.
Harrow, J. and Shaw, M. (1992), 'The manager faces the consumer'. In Willcocks, L. and Harrow, J. (Eds.), *Rediscovering Public Services Management*. McGraw-Hill, London.
HM Treasury (1991), *Competing for Quality. Buying better public services*. Cm 1730. HMSO, London.
Laughlin, R., Broadbent, J. and Shearn, D. (1992), 'Recent Financial and Accountability Changes in General Practice: An Unhealthy Intrusion into Medical Autonomy?' *Financial Accountability & Management*, Volume 8, Number 2, Summer, pp.129–148.
Lawton, A. and Rose, A. (1991), *Organisation and Management in the Public Sector*. Pitman, London.
Metcalfe, L. and Richards, S. (1990), *Improving Public Management* (2nd edn). Sage, London.
Mayston, D. (1992), 'Foreword. Developing a conceptual framework for public sector financial reporting'. *Financial Accountability & Management*, Volume 8, Number 4, Winter, pp.225–226.
Patton, J.M. (1992), 'Accountability and Governmental Financial Reporting'. *Financial Accountability & Management*, Vol.8, Number 3, Autumn, pp. 165–180.

Peters, B.G. (1984), *The Politics of Bureaucracy* (2nd edn). Longman, New York.

The Prime Minister, (1991), *The Citizen's Charter. Raising the Standard.* Cm 1599. HMSO, London.

CHAPTER EIGHT

CRISIS MANAGEMENT IN THE PUBLIC SECTOR: LESSONS FROM THE PRISON SERVICE

Denis Smith

Introduction

The announcement, in October 1992, of the closure of a significant number of mines and the disclosure, a few days later, of a number of hospital mergers and closures marked a milestone in the apparent demise in the public sector. Whilst the public sector is currently portrayed as being in the midst of crisis, such a statement needs to be assessed fully in the light of recent research on crisis management. Outside the public sector, organisational response to crisis has become an important management issue throughout the latter part of the 20th Century. What has become apparent is that organisations need to consider the range of crisis events that can befall them and develop their crisis prevention strategies accordingly. This must be achieved prior to the onset of crisis events in order to ensure that the potential damage arising from such events is limited. Whilst most of the attention to date has focused on the private sector, and particularly on those industries that deal with hazardous processes and technologies, it is recognised that all organisations can find themselves in crisis. Immunity from the trauma of such events is not guaranteed and the public sector is coming under increasing scrutiny with regard to its levels of crisis preparedness. Following recent events, the media has begun to portray various elements of the public sector as organisations in the midst of crisis (see Hood and Jackson, 1992).

Set against such a background of crisis, the public sector is also the 'home' of a number of organisations which exist either to manage crisis or to ensure that organisations facing such events can recover from the intense trauma that accompanies them. The emergency services, for example, serve as rescuers within the crisis management process, with the Fire and Ambulance services adopting an important role in rescue and recovery. In disaster situations, the emergency services, hospitals and social services all play an important role in damage limitation, rescue and recovery. At events such as Lockerbie and the Towyn floods, the local authority was a key player in managing the aftermath of the disaster. The public sector also plays host to the emergency planning function which seeks to co-ordinate the response to major crisis events; to help provide training and planning to deal with the intense emotional and physical energy flows that accompany such trauma; and to ensure that the various elements involved in the process of rescue and recovery are able to interact with each other in an effective manner (see Gainsford, 1992). Given this apparent paradox within the sector and its level of perceived crisis preparedness, it is important to ask what is the state of crisis management within the public sector?

Moving beyond the bland political and media statements of a sector which is facing crisis, much of the supposed evidence to support a prognosis of the public sector in crisis has not been subjected to a rigorous analysis within the context of the academic research on crisis management. The purpose of this chapter is to explore briefly the implications of crisis management within the public sector generally, and the Prison Service in particular, by reference to a series of recent events. After reviewing the nature of crisis management, the chapter goes on to assess whether these organisations are crisis prone, as implied by the media, or crisis prepared as implied by senior managers and government ministers. The chapter concludes by assessing the managerial implications of crisis management across the public sector. It is important to state at the outset, that this is a speculative assessment of crisis management within the public sector. There is a need for a systematic review of the sector but that task falls beyond the scope of this chapter.

Managing on the edge: The nature of crisis management
The term crisis is difficult to define in an unitary manner and a multitude of definitions exist according to the particular paradigmatic context of the discussion (Smith, 1990). One of the more useful definitions is that provided by Shrivastava and colleagues (1988) who argue that a crisis can be seen as, an event which threatens the strategic goals of an organisation and unfolds through the complex morass of stakeholders and shareholders. Here, the organisational and techno-logical aspects of the event are important elements in determining the scale, rapidity of onset and escalation of the crisis event. Within this

setting the management of crises takes on a strategic dimension and should not be seen in a narrow, reactive context (Smith, 1992a). In order to adopt such a strategic view of the crisis process, it is important that managers recognise the extent of those events that can affect them. For Greiner (1972), crises arise as a natural function of the growth and development of organisations and can be seen to punctuate phases in organisational growth cycles. As such, it is possible to argue that there are two basic groups of crises. The first are those chronic events which emerge out of the modus operandi of organisational life. Examples of such crises include the current series of environmental degradation issues facing organisations which result from decades of neglect and poor environmental practice. Other examples arise as a result of the growth of the organisation itself and the associated need to develop effective control and communication processes to ensure that all components of the organisation strive towards the same goal. Crisis events, such as those relating to leadership and direction, have a certain inevitability according to Greiner. The second group consists of the more acute shock type events that are characterised by disasters. The 1980s provide us with a catologue of such events including, Lockerbie, Kegworth, Hillsborough, the Herald of Free Enterprise and Bhopal. These events may be preventable, according to some writers (Pauchant and Mitroff, 1992), and their destructive potential necessitates that steps are taken to develop contingencies which seek to cope with the demands associated with their occurrence. Neither group of crises is mutually exclusive and both can arise from the culture, values and management style that are prevalent within the organisation (see Kets de Vries and Miller, 1987). Whilst there are steps that the organisation can take to prevent crises (Pauchant and Mitroff, 1992), the argument that Greiner develops indicates that unless active steps are taken to anticipate and prevent such events then many of them will occur as a matter of course. Indeed, the belief that the organisation is immune from crisis is a sure sign of a managerial malaise that will eventually generate an organisational climate that will result in an event occurring. Such a *crisis prone* culture is surprisingly common within organisations (see Mitroff et al, 1989; Pauchant and Mitroff, 1988; 1992) and is an important incubatory element in crisis generation (Smith, 1992a). In order to develop our discussion of the management of such events, it is first necessary to generate a framework within which they can be analyzed.

The process of crisis management can be considered in three distinct phases (Smith, 1990; 1992b) (figure 8.1). The first, termed the *crisis of management*, occurs as a result of the values and beliefs of managers, the communications processes within the organisation and the decision making procedures that operate at all levels of the hierarchy (Smith, 1990). It is here that organisations can be considered to be crisis prone and that the process of crisis incubation can be seen to operate. The second phase can be termed the *operational phase* of the crisis. Here, relatively small trigger events can propel the organisation into the throes of a crisis by exploiting the incubation process that had occurred within the previous phase. The systems that are in place within the organisation are important in determining the speed and extent of the crisis. Perrow (1984) argues that the sheer complexity of technological systems create problems for managers by virtue of the extent of *tight coupling* and *interactive complexity* that exists within them. These facets of the system will ensure that a failure will cascade throughout the organisation and result in damage or further failures beyond the immediate initiating event. The speed of this interactive complexity of failures will be determined by the extent of the coupling within the various parts of the system. The closer the coupling the less time will be available to ensure that remedial action or containment can be initiated. The final phase, the *crisis of legitimation*, occurs as a result of the attempts to determine causality for the crisis, usually in the form of scapegoating, to reassure clients and other stakeholders that the crisis event cannot be replicated and that the problem has been exorcised. An important, although often absent, aspect of this legitimation process is the move towards organisational learning. This process should ensure that the 'resident pathogens' (Reason, 1987) within organisational design are recognised and isolated and that some evolution occurs within the organisation to prevent other similar events from having the same impact upon it.

For Pauchant and Mitroff (1992) an organisation's susceptibility to crisis needs to be considered in a number of stages. They argue that we can only understand the way in which an organisation works by peeling back its various layers, using the analogy of an onion to illustrate how important it is to move beyond a superficial examination of crisis. The resulting onion model is shown in figure 8.2 where it can be seen that there are effectively two main blocks of organisational characteristics. The first encompasses the strategy and structure of the organisation. Both of these are easily observable and serve to stand as visible

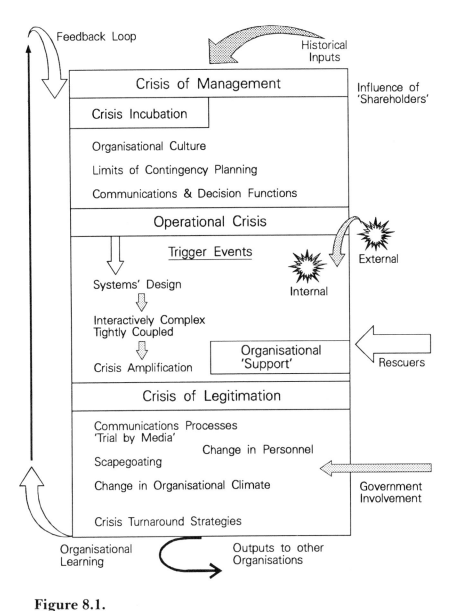

Figure 8.1.

The Three Phases of Crisis Management

examples of an organisation's abilities with regard to crisis prevention and recovery. The responses made to crisis events are often well reported in the legitimation phase and organisations that fail to develop effective strategies prior to an event will be called to task in the wake of the crisis. However, this layer of the onion model is about more than simply developing reactive strategies to crises. Organisations need to be aware that the strategies that they embark upon way well place them in a position of becoming crisis prone at a later date and that there is a need to constantly review their strategic position with regard to changes in the organisational climate and external environment. The next layer of the onion deals with the importance of structure within the process. Whilst there are obvious aspects of structure which impinge upon crisis management, such as the provision of crisis decision units, there are also more subtle aspects of the relationship. Pauchant and Mitroff (1992) argue that,

> '. . . an organization's structure is much more than tangible elements such as established norms, rules about authority and power, and formal hierarchy. We also include . . . *symbolic* functions, that is, how the formal structure of an organization reveals the perceptions of its members' (p. 50).

It is these structural considerations that provide the skeletal basis for the more human issues which lie at the heart of the onion model.

As we move beyond the superficial layers of the model, both layers 1 and 2 can be seen as deep seated and are therefore invisible to many observers. Layer 2 deals with the culture of the organisation – in essence its cultural web (See Johnson and Scholes, 1988) – and the key assumptions that form the basis of the organisational psyche. There are considerable problems inherent in attempting to define the nature of corporate culture. For some its nature defies strict definition and it can be seen in terms of an ink blot, the contents of which are largely in the eyes of the beholder (see Hampden-Turner, 1990). For Pauchant and Mitroff (1992) whilst the culture of an organisation,

> '. . .includes a number of visible items such as technologies, products, and services, we emphasise . . . the less visible part of this culture: the basic assumptions held by its members about themselves and their organization, their environment . . . These beliefs are largely un-conscious and rarely articulated. In effect, culture is the set of unwritten rules that govern acceptable behavior within an organization' (p. 81).

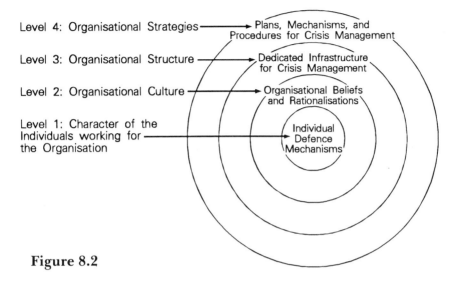

Level 4: Organisational Strategies ⟶ Plans, Mechanisms, and Procedures for Crisis Management

Level 3: Organisational Structure ⟶ Dedicated Infrastructure for Crisis Management

Level 2: Organisational Culture ⟶ Organisational Beliefs and Rationalisations

Level 1: Character of the Individuals working for the Organisation ⟶ Individual Defence Mechanisms

Figure 8.2

The Onion Model of Management

Source: Pauchant and Mitroff (1992) p.49

The important aspect of culture concerns its relationship to learning (Hampden-Turner, 1990) and, within the context of crisis management, that process of learning is a central pillar of developing a crisis prepared organisation. The final, and deepest, level of the onion model concerns the existential nature of crises and the importance of individual defence mechanisms therein. The core values of individuals (as opposed to a set of collective values and assumptions) lie at the heart of developing a crisis prepared organisation:

> '. . . crisis management is not primarily a set of tools and mechanisms to be implemented in organizations. It is rather a general mood and a set of actions by managers who are not too 'emotionally bounded' . . . to develop an effective crisis management effort requires much more than the search for self-interest.' (Pauchant and Mitroff, 1992 p. 62).

The onion model thus provides a framework for assessing the crisis preparedness of the organisation by examining both each level in turn and also assesing the interactions between each level. As such the model can be seen to operate within each of the three phases of crisis management outlined earlier and will form the basis of the empirical discussion later in this chapter.

Turning around the organisation in crisis.

Returning to the broad framework of crisis management it can be argued that, within the process of legitimation, organisations will need to attempt to effect turnaround if demise is to be avoided (see Slatter, 1984). Again it can be argued that the turnaround process will exist in three distinct phases: defence, consolidation and offence (see figure 8.3) (Smith and Sipika, 1993; Sipika and Smith, 1992a). A failure to recover in any of these turnaround phases will result in 'endgame', or organisation demise. Again it is necessary for managers to think through the strategies for recovery well in advance of the crisis event, as an ad hoc approach to dealing with the demands of the crisis can lead to major organisational difficulties.

An example of such problems can be found in the case of benzene contamination within Perrier's bottled water. Here the organisation was not prepared for the demands of the crisis and failed to deal effectively with the increased demands for information that arose from the media (Sipika and Smith, 1992b). For Pan Am, the problems that they faced as a result of the Lockerbie explosion must be seen as but one in a whole series of crises that befell the company (Sipika and Smith, 1992b). Whilst many observers have attributed the terrorist bombing as being the root cause of the company's eventual collapse, it has been argued that the Gulf war, along with a series of divestment decisions, resulted in the downward spiral of crisis from which the company was unable to recover (Sipika and Smith, 1992b). For the Local Authority, the crisis took a different form as they had to deal with the trauma and disruption caused by the damage on the ground. In the defensive phase of the turnaround process, organisations need to ensure that they communicate with their various stakeholder groups and other interested parties. Within this context, the contingency plans that the organisation has in place prior to the event will be of critical importance in determining its initial response in setting up chains of command, organisational structures and decision making procedures to cope with the high level of demand that is inevitably generated by a crisis event. In the process of consolidation, the organisation will usually pay attention to the cost elements of the crisis and will attempt to regain some measure of control over its markets, information flows and investment. The final phase, that of offence, is marked by changes in

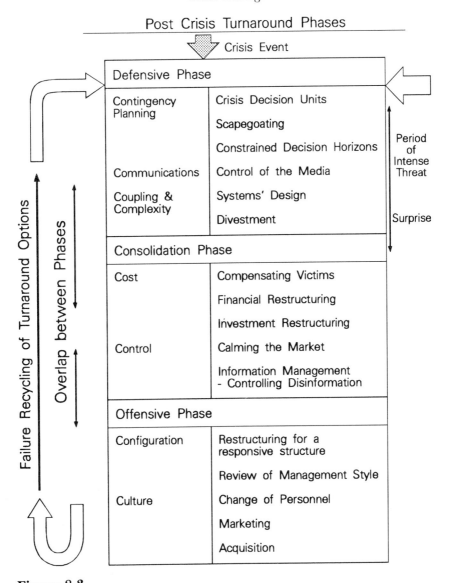

Figure 8.3

Post Crisis Turnaround Strategies

Source: Smith and Sipika (1992)

the organisation's structure and culture which are necessary prerequisites in order to facilitate learning within the organisation. Here also, the organisation embarks upon an aggressive marketing strategy in an attempt to regain market share and to increase profit margins or, in the case of the public sector, to restore public confidence in the service. Inherent within this whole process is the importance of learning and this now needs to be discussed in more detail.

The 7Cs of crisis management: Organisational learning in the wake of crisis.

This process of learning from crisis is an important, but largely neglected, area of research. Whilst considerable research has been undertaken in the area of organisational learning (see Pedler et al, 1990; Senge, 1985) this work has not been applied to organisations in crisis. The final phase in our emerging model of crisis management can thus be seen as organisational learning (Smith, 1990). Figure 8.4 illustrates the interaction of certain elements of the learning process in providing a feedback loop into the crisis of management phase. In certain cases it is not learning per se but facilitating the necessary *unlearning* that will be of importance as organisations seek to change their core values, beliefs and assumptions. The learning phase also equates with the process of recovery within the context of turnarounds, although it can be argued that final recovery can exist without learning in what can be termed the 'Titanic syndrome'. Here organisations that feel immune to crisis, assume that the threat of 'minor' events do not constitute a challenge to organisational survival and that recovery from such events proves how invulnerable the organisation is. However, what appears to be a minor event can be just the tip of the crisis iceberg and may provide a trigger that will precipitate a major crisis throughout the organisation. Here a failure to learn, is a precursor to crisis at another point in time.

The notion of organisational learning is therefore a powerful one for crisis management and it is closely related to the notion of a crisis prepared organisation as outlined by Pauchant and Mitroff (1992). Within the context of our present discussions, the learning organisation can be seen as an,

'. . . organisation that facilitates the learning of all its members and continuously transforms itself' (Pedler et al, 1991 p. 1).

Another definition of the concept is offered by Senge (1990) who sees the learning organisation as,

'. . . an organization that is continually expanding its capacity to create its future. For such an organization, it is not enough merely to survive. "Survival learning" or what it is more often termed "adaptive learning" is important – indeed it is necessary. But for the learning organization, "adaptive learning" must be joined by "generative learning", learning that enhances our capacity to create' (p. 14).

As part of the learning process, a number of factors assume considerable importance in developing the crisis prepared (that is, learning) organisation. These can be considered as the process of systems

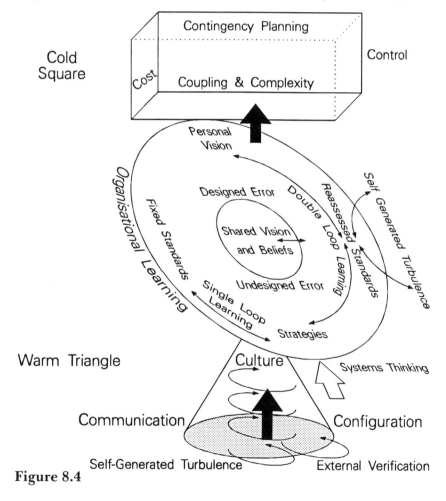

Figure 8.4

Organisational Learning and Crisis Management

thinking, personal and shared vision, shared assumptions and beliefs and team development (Senge, 1990). To these facets of the learning organisation we can merge Pauchant and Mitroff's Onion Model layers, namely: core beliefs, shared assumptions, strategies and structure. It is the interaction of these elements that produces learning within organisations. In the feedback loop for learning, the process of reinforcement is of importance in establishing an effective learning environment. Within the context of crisis management, this reinforcement can be either positive or negative. Here positive reinforcement is seen to occur when the organisation learns from the experience of others and challenges the core assumptions and beliefs, or dominant paradigm, of the organisation. In so doing, the organisation moves towards a crisis prepared state. Negative feedback occurs within the organisation which fails to recognise, pick up and act upon the signals that exist within its environment. In so doing the organisation begins to incubate crises through its 'cultural web'[1]. The denial of the worst case, in the face of conflicting evidence, provides a barrier to effective learning as does the power of technocracy which can lure organisations into a feeling of security.

The question that remains is, 'What drives the process of crisis management?' Smith (1992a; 1992b) has argued that there are seven key aspects of organisations that serve both to precipitate crises and to aid organisations in their process of recovery. These 7Cs of crisis management have already been referred to in passing but now need to be examined in more detail, as they provide the driving force behind the crisis management model developed in this paper. The 7Cs can be considered to relate closely to the cultural web of the organisation and, as such, are part of the organisational paradigm. Smith (1992a; 1992b) has illustrated the role of the 7Cs in precipitating crisis events and determining the effectiveness of the organisational response in the wake of such incidents. It is possible to see the 7Cs in terms of their 'warm' (i.e. human) or 'cold' (i.e. technical) natures (see figure 8.5). For coupling/complexity, control, cost and contingency planning, the solutions to an organisation's crisis management problems are technocratic – expertise is available to meet the demands of the event both in terms of the ability to prevent events and to respond to them after they occur. Whilst this 'cold square' may offer a solution to the range of problems facing organisations it is important also to deal with the

[1] For a full discussion of the notion of the cultural web see Johnson and Scholes (1989) and for its relationship to crisis management see Smith (1992b).

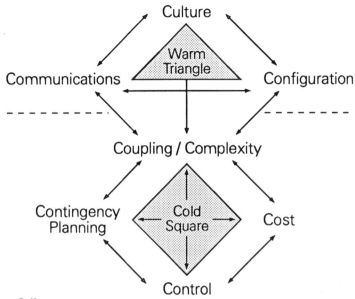

Figure 8.5

The 7Cs of Crisis Management

Source: Smith (1992a; 1992b)

'warm triangle' of culture, communication and configuration. Figure 8.6 illustrates the dichotomies that exist between the two groups. The cold square represents the power of analysis, technocracy and control whilst the warm triangle is related to notions of organisational democracy and participation, the evaluation of wider issues other than purely technical analysis and the question of implementation which are so essential to ensuring the effectiveness of a crisis prepared strategy. The reality is that both warm and cold elements are essential to ensuring that the organisation is effective in dealing with the demands of crisis. However in practice, many managers tend to focus on a sub-set rather than the whole, with the result that the emphasis is often on the 'cold' elements of the framework (see Hampden-Turner, 1990; Pascale and Athos, 1981; Peters and Waterman, 1982)[2]. It has been argued elsewhere, that the interaction of these elements of the crisis management framework can be instrumental in determining the onset

---

[2] Whilst these authors are referring to the McKinsey 7S framework (developed for use within business policy), the points made are directly transferable to the discussion to the role of the 7Cs within crisis management.

of a crisis and also in preventing an organisation from being able to respond effectively to the demands of the event (Smith, 1992a; 1992b). The final model of crisis management is shown in Figure 8.7 where it can be seen that the process is continuous and driven by the 7Cs. Crises originate and become incubated in the crisis of management phase, move through the operational period and into the crisis of legitimation. At this point the process of turnaround management becomes important and this leads into organisational learning.

To-date, this paper has been concerned with developing a broad theoretical framework for the understanding of crisis causation and development. Given the sheer complexity of crisis

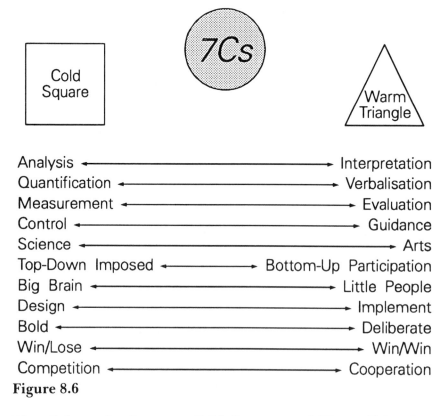

Figure 8.6

The dichotomies between Cold Squares and Warm Triangles within the 7Cs of Crisis Management

Source: Adapted from Hampden-Turner (1990) p. 211 (after Pascale and Athos (1981); Peters and Waterman, 1982)

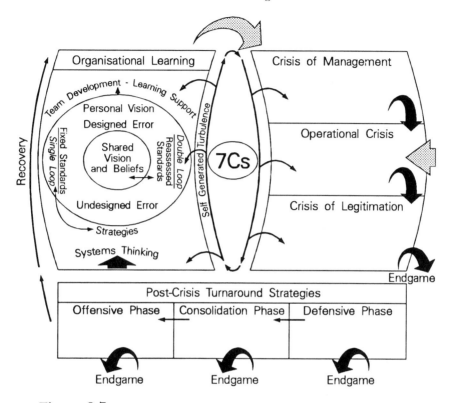

Figure 8.7

The Model of Crisis Management

events, it is important to develop an understanding of the forces that are at work surrounding such events. Given the particular focus of this book, it is now necessary to apply elements of this framework to a public sector organisation in an attempt to add some empirical evidence to the theoretical expositions. As stated at the outset of this paper, the public sector has been the subject of media attention in recent years concerning its supposed crisis prone nature. The choice of the Prison Service to illustrate the issues facing the public sector needs to be explored briefly at this point. Within the context of the current discussions, the Prison Service has much in common with the chemicals industry: both handle 'substances' which are deemed to be hazardous and which cannot be released into the environment; both activities tend to create unease amongst local publics concerning their location; and in both areas the issues of containment and control are of

critical importance to management as is the process of crisis management itself. Given the discussion of the theoretical basis of crisis
management outlined in the first part of this paper, it is now possible to
discuss the state of crisis preparedness within the public sector by
reference to the Prison Service, although it is accepted that no single
organisation can serve as a microcosm of the public sector. The Prison
Service, along with the NHS, has shouldered the brunt of media
concerns over public sector crises and serves to illustrate the
importance of the theoretical frameworks detailed earlier.

Blowing the lid off: Crisis management in the Prison Service.
The riots at Strangeways gaol and the media coverage of that event
created a poignant image of an organisation that was deep in crisis. The
prison was taken over by inmates on the 1st April 1990 and the Home
Office effectively lost control of the situation. The resultant strategy
employed by the Prison Service was one of containment and control
rather than attempting to retake the prison during the early stages of
the crisis. The ensuing roof top occupation (which lasted for some three
weeks until the 25th April), the rumours of murders amongst the prison
population and the apparent inability of the prison staff to regain
control of the establishment, all contributed to the image of organisational malaise. The cost of the occupation was considerable: £60
million to rebuild the prison and £20 million to house the prisoners in
Police cells (Rouse, 1992). The Strangeways riot was not the only one to
occur during this period. There were also disturbances at Glen Parva,
Dartmoor, Bristol, Pucklechurch and Cardiff (Woolf, 1991) and this
served to compound the image of crisis further.

The riot at Strangeways shows the significance of the stages of crisis
management outlined earlier in this paper. The crisis of management
phase can be seen to exist in terms of prison overcrowding and low staff
morale. The operational phase is illustrated by the period of the riots
and the inherent confusion and concern that accompanied them. The
crisis of legitimation and the associated 'turnaround' of the prison
followed into 1992. When Strangeways prison was eventually regained
by the prison staff, the attention of the media turned away from the
local management of Strangeways towards the Prison Service itself.
Had the culture of the organisation and the ways in which the various
prison establishments were managed contributed to the causation of
the riots throughout a number of prisons? Put simply, was the
organisation in crisis? The problem for an analysis of crisis manage-

ment within the Prison Service centres around the large number of individual prisons, their different functions (i.e. high security, open, local, remand and young offender) and the role of the Home Office as both a unifying force and potential causal agent in crisis generation at the local level. In generating the crisis portfolio for the service, these relationships provide an important backcloth to the development of the Prison Service's image.

An assessment of the media coverage associated with the Prison Service, in the period after the 1991 disturbances, raises a number of issues that have been used as being indicative of crisis. By classifying these events as lying upon two axis – human-technical and internal-external – it is possible to identify four major groups of events and these are shown in Figure 8.8. Of these events, those which are external and human based (Cell 1) have attracted considerable attention in the media. The drive towards privatisation has created considerable anxiety amongst prison officers (Carvel, 1991a). The development of the UK's first private prison, and the threat of further privatisation within the service, created concerns amongst prison staff. The move towards privatisation marks an 'external' threat in the sense that the government, as principal stakeholder in the service, was driven by its own ideology concerning market forces within the public sector rather than necessarily being driven by the needs of the service itself. Another negative aspect of government policy which created a problem for the Prison Service arose out of the community charge. The attempts to take defaulters to court and the riots that occurred in support of such opposition gave the appearance of a judicial system in turmoil. The cut-backs in the prisoner education service also gave rise to concerns about the heightening of anxiety and restlessness amongst the prison population. The erosion of the education provision is simply another indicator of prison conditions. The issue of conditions had been an element in the riot at Strangeways gaol and had also been a central issue raised by the Woolf report. In Cell 2, which sees events structured around the technical-external axis, the most obvious event to fall into this category is the copy-cat riots that followed in the wake of the Strangeways' disturbance. The importance of the media coverage in the wake of such events can be seen in terms of acting as a trigger for operational crises at other prisons and moving those organisations into the operational phase of a crisis.

In Cell 3, characterised by internal and human causes of crisis, we can identify those events which have been dominant issues to the lay

Cell 1	*Human/Social/Political*	Cell 3

□ Under capacity/overcrowding	□ Drug abuse amongst inmates
□ Unemployment/social conditions and criminal behaviour	□ Lack of effective officer/governor training
□ Privatisation	□ "Fresh start"
□ Social riots	□ Prison security
□ Negative external reports	□ Prison disturbances
	□ Cutbacks in prisoner education
□ Instantaneous adverse media coverage of events	□ Financial provision (prisons as cost centres)
□ Copycat disturbances (riots)	□ Communications failures
	□ Equipment shortfalls
	□ Poor design of gaols
	□ Prison conditions

External (left side) *Internal* (right side)

Cell 2   *Technical/Economic*   Cell 4

Figure 8.8

Crisis Portfolio Matrix for the Prison Service

(adapted from Pauchant and Mitroff 1992)

observer. These include, drug abuse, the incidence of HIV amongst inmates, prison disturbances and the whole issue of prison escapes. The escape of prisoners from high security prisons had implications beyond the individual prison and raised questions about government policy (Carvel and Campbell, 1991). At a more subtle level, but easily identifiable by insiders to the system, there exist a range of issues which centre around the management development and training needs of officer and governor grades. In particular, the Fresh Start programme (aimed at restructuring and revitalising the service) was heralded as a major attempt to redress the problems experienced by staff and to move the Prison Service towards, if not into, the next century. Concerns over the success of the restructuring and training processes associated with Fresh Start have combined with other problems to undermine morale within the service (Carvel, 1991b; 1991d). In the final category, Cell 4, the Prison Service can be seen to face a series of events that are held to be common across the public sector. The move towards cost centre status combined with equipment shortfalls and communication and data handling failures could apply to any public sector organisation. The poor design of gaols and the conditions within them have attracted much adverse attention in the media in the wake of the Woolf Report. Conditions within the UK's Victorian prisons attracted the attention of the Council of Europe's torture committee who were highly critical of conditions in Brixton, Wandsworth and Armly prisons (Carvel, 1991a; 1991c; 1991e; Wainwright, 1991). Similarly, reports from other external agencies and prison inspectors pointed to the less than favourable conditions under which prisoners were kept (Carvel, 1991c; 1991g). Problems associated with the suitability of conditions in prisons were not just restricted to the Victorian establishments. The governor of the UK's newest maximum security prison at Full Sutton, built at a cost of some £28 million, was apparently vocal in his criticism of the design according to newspaper reports (Carvel, 1991f).

In order to explore the state of crisis management within the Prison Service in more detail, a survey of prison governors was undertaken in an attempt to assess the levels of crisis preparedness in the various layers of Pauchant and Mitroff's onion model. The results of this survey are shown in Figure 8.9. Before discussing the implications of these results it is necessary to make a number of observations. The questionnaire developed by Pauchant and Mitroff[3] (1992) was intended for use within public sector organisations in North America. As a consequence, it was necessary to undertake some minor modifications to 'translate' it into the UK context. In addition, the language used was largely private sector and this caused some concern amongst a small number of respondents who felt that profit and other aspects of the corporate world did not apply to the Prison Service. The reaction may be more easily understood when one considers that the survey was carried out at the time of the opening of the UK's first private prison. Whilst Pauchant and Mitroff (1992) acknowledge that their question naire does not provide a scientific assessment of an organisation's level of crisis preparedness, it does serve to provide a base upon which to build improvement strategies. By identifying such a profile for any organisation it is possible to audit managers' perceptions of the state of

---

[3] The questionnaire used by Pauchant and Mitroff is given as an appendix to their book, *Transforming the Crisis Prone Organisation*.

crisis management and this can then serve as a basis for further action within each level of the onion model. In addition to the broader national survey, some in-depth assessments were undertaken in a number of prisons. This involved prison officers as well as governor grades and serves to provide a limited insight into the broader assessment of the organisation (Rouse, 1992). In order to provide a 'control group', against which to test the governor sample, the survey was also carried out with a number of practising corporate and public sector managers who were themselves expected to deal with crisis events.

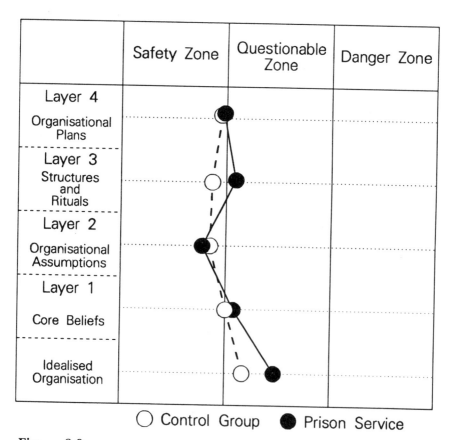

Figure 8.9

Onion Profile for the Prison Service

The survey showed that, despite adverse media attention, the Prison Service could generally be considered to be taking the process of crisis management seriously and was not crisis prone as suggested by media reports. Whilst there were undoubtedly areas that needed further attention, the service had improved its decision making and communications processes and was making structural changes deemed necessary to both help prevent and cope with the trauma of crisis events. The responses, derived from 59 governors within England and Wales, suggest a profile that is crisis prepared in levels 4 and 2 of the onion and in the questionable zone in terms of levels 3 and 1 (see Figure 8.9). This suggests that governors see the strategies and plans that are employed within the service as contributing to its overall state of crisis preparedness and that organisational assumptions also contribute to this profile. In terms of the core beliefs and structure/rituals of the Prison Service, it emerges that governors see the potential for further improvements, although at both levels the results are marginal. Governors did see the opportunity for change in terms of the Prison Services' relationship to the 'ideal' crisis-prepared organisation and the responses here put the service in the questionable zone. However, this in itself is reassuring as it suggests that the governor grades within the service are not complacent and see the potential for continuous improvement and learning. Overall, it can be argued that, contrary to media speculation, the Prison Service is more crisis prepared than crisis prone.

This view is supported by in-depth interviews carried out by Rouse (1992) at local riot-affected prisons in Manchester and throughout Leicestershire. These interviews, carried out in 1991, used the Pauchant and Mitroff questionnaire across the range of grades within the service, thereby providing an assessment of differences in perception between management and staff. The results suggested that there was a significant degree of commonality across grades and between the prisons that were studied (Rouse, 1992). Again, the results showed that staff saw the service as being in the safety zone, both for assumptions (layer 2) and in terms of overall strategies (layer 4) with core beliefs (layer 1) and structures (later 3) being in the questionable zone by a small margin. In terms of an idealised organisation, staff from both prisons again saw the service as being in the question mark zone and requiring further attention. Whilst the numbers sampled in each prison were small, the results do add some support to the overall argument that the Prison Service is not crisis prone as suggested by the media. Indeed, in-depth interviews with staff at riot-affected prisons also bears testimony to this argument (Rouse, 1992). Whilst staff accept that there have been problems within individual prisons, they argue that the service has attempted to incorporate its learning from such events into local management strategies. Rouse did, however, identify a number of key areas of concern and these centred around the configuration of the service and communications therein. A particular problem area concerns the relationship between headquarters and the various regions – a problem that faces many public service organisations. Given the climate generated by Government policy on privatisation, issues over staffing levels (compared to the increasing prison population) and the opening of the UK's first private prison were also high amongst the concerns of prison staff (Rouse, 1992).

By using the 7C framework Rouse and Smith (1992) identified those elements of the Prison Service that may give rise to potential problems in the future. The main points to emerge from this analysis are shown in Table 8.1. There have been concerns expressed over the levels of morale within the service and the extent of communication and co-operation between the various grades (Woolf, 1991). There have also been problems over the extent of communication between headquarters and individual prisons and this reflects upon the hierarchical nature of the service. The Woolf Report is critical of the relationship between the regions, individual governors and headquarters in terms of its effect upon the perceived lack of power that individual governors have to affect change at the local level and the lack of support that governors receive under conditions of crisis (see paragraphs 1.145 and 1.154 of the Woolf Report). The issue of control is also important as the conditions under which prisoners are kept and the design of certain Victorian prisons make control outside of the cells themselves difficult. The levels of contingency planning within the service were criticised by Woolf and the need for regular updating of those plans was emphasised. The listing of factors in Table 8.1 serve to illustrate the importance of using the 7Cs in an auditing framework and one might argue that if these issues are not addressed then the Prison Service may be incubating crises for the future.

For the Prison Service, the media hype concerning its crisis prone nature is not supported by the views of senior managers within the Service. What emerges is that, whilst the Service is destined to have to deal with a range of potential crisis events, it is generally well prepared

Culture	□ Need for a recognition of the likelihood of crises at all levels of the organisation.
	□ Need for strong leadership during conflict situations.
	□ Lack of trust and confidence in Headquarters.
Control	□ Design of prisons and the numbers of prisoners require that inmates spend long periods of time in cells.
	□ Inability to isolate disturbances in some prisons due to design factors.
Communications	□ Need to improve internal communications and external liaison.
	□ Revise methods of communications with Headquarters, especially within operational crises.
	□ New initiatives to be channelled through one source (Lygo Report).
Configuration	□ Need for a tighter relationship between the prison service and the judicial system.
	□ Need to redesign away from a hierarchical structure.
	□ Need for more local prisons.
Contingency Planning	□ Training for riot situations increasing.
	□ Need to undertake crisis simulations on a wide scale within the service.
	□ Need to implement the recommendations of the Woolf Report.
Cost	□ Public sector cut-backs and need for efficiency measures.
	□ Revision of staffing levels to accommodate increased occupancy levels.
Coupling & Complexity	□ Revision of prison design and adaptation of existing prisons to allow for isolation and containment of riot affected areas.
	□ Installation of electronic gates to facilitate containment and control.

Table 8.1

The 7Cs of Crisis Management applied to the Prison Service

Source: Rouse and Smith – 1992

to deal with such events. In particular, the service has shown that it has the potential to learn from crisis, with a series of reforms following in the wake of the 1990s disturbances. However, in common with all public sector organisations the Prison Service is heavily dependent upon government policy and vulnerable to public spending cutbacks. Whether the Service will be able to implement the recommendations of the Lygo and Woolf reports will be determined by the government's willingness to pay for an improved service. All that prison governors can do is to ensure that their own prisons are individually prepared for the demands of crisis. Such a policy would require a significant shift in the culture of the organisation and a relaxing of the hierarchical bureaucracy of the Prison Service to facilitate greater local freedoms to innovate within broad policy frameworks. Where the Prison Service needs to develop crisis preparedness strategies, in common with other public sector organisations, is in terms of data protection and handling, communications strategies for dealing with the media, and in terms of cultural and organisational change in order to cope with a more dynamic external policy environment.

Conclusions

This paper has sought to outline the nature of the crisis management process and has applied the principles of the process to public sector management by examining the Prison Service. The arguments developed here do not correspond to a systematic review of the state of crisis management within the service, but merely a brief snapshot of the state of play in an organisation that has experienced more than its fair share of crisis during the early part of the 1990s. It is argued that the case of the Prison Service illustrates the potential for the application across the public sector, although it is important to note that each public service organisation will have its own distinct crisis portfolio and profile. Indeed, by its very nature, the Prison Service seems destined to experience the potential for crisis events and, as such, may not be typical of the public sector as a whole. The complexity of the issues prevents a comprehensive account of the nature of crisis management within the public sector and consequently the paper has merely highlighted some of the key points. The implications from this discussion are that organisations can prepare for the demands of crisis events. It is important that organisations undertake an assessment of their crisis portfolio and audit their procedures on a regular basis. This auditing process must go beyond the development of contingency plans, to include an assessment of the organisation's capabilities in all four layers of Pauchant and Mitroff's onion model.

The implications for management are clear within each of the layers. There is an obvious need to establish an effective crisis decision unit to cope with the initial demands of such an event (Smart and Vertinsky, 1977), leaving management free to continue to deal with the daily requirements of the organisation. Such units must have the authority to make decisions without referral to senior management. For complex technical systems, the organisation must ensure that it has de-coupled the system, thereby preventing a recurrence of the chain of events. The strategies that organisations have in place must go beyond the immediate requirements of the event and should take account of the need to effect turnaround after the operational phase of the crisis.

At the deeper levels of the onion model it is important that organisations pay attention to those aspects of the 7Cs that fall within the warm triangle – communications, culture and configuration. Here it is essential that organisations learn from their own and others' experience of crisis by external verification and validation of their strategies. Given the view expressed by Greiner (1972) that most crises are inevitable, the learning process becomes of central importance to organisational survival. In order to facilitate learning, managers should examine their own organisations by reference to the 7Cs and use them as a framework for crisis auditing.

This chapter represents an attempt to highlight the process of crisis management which can be utilised within the public sector. It does not represent a systematic attempt to detail the various implications of the process for the public sector – the sheer complexity of the problem goes beyond our current brief. What this chapter has done is to outline a model of crisis management and to suggest ways in which its basic principles can be applied to public sector organisations. The basic argument developed here is that all organisations will face crisis at some point in their existence and should prepare themselves accordingly.

References

Carvel, J. (1991a) 'Prison officers prepare action', *The Guardian*, Friday May 17, 1991 p.3.

Carvel, J. (1991b) 'Potent mixture in degrading jail system', *The Guardian*, Friday December 13, 1991 p. 2.

Carvel, J. (1991c) 'Fraggle Rock jail screams out for reform' *The Guardian*, Wednesday December 11 1991 p. 6.

Carvel, J. (1991d) 'Ministers' pledges 'do not impress staff or inmates', *The Guardian*, Friday December 13, 1991 p. 2.

Carvel, J. (1991e) 'Britain accused of inhuman treatment of prisoners', *The Guardian*, Friday December 13, 1991 p. 20.

Carvel, J. (1991f) 'Jail inspectors frustrated by report delays' *The Guardian*, Thursday December 19, 1991 p. 2.

Carvel, J. (1991g) 'Meagre progress on prevention of suicides in prison', *The Guardian*, Monday December 30 1991, p. 2.

Carvel, J. and Campbell, D. (1991) 'Baker admits not telling all on jailbreak', *The Guardian*, Wednesday December 11 1991, p.6.

Gainsford, R. (1992) 'Peacetime emergency planning in Britain – A County Emergency Planning Officers' Society viewpoint', in Parker, D. and Handmer, J. (Eds.) (1992) *Hazard management and emergency planning: Perspectives on Britain*. London: James and James. pp. 31–42.

Greiner, L.E. (1972) 'Evolution and revolution as organisations grow' *Harvard Business Review*, July/August, reprinted in, Asch, D. and Bowman, C. (Eds.) (1989) *Readings in Strategic Management*. London: Macmillan. p.373–387.

Hampden-Turner, C. (1990) *Creating corporate culture: From discord to harmony*. Reading, Mass.: Economist Books/Addison-Wesley Publishing.

Hood, C. and Jackson, M. (1992) 'The new public management: A recipe for disaster?', in, Parker, D. and Handmer, J. (Eds.) (1992) *Hazard management and emergency planning: Perspectives on Britain*. London: James and James. pp. 109–125.

Johnson, J. and Scholes, K. (1988) *Exploring Corporate Strategy*. London: Prentice Hall.

Lygo, R. (1991) *Management of the Prison Service*. London: HMSO

Kets de Vries, M.F.R. and Miller, D. (1987) *Unstable at the top: Inside the troubled organization*. New York: Mentor.

Mitroff, I.,Pauchant, T., Finney, M. and Pearson, C. (1989) 'Do (some) organisations cause their own crises? The cultural profiles of crisis-prone vs. crisis-prepared organisations'. *Industrial Crisis Quarterly* Vol 3 No 4. pp.269–283.

Pascale, R.T. and Athos, A.G. (1981) *The art of Japanese management*. New York: Simon Schuster.

Pauchant, T.C. and Mitroff, I.I. (1988) 'Crisis Prone Versus Crisis Avoiding Organisations; Is your company's culture its own worst enemy in creating crises?' *Industrial Crisis Quarterly*, Vol 2 No 1.

Pauchant, T.C. and Mitroff, I.I. (1992) *Transforming the crisis prone organization.*

Pedler, M., Burgoyne, J. and Boydell, T. (1991) *The learning company: A strategy for sustainable development.* London: McGraw Hill.

Perrow, C. (1984) *'Normal Accidents: Living with High Risk Technologies'.* New York: Basic Books.

Peters, T. and Waterman, J. (1982) *In search of excellence.* New York: Warner Books.

Reason, J. (1987) 'Cognitive aids in process environments: prostheses or tools?' *International Journal of Man-Machine Studies*, 27, pp.463–470.

Rouse, P. (1992) *Crisis management in prisons: Are prisons crisis prepared?* Unpublished MBA dissertation. Leicester Business School, De Montfort University, Leicester.

Rouse, P. and Smith, D. (1992) 'Keeping the lid on: Crisis management in the Prison Service'. *Mimeo.* Liverpool Business School.

Senge, P. M. (1990) *The Fifth Dimension: The art and practice of the learning organization.* New York: Doubleday.

Shrivastava, P., Mitroff, I., Miller D., Miglani, I. (1988) 'Understanding Industrial Crises' *Journal of Management Studies* July Vol 25 No4, p.283–303.

Smart, C. and Vertinshy, I. (1977) 'Design for crisis decision units' *Adminstrative Science Quarterly*, 22 pp.640–657

Smith, D. (1990) 'Beyond contingency planning – Towards a model of crisis management'. *Industrial Crisis Quarterly.* 4(4). pp. 263–275.

Smith, D. (1992a) 'The Kegworth aircrash – A crisis in three phases?' *Disaster Management.* 4(2) pp.63–72.

Smith, D. (1992b) 'The strategic implications of crisis management: A commentary on Mitroff et.al.', in Shrivastava, P., Huff, A. and Dutton, J. (Eds.) *Advances in Strategic Management.* Volume 8. pp.261–269

Smith, D. and Sipika, C. (1993) 'Back from the brink – A model of post-crisis turnaround strategies'. *Long Range Planning*, pp.28–38

Sipika, C. and Smith, D. (1992a) 'Message in a bottle: Crisis communication at Perrier', Paper presented at the 4th. International Disaster Management and Limitation Conference, University of Bradford. September.

Sipika, C. and Smith, D. (1992b) 'From disaster to crisis – The failed turnaround of Pan American Airlines'. Paper presented at the conference 'Crisis management in the 1990s', Home Office Emergency Planning College, Easingwold. September 1992.

Wainwright, M. (1991) 'Armly gets a little better'. *The Guardian*, Friday December 13, 1991 p. 2.

Woolf, H. (1991) *Prison Disturbances, April 1990.* (Parts I and II). Cm 1456. London: HMSO.

Acknowledgements

I would like to acknowledge the comments made on an earlier draft of this paper by Dr Des Hickie, Josephine McCloskey and Dr Steve Tombs from the Centre for Risk and Crisis Management, Liverpool Business School. Of course, the usual provisos concerning the possible errors of interpretation on the part of the author remain valid.

CHAPTER NINE

LOCAL GOVERNMENT

David Gardner

Introduction – The Scale and Structure of Local Government

Local government is a vitally important part of the UK economy, representing a quarter of total public spending, or 13% of Gross Domestic Product over recent years. It consists of 468 local authorities in England and Wales :- 47 Shire County Councils, 333 Shire District Councils, 36 Metropolitan Boroughs, 33 London Boroughs and 19 Joint Authorities (single-purpose authorities administered jointly by the Metropolitan Boroughs in each Metropolitan area). In Scotland, there are 9 Regional Councils, 53 District Councils within the Regions' areas, and 3 all-purpose Island Councils. Northern Ireland has 'a much more limited form of local government' (Henley 1989).

The agencies of local government are the major providers of services of a local nature, responsive to local needs. The distribution of services over the major authorities is shown in Table 9.1 below.

The economics of local service provision and the means of financing that provision will be considered first, reflecting on the many changes that have taken place over the post 1945 period in an area which has been at the heart of political controversy. It will be followed by a discussion, in greater detail, of existing and proposed funding arrangements, considering how they reflect the changing relationship between local government and the centre. How local authorities manage the provision of specific services and the deployment of their funds in support of that provision is outside the scope of this chapter. The effects of legislation in the 1980's requiring the use of compulsory competitive tendering, and more recent moves towards authorities assuming an enabling role whereby most if not all direct service provision is carried out under the direction of local authorities by private contractors, will not therefore be considered here.

Table 9.1

Main Local Authority Services as at 1 April 1990

Service	London	Met.		Shire		Scotland	
	LBC/Joint	MBC/Joint		CC	DC	RC	DC
Strategic planning	*	*		*		*	
Highways & Traffic	*	*		*			*
Housing	*	*			*		*
Building Regs.	*	*			*		*
Trading Standards	*	*		*		*	*
Refuse Disposal	*	*		*			*
Refuse Collection	*	*		*	*		*
Transport			*	*	*	*	
Police	Central Govt	*	*		*		
Fire	*		*	*		*	
Education	*	*		*		*	
Social Services	*	*		*		*	
Libraries	*	*		*			*
Leisure	*	*			*		*
Environmental Health	*	*			*		*

Source: After Henley et al, 1989, p94.

The Economic Rationale of Local Government
 – Local or Central Provision of Local Services

The case for the provision of public services by locally accountable agencies contains both political and economic strands (Brown & Jackson, 1990 Ch9). The political arguments are, first, that local government's existence, on the one hand, inhibits the development of a top heavy bureaucracy of purely central provision, whilst, on the other, provides a separation of functions in such a way that central government acts as a natural check on local government, acting to curb the excesses of extremist local authorities. Secondly, it is held that local government provides a local focus for political interest and activity – a training ground for politicians – and a counterweight to national government, reducing the chances of political domination by the centre against local wishes, by allowing democratic accountability at both levels.

The economic case starts with the view that, by permitting each local area to apply its own values to government policies, and to respond to expressions of local preference, the existence of local government assists in attuning service provision more closely to people's wants, and in providing a better measure of their effects on markets and opinions. Individual choice is catered for and a greater coincidence of people's wants and services provided should occur more than would be the case with purely central provision. Tiebout (1956) proposed a 'spacial shopping' model, which tried to explain how semi-public goods – those which are unsuitable for market provision and provision by central government –are distributed at sub-national level in accordance with expressions of people's preferences when they 'vote with their feet' and move to one of a large number of providing authorities, each offering a different tax and service package of such goods. In doing so, he was building on the work of Samuelson(1954) in explaining the level of provision of pure public goods at national level. There were many restrictive assumptions in Tiebout's model which divorced it from reality, but it did show the justification for local service provision on welfare grounds and strongly suggested that people's preferences for semi-public goods, like education and social services, would be more closely met at sub-national level than by the state centrally. In advanced economies, geographical mobility is a way of life. The choice of local authority, and its services and tax levels is, *inter alia*, an important determinant of where people opt to live. (see Oates, 1969) A further economic argument is that, for some services, local rather than central provision is more efficient. Buchanan (1965) offered an explanation for this in the 'Theory of Clubs', which offers a means of identifying the optimal size of providing authority for semi-public goods. It recognises a trade-off between 'cost-sharing' arising from providing a service of a given cost to an increasing number of people, and a 'crowding factor' arising from diseconomies of scale, whereby individuals' enjoyment of the service is reduced by an increasing number of recipients. Mueller (1979) p131 expands on Buchanan's explanation: 'The optimal size is where the marginal cost of an additional member through enhanced crowding just equals the reduction in other members' dues from spreading fixed costs over one extra member.' Whilst local authorities provide several services, and there is likely to be a different optimal scale for the provision of each, the Clubs Theory shows how more efficient provision is likely at sub- national level, and supports the justification for local providing agencies for semi-public goods.

However, despite the strength of these arguments, there is a compelling political and economic case for the centre having a strong role in overseeing and directing local government. After all, final legal power within the UK rests with central government. Local authorities can only act within legal powers that the state chooses to bestow.

National interests dictate how many local services should be provided. Local authorities need to be required to fulfil their statutory duties to provide services within centrally prescribed guidelines and monitoring. Education provision illustrates this. A widely held conviction, that a measure of uniformity of treatment for people receiving a local service is necessary, further justifies actions by the centre in using statutory controls and grant aid. In providing certain services, local authorities may not share the enthusiasm of the government of the day, for example in selling council houses in the early 1980's. Central government must, in these circumstances, have the power to enforce its legislative decisions, and to provide 'encouragement'. Local authorities depend on the centre for revenue raising powers, which are delegated very sparingly, limiting the means at local government's disposal to fund ever increasing services required by the state. This often requires that central government is obliged to provide additional financial help, usually in the form of grant assistance.

It is necessary for the management of the economy that the policies of local and central governments are consistent. For example, local authority borrowing must not be of such a scale and direction to have the potential to disturb money markets and interest rates and disrupt national monetary policy. Central government must retain regulatory powers. Local activities which can lead to income redistribution, must not be able to clash with the larger scale redistributive activities of the centre, if the latter are to be effective.

Finally, a group of arguments concern the movement of people and service benefits across local authority boundaries. People generally have interests in local authorities other than the one in which they reside, often living, working, and enjoying leisure in different areas. People have mobility potential and are keen to ensure that services are of an acceptable standard in areas into which they might move. Central government, therefore, has a standards maintenance role to safeguard people's wider interests. Further, there is a range of services the impact of which crosses local authority boundaries. Examples might include a leisure centre in one area, attracting custom from and providing benefits to another; or pollution control measures in one authority which might benefit those downstream of it. These 'spillovers' cause difficulties in setting the size of authority spending as people will only pay for benefits within their own areas, gladly accepting benefits that 'spill in' from neighbouring areas, free of charge. Authorities take account of spill-in benefits in scaling down their own spending. If all authorities do this, the net result is service underprovision. Pauly (1970) produced a model of the decision making processes of neighbouring authorities, involving a spiral of downward adjustment in provision levels. If people are not to be left short of service, an incentive is needed to induce authorities to maintain provision, only available from a higher tier of government, namely, the state. It is clear that the arguments support a balance whereby local authorities provide local services (consisting of semi-public goods), but central government has a major role in empowering, regulating, and encouraging provision.

Funding from the Centre – Exchequer Grants
Over the financial year 1991/2, 47% of local authority net revenue funding was provided in the form of grants from central government (16% out of V.A.T. to cover the cost of reducing Community Charge bills), more if the distributed proceeds of the National Non-Domestic Rate are added. Grants are therefore a vital feature of local government finance. There are strong arguments for the use of exchequer grants, many related to the justification for central government involvement with local government considered above. The fundamental need for grants stems from the tax base of local government, which is narrow and lacks the flexibility of that of central government, consisting of just one tax. Up to 1990, Local Rates had failed to keep pace with the effects of inflation on local government expenditure. An early identification of this occurred in the Green Paper *The Future Shape of Local Government Finance* in 1971. Additionally, rates were not equitable in their distribution. Since 1990, the Community Charge has attempted to keep up with local expenditures but is very inequitable, being a lump sum tax per capita taking little account of ability to pay. It is appropriate for central government to make a contribution from its broader based, more equitable taxes, so that local government's revenue resources can match its spending needs, and 'fiscal imbalance' (Ridge & Smith, 1991, pp15–16) is overcome. It is likely that there will be users of statutory local services who fall outside the catchment of local taxes (fewer under a poll tax than a property tax), and make no contribution towards the costs, whilst still paying national taxes. It is appropriate that central government transfers some of its resources to local government in the form of grants. There are clear instances where central government legislation has deprived local authorities of tax revenues. One of the

earliest and best documented examples was the 1929 Local Government Act, which derated agricultural land and buildings. It therefore
seems fair that government compensates local authorities for their lost
income using grants.

Many local government services are of national concern, necessitating a central government influence which justifies a central contribution towards their costs, as in the case of education and the police. For
other services, an external stimulus is needed to encourage service
development, as in housing construction and sales. Grants provide a
suitable medium for this. In some instances, central government wishes
local authorities to provide a national minimum standard of services. A
grant might be used to top up the cost difference between supplying for
local needs and for central requirements. However, Ridge & Smith
(1991) highlight difficulties in designing a grant which can achieve this
and avert a 'free-rider' situation with local authorities. The tax base of
local authorities varies considerably nationwide, and, along with it, the
means to provide local services. Government's aim is uniformity of
provision; it therefore needs to contribute to poorer authorities to
equalise taxable resources. Similarly, service needs of local authority
areas differ. For instance, some have ageing populations requiring
more social services, and others have decaying urban areas requiring
regeneration. There are grounds here for government compensating
local authorities for differing demands on their resources. A great deal
of research has been undertaken into the justification for, and the
design of, suitable equalisation grants, notably by Feldstein (1975) in
the USA. However, there are those who argue that local variations in
needs and resources are taken into account by the market or
'capitalised' , along with local tax differences, in property prices
(Oates,1969; Epple et al,1978), although the research is inconclusive.
Barnett & Topham (1980) argue that equalisation grants will be
unnecessary or even counter-productive if this 'capitalisation' in
property prices occurs in full.

Finally, the role of spillovers and externalities has been discussed
earlier, together with the need for the state to intervene to provide
incentives to local authorities and avert underprovision. Williams
(1966) suggested a scheme using grants to achieve this, and there is
general recognition of such a need, especially for grants which match
spending by the local authority (Ridge & Smith, 1991, p17).

The principles governing the form that grants might take will now be
considered. Two statements of such principles exist. In 1929, when the

UK's first grant system was introduced, a White Paper specified that it should:–

– ensure that a fair contribution should be made from the Exchequer towards the cost of local services.
– ensure that local authorities have complete financial interest in their administration.
– be adaptable to the needs of local authority areas.
– permit freedom of local administration and initiative.
– and provide for sufficient general control and advice from central government to ensure a reasonable standard of service.

In 1954, the then Institute of Municipal Treasurers and Accountants (now CIPFA, the Chartered Institute of Public Finance and Accountancy) published a paper broadly concurring with central government's principles but with more emphasis on local initiative and less on detailed central government control.

Options available in designing a grant system can now be considered. Perhaps the earliest type of grant was a service specific Unit Grant, an amount per measured unit of service provided, for example, per school place created. This type was first used in the mid-nineteenth century to encourage early development in the health and education services. It is claimed that it promoted economy and required little detailed control by the centre. However, it was sometimes difficult to determine appropriate units of service which could accommodate peculiar local circumstances and, despite its origins, it was inappropriate as an aid to the introduction of new services in that, until service provision commenced, no grant was paid. In the UK these grants are historical.

A second type is the specific Percentage Grant, closely resembling the Matching Grant identified in research by McGuire (1973). This involves government paying to each local authority a predetermined proportion of the agreed costs of a service or part-service, a UK example being the 50% grant paid by the Home Office for the police service. In its favour, it is argued that such a grant is simple and intelligible, and serves to encourage local initiatives. It provides an incentive to develop a service, and to enhance standards of provision, with the added advantage that it is directly related to service costs, taking account of both price rises and service expansion.

However, percentage grants are inequitable between authorities, in that rich ones that can afford to pay for more service receive more grant than poorer ones that can only afford a rudimentary service, yet may have greater needs. In addition to requiring detailed government control, a percentage grant is normally open-ended, being demand led, which makes it hard for government to budget precisely for the amount payable at the start of a particular year. The grant can be made close-ended but this reduces several of its advantages and necessitates a form of rationing. A complex claims procedure is needed at local and central levels and it is not surprising that, in the UK, government has sought to reduce the number of such grants by absorbing them into its general/block/formula grant.

The third and most widely used form of grant is the General, Formula, Lump-sum, or Block Grant. It involves payments being made to local authorities on the basis of a formula, which reflects the authorities' characteristics to show its needs and/or its resources. The Revenue Support Grant in the UK is a current example. A formula grant is suitable where services are fairly evenly distributed, with no major variations in provision between authorities, when the grant serves as a reward for efficiency. The grant permits the authority some freedom to choose how it should be spent, within its statutory powers, and requires minimal oversight by the centre. The grant is closed-ended, the amount payable being predetermined, providing certainty in government budgeting. However, the formulae for distribution are, by necessity, complex to take account of variances in authorities' circumstances, but, even then, cannot be adapted to extreme needs. It is difficult to define criteria for payment which are equitable and universally acceptable. There is always the risk that government might manipulate the distribution criteria for political purposes.

In the UK, since 1990, the Revenue Support Grant has been the major Exchequer contributor to local revenues, representing a considerable simplification over its unwieldy predecessor, the Block Grant. It involves paying to local authorities an amount judged by government to meet a proportion of the cost of services assumed to be provided according to government's measures of need (Standard Spending Assessments). It also assumes that they are partly funded by the centrally determined National Non-Domestic Rate and an assumed average level of local taxation, currently the Community Charge. In addition, there are still a number of Specific Percentage Grants, such as the Police Grant, and Derelict Land Reclamation Grants, which amount to about 23% of total grants paid to local government.

Local Taxation

In the UK, in recent years, local taxes have contributed 38% (22% in 1991/2 after subsidy from VAT) of total local authority revenues. If the National Non-Domestic Rate (NNDR) is added, for comparability purposes, this figure reaches approximately 60% (38%). Massive changes have taken place, with the switch from rates to Community Charge/NNDR in 1990 (1989 in Scotland), and a further upheaval is under way, with the introduction of the property-based Council Tax in 1993 replacing the ill-fated Community Charge. Amid these changes, it is worthwhile to consider what purposes local taxation is intended to serve. Perhaps the clearest statement of these is found in the evidence of CIPFA to the Layfield Committee of Inquiry into local government finance, in 1976. CIPFA stated that local taxes should display:-

- certainty, convenience, clarity, and economy.
- buoyancy ie, keep pace with the effects of inflation on local spending.
- low administrative costs, with no duplication of existing administrative machinery.
- and they should be 'genuine' local taxes – locally operated, the burden falling on the local electors, and with local power to determine the tax rate.

Ridge & Smith (1991, Ch5) demonstrate that they are valid today when they identify Administrative Feasibility, Economic Efficiency, Equity, and Accountability, as the key issues. More recently, Isaac (1992) pp27–39 has added the speed of introduction, and maintaining the confidentiality of personal information as further criteria.

It is important, therefore, to determine which taxes are appropriate to UK local government. Up to 1990 (1989 Scotland), local taxation needs were met by local rates, applied to individual households and the business community, raising, in its later years, 35% of total revenue needs of which over 55% was collected from businesses. Rates were a local tax on the occupation of fixed property determined annually by each local authority. The tax base was 'rateable value', the market rent that a property would generate if let on the open market less the notional cost of repairs and insurance, and was determined by the Inland Revenue (local assessment committees in Scotland). A re-valuation should have taken place every five years, but this seldom occured. This meant that rateable values (RV's) were too low, forcing local councils to compensate, usually reluctantly, with a higher rate in the pound of RV. The tax base was far from comprehensive, with many exempted properties. Business property bore the rate in full. Domestic ratepayers (49% of RV's) received a reduction for which the local authority was compensated by grant. It should also be noted that, since 1984, government have had powers to place a ceiling on the rate poundage of authorities, individually or generally, known as 'rate capping'.

Local rates had several positive features, developed and proven over many years. Their yield was relatively certain and stable, an advantage for local authority budgeting. That yield was considerable, putting it on a par with national taxes such as VAT. With an immobile tax base, fixed property, it was hard to evade, whilst instalment payment provision made it convenient to pay. These contributed to low collection costs, with very little policing required. Subject to the constraint of 'capping', the tax was genuinely local, a safeguard for local government's independence from the centre. With its rebate system providing relief to those on low incomes, the tax was fairly equitable, when viewed nationally, in terms of tax paid as a proportion of household incomes (Smith & Squire, 1987), with some progression over the lower tail of the income distribution (Brown & Jackson, 1990).

However, the tax had fundamental weaknesses. It lacked buoyancy; its yield consistently failed to keep pace with inflation of local government spending, due largely to valuation difficulties (infrequent revaluations and a shortage of rental information), and a political reluctance to sanction large poundage rises. In the case of rates on domestic properties, the tax was clearly inequitable – regressive between households (Smith & Squire, 1987), and between areas, with poorer areas needing to levy higher rate poundages. Rates taxed improvements to property, providing a deterrent, and they failed to tax up to 4m earning non-householders with ability to pay, who used local services, but did not pay rates, undermining the accountability of local authorities for their spending decisions. These weaknesses, fuelled by the high inflation rates of the 1970's, and the political reaction to a delayed revaluation in Scotland in the 1980's, pushed government into the abolition of domestic rates in 1989 and 1990.

With regard to non-domestic rating, there were further problems. Rates did not reflect a firm's ability to pay, ignoring profitability. They served to discourage and distort investment decisions, hitting capital intensive concerns hardest (Bennett, 1986). They entered export prices and, along with other costs damaged international competitiveness.

They undermined local accountability by subsidising the cost to local electors of extra local spending. Most seriously, their burden was very uneven across the country, with alleged major consequences for locational decisions, though Mair (1987)argued that this effect was very limited. Often, the highest rates were levied in areas most in need of additional employment opportunities. This uneven distribution made it necessary for a resource equalisation element to be built into the exchequer grant, which served to confuse public understanding of the link between spending and local household tax bills (Ridge & Smith, 1991). These issues led government to take local business rating out of the jurisdiction of local authorities. In 1990 (1989 Scotland), the NNDR was introduced, replacing locally operated business rates. The poundage of the NNDR is determined annually by government for the country as a whole and raised in line with the Retail Price Index each year. The rateable values of businesses were revalued in early 1990, and will be again in 1995. The national proceeds are pooled and redistributed to each local authority on a population basis, removing the need for resource equalisation through the grant system.

A most striking effect of this measure is that it leaves only 22% of local revenue needs (from 1991/2) to be collected using a tax, the rate and yield of which are determined by decision of the local authority, namely the Community Charge up to 1993. This means that, given tight control by the government of central funding (grant or NNDR distribution), the full effects of decisions made to increase spending by a local authority above government targets are focused on the Community Charge/Local Taxpayer, and hence, on the electorate – the so-called 'gearing effect', designed to increase accountability, subject to government's powers to cap local taxes. A 5% increase in an authority's spending means a 23% rise in its Community Charge, as other income sources would not change. According to Jackman (1987), this ignores the fact that the benefits of spending a marginal increase in local tax revenues also fall on businesses to the tune of an estimated 15%, yet businesses are not likely to be required to meet the cost. Perhaps remedial action is needed here to share out the burden, yet government intends to continue this arrangement into the new Council Tax regime. The consequences are amplified by the fact that local taxes have now been made ultra sensitive to changes in the basis of grant distribution, either through changing inflation assumptions (Ridge & Smith, 1991), or as a response to political pressures (Smith & Squire, 1986).

The Community Charge

In 1990 (1989 Scotland), the Community Charge replaced local domestic rates. It is a flat rate tax, determined annually, locally, on all eligible adult residents of each local authority in England, Scotland, and Wales. It is a 'Poll Tax', and as such, is simple in concept, aimed primarily at ensuring that more who vote for and consume local services pay something towards their cost. It is an attractive concept from an accountability standpoint, involving a considerable broadening of the tax base, whilst increasing the perceptibility of local taxation through individual billing. Arguably, it is attractive from an economic efficiency viewpoint, in that, a lump sum tax is held to be allocatively neutral – not altering resource allocation –, though it should be clear that personal spending decisions are likely to be affected by this tax, especially those of the less well-off. However, equity is the fundamental failing of Community Charge. No tax is less equitable than a lump sum. The switch from rates involved gains for the better-off, and losses for the less well-off, with a tax which is seriously regressive. The administrative complexity of the tax also contributed to its downfall. It proved very costly to establish and maintain a register to track eligible adults for billing, costs which were supplemented to a great extent by the costs of separate billing, and a major campaign of non-payment, necessitating complex and very ineffective recovery procedures, the costs of which falling on those who did pay. The resulting unpopularity of this tax contributed to the displacement of the Prime Minister, Margaret Thatcher, and led to a commitment by her successor, John Major, to replace it with a less contentious measure, and, in the interim, to reduce the burden on the payer with a contribution from the exchequer (£14bn in 1991/2) funded by an increase in the rate of VAT from 15% to 17.5%.

After the Community Charge – The Way Forward in the 1990's

The Conservatives legislated for a new Council Tax to operate from 1993. It is based on property capital values, determined by approved estate agents/valuers, making use of a system of banding. The valuer determines which of eight bands of predetermined value a property falls in . A different rate of tax determined by the local authority, is applied to each band. The household rather than the individual will be the tax unit, with single person households receiving a 25% discount, and a rebate system maintained for those on low incomes. Given the outcome of the 1992 General Election, this is likely to be in place for some time. The Labour Party, however, favour a return to the old domestic rates as a short term expedient, pending the introduction of a scheme of 'fair rates' reflecting capital values and the occupier's income. Both major parties therefore favour some form of Property Tax. It is appropriate to examine the related arguments.

There are strong economic efficiency arguments for property taxation. Adam Smith (1776) argued for a tax on land rents, because it would cause no economic distortion, as it would be borne by landowners out of fortuitous surpluses which were not the fruits of endeavour, but of events such as demographic changes. Taxes on buildings, however, require consideration of short and long run effects, as they can be built, or removed, or relocated over time, along with investment in them. In the short run, supply is fixed, so the consequences of a buildings tax are the same as those for land, namely lower profits to owners, and lower property prices, through capitalisation (after Muth 1960 and Reid 1962). The burden falls on current property owners with no distortion of their decisions. In the long run, however, tax on buildings will lead to owners switching investment out of buildings, resulting in higher rents, whereby the tax is passed to the property consumer. Further, if rents are controlled there may be scope for passing the tax to the tenant even in the short run.

It has been argued that if benefits from the spending of tax proceeds are distributed as per the tax, in accordance with properties, these would offset any allocative consequences of the tax, but there is little evidence to suggest such a benefit distribution.

The case for taxing property on neutrality grounds is therefore rather tenuous. It is undermined further by locally set and varying tax rates (Ridge & Smith, 1991, p49). The uneven distribution of taxable resources, even with uniform rates, would result in either population movement to low tax areas (Blake, 1979), or, as a necessary result, the establishment of equalisation grants.

The only real efficiency case for property taxation consists of two arguments. Firstly, in the UK, property is favourably treated compared with other durable goods (subject to VAT), especially owner-occupied property, with mortgage tax relief and no taxation of imputed rent income, suggesting a need for tax to minimise distortion of markets (Muellbauer, 1990). Secondly housing consumption is not specifically taxed, leading to over consumption compared with other durables, and a need for tax on property to render the whole tax system neutral towards consumption.

The equity issues surrounding property taxes stem from the traditional efficiency analysis above which shows that, in the long run, landlords pass the tax on to tenants in rent, with regressive consequences. However, it is clear that different tax rates among local authorities provide an opportunity for shifting the tax burden (Harberger 1962, and Mieskowski 1972). If owners' capital moves from high to low tax authorities, property supply will increase and rents fall, lowering the return on capital to owners. As higher income earners hold more property than low income earners, this result would increase the progressiveness of the tax. Empirical evidence of the old UK rating system, however, shows it to be solidly regressive up to 1966, and even after the introduction of rebates, progressiveness only extended over the lower income ranges. It is likely that any property tax base will show generally regressive characteristics. There is no equity case therefore for property taxation.

Perhaps the strongest case for property tax is its ease of administration (Green Paper 1981, and Layfield 1976). Its base is immobile and readily identifiable, whilst its definitions are far clearer than for other tax bases. Its yield is predictable and stable (not subject to boom or recession), due to the freedom of authorities to fix the tax rate to compensate for inflation. This is a valuable aid to budget balancing, and compares favourably with the variable yield of an income tax. The yield is attributable to all sizes of local authority units, because the location of property is unambiguous. This contributes to the fact that evasion is very difficult. The tax is simple in concept and comprehensible. Its operation is stable over time, its operating costs low compared with yield. It has none of the confidentiality of information problems associated with a local income tax.

There is a further case for property taxes in their contribution to local authority accountability. Rates were very perceptible. The annual demand draws the tax to the payers' attention very severely. As local authorities had to pass increased costs on to all ratepayers through rate poundages, according to Layfield (1976), rates promoted accountability. However, in the Green Paper (1986), government criticised the lack of accountability of domestic rating. Only half the electorate were billed for local rates, and hence, there were incentives for those who did not pay to vote for higher spending. However, this charge ignores the fact that, whilst the head of household is billed, households usually consist of two adults, both of whom have an interest in obtaining value for money for their taxes. According to Smith (1991), the government's analysis is an oversimplification and accountability under domestic rating is not as low as was argued.

It would appear that the preferred replacement for the Community Charge, a Property Tax, whilst strong administratively, is weak on efficiency and equity and unclear in terms of accountability. Moreover, the Government do not appear to have paid sufficient heed to a number of implementation difficulties likely to face the new Council Tax. It is now clear that, given that in parts of the South-East almost everyone will reside in a property in one of the highest bands, whilst in parts of the North most will be compressed into the lower bands, the tax provides little recognition of ability to pay within certain areas. 'It runs the danger of becoming perceived, like the Community Charge, as a flat rate tax with little redistributing impact' (Stoker, 1992, p68).

The provision of discounts to single householders will probably require authorities to carry out checks and set up a register, a costly exercise which is potentially as unpopular as that associated with the Community Charge. House buyers could be somewhat surprised when properties are revalued on sale, especially when other houses in the same street carry a lower value as they have not changed hands. These measures are likely to generate a further wave of protest and a welter of appeals which could clog the system up again. 'In short, the sort of anomolies, implementation dilemmas and inequities that dogged the poll tax seem likely to surround the new Council Tax.' (Stoker, 1992, p68).

If that turns out to be the case, and the Council tax results in as much ill-will as its predecessor, its life might be just as short, and a further form of local tax may need to be found. Perhaps the most likely candidate, given the general lack of enthusiasm for a Sales Tax, is a Local Income Tax (LIT) along the lines of that advocated by the Liberal Democrat Party, which is not without its supporters in the other major parties.

A U.K. LIT. could realistically take one of two forms : it could be assessed by the Inland Revenue and collected by the local authority using Inland Revenue information, or it could be collected by the I.R. at rates prescribed by the local authority. The latter is preferred, as it maintains the confidentiality of personal tax information, and minimises the duplication of administrative machinery. Other options are possible where either the local authority has no discretion over the tax rate or where the authority undertakes assessment as well as collection (Isaac 1992 pp8–10). Neither of these adequately meets the local tax criteria described earlier.

A LIT. is capable of generating a substantial yield (in the U.K., a 4.5% LIT. could replace the yield of rates), which, given that incomes tend to rise faster than prices, would be very buoyant. The tax takes account of peoples' ability to pay; it does not tax the less well-off; it extracts a payment from earning non-householders; and it does away with the need for a rebate system. It may well stimulate greater interest in local government affairs, as the periodic payslip would regularly remind people of their contribution. The tax collecting authorities regard the tax as a technically feasible proposition.

However, there are major problems to be overcome. One is that a decision would have to be made on whether tax would be collected by the authority of residence or of employment. Either would result in a very uneven distribution of tax yield. This could be worsened by the tax being collected at company headquarters, concentrated around capital cities, rather than at branches. Many argue that LIT. would place too great a proportion of taxation on the base of income, effectively narrowing the overall tax base. It is also argued that it would reduce the government's manoeuvrability in economic management by providing local authorities with a means of offsetting national tax changes. However, there are precedents in that local income taxes are in operation in a number of countries, notably Sweden.

It is clear, therefore, that a Local Income Tax, whilst very effective in achieving equity and good revenue raising, is likely to be weak on efficiency and accountability and suffers serious administrative short-comings at least as severe as the Council Tax (Ridge and Smith, 1991). None of the available options wholly meets the criteria set by Layfield (1976) and Ridge and Smith (1991), though a property tax gets closer than the alternatives.

Perhaps what has been missing from attempts to find a suitable local tax, and has been from all recent inquiries into local government finance, is a simultaneous review of financing mechanisms and the structure of local government. The 1972 Local Government Act structural changes perpetuated existing financing arrangements whilst subsequent legislation has altered the local tax and exchequer grant regimes with minimal attention to the structures they finance, and without obvious regard to the funding needs of different structures. CIPFA (1985) issued a discussion paper which sought to relate proposed local taxes to different tiers of local government. This however attracted little attention as it was overshadowed by the 1986 Green Paper *Paying For Local Government*. Government has initiated a further structural review with the establishment in 1992 of a Local Government Commission in the light of Government assuming responsibility for a greater share of local government finance, and the development of the enabling role for local authorities following compulsory competitive tendering. The time is right to widen its brief to take on board the financing needs of the new streamlined local authority structures that are likely to be implemented as a consequence of the Commission's work, perhaps seeking to match groups of local services of similar optimal scale (Theory of Clubs, Buchanan, 1965) with the most appropriate form of local taxation for each.

References

Barnett R. and Topham N. (1980) 'A Critique of Equalising Grants to Local Government' *Scottish Journal of Political Economy* Vol 27.
Bennett R. (1986) 'The Impact of Non-Domestic Rates on Profitability and Investment' *Fiscal Studies* Vol.7, No.1.
Blake D.R. (1979) 'Property Tax Incidence: an Alternative View' *Land Economics* 55, No.4.
Brown C.V. & Jackson P.M. (1990) *'Public Sector Economics'* 4th Ed, Basil Blackwell, Oxford.
Buchanan J.M. (1965) 'An Economic Theory of Clubs' *Economica*, pp1–14.
CIPFA (1985) *'Financing Local Government'* Discussion Paper.
Department of the Environment (1971) *'The Future Shape of Local Government Finance'* Cmnd 4741 HMSO, London.
D.of E. (1981) *'Alternatives to Domestic Rates'* Cmnd 8449, HMSO, London.
D.of E. (1986) *'Paying for Local Government'* Cmnd 9714, HMSO, London
Epple D. Zelenitz A. and Visscher. (1978) 'A Search for Testable Implications of the Tiebout Hypothesis' *Journal of Political Economy*, 6, pp406–426.
Feldstein M.S. (1975) 'Wealth, Neutrality and Local Choice in Public Education' *American Economic Review*, pp75–88.
Harberger A.C. (1962) 'The Incidence of Corporate Income Tax' *Journal of Political Economy* Vol.70, pp215–240.
Henley D., Holtham C., Likierman A. and Perrin J. (1989) *'Public Sector Accounting and Financial Control'*, Van Nostrand Reinhold.

Isaac A.S.J. (1992) *'Local Income Tax - a study of the options'*, Joseph Rowntree Foundation, York.

Jackman R. (1987) 'Paying for Local Government; an appraisal of the British Government's Proposals for Non-Domestic Rates' *Government and Policy* Vol.5, No.1.

Layfield F. (1976) *'Report of the Committee of Inquiry into Local Government Finance'* Cmnd 6453, HMSO, London.

Mair D. (1987) 'The Incidence of Business Rates: Preliminary Estimates' *Government and Policy* Vol.5, No.5.

McGuire M. (1973) ' Notes on Grants in Aid and Economic Interactions among Governments' *Canadian Journal of Economics*, No.6, pp207–221.

Mieskowski P. (1972) 'The Property Tax: Excise Tax or Profits Tax' *Journal of Public Economics* Vol.2, pp73–96.

 Muellbauer J. (1990) *'The Great British Housing Disaster and Economic Policy'* London, IPPR.

Mueller D. (1979) *'Public Choice'* Cambridge.

Muth R. (1960) ' The Demand for Non-Farm Housing' in *'The Demand for Durable Goods'* Harberger A.C.,Ed, Chicago.

Oates W.E. (1969) ' The Effects of Property Taxes and Local Public Spending on Property Values: An Empirical Study on Tax Capitalisation and the Tiebout Hypothesis' *Journal of Political Economy*, 77, pp957–971.

Oates W.E. (1972) *'Fiscal Federalism'* , New York, Harcourt Brace.

Pauly N.V. (1970) 'Optimality, Public Goods and Local Governments - A General Theoretical Analysis' *Journal of Political Economy*, pp572–585

Ridge M. and Smith S.R. (1991) ' Local Taxation - The Options and The Arguments' *Institute of Fiscal Studies Report* No. 38, London.

Reid M.G. (1962) *'Housing and Income'* Chicago.

Samuelson P.A. (1954) 'The Pure Theory of Public Expenditure' *Review of Economics and Statistics*, 36, pp387–389.

Smith A. (1776) *'The Wealth of Nations'* London, Methuan, 1961.

Smith S.R. (1991) ' Economic Policy and the Division of Income Within The Family' *IFS Report*, No.37.

Smith S.R. and Squire D.L. (1986) 'The Local Government Green Paper' *Fiscal Studies* Vol.7, No.2.

Smith S.R. and Squire D.L. (1987) 'Local Taxes and Local Government' *IFS Report* No.25, London, IFS.

Stoker G. (1992) *'Local Government'* in 'Public Domain', Terry F. and Jackson P. Eds, Chapman and Hall.

Tiebout C.M. (1956) 'A Pure Theory of Local Expenditures' *Journal of Political Economy*, 65, pp416–424.

Williams A. (1966) 'The Optimal Provision of Public Goods in a System of Local Government' *Journal of Political Economy*, 65, pp13–33.

CHAPTER TEN

NATIONAL HEALTH SERVICE

Anita Carroll and John Wilson

Introduction

The National Health Service (NHS) is the largest of all the public services in the United Kingdom (UK). It accounts for approximately 13.3% of the total UK public expenditure budget in 1991–92 (Command 1920 1992, Table 2.2), and has approximately 970,000 employees (Command 1920 1992, Table 8.6). The political importance of the NHS was emphasised during the 1992 general election campaign when all three major parties proposed health policies designed to convince the electorate of their commitment to the future of the service. The re-election of the Conservatives means that the measures included in the NHS and Community Care Act 1990 will continue to be implemented and developed well into the 1990s despite controversy over the pace of implementation, desirability and effectiveness of these reforms.

This chapter explores Conservative policy towards the NHS. Its rationale is assessed within an historical context and critically evaluated. Finally, comments are made as to the possible nature of the NHS at the end of the 1990s.

Background

Conservative policy towards the NHS represents the most radical programme of innovation since it was established in 1948. There have, of course, been changes in the last forty-five years. These have involved a combination of organisational, financial and managerial measures but they have not provoked the same degree of controversy as current policy. This reflects the nature of the programme and its degree of departure from the *status quo* but it also reflects the politicisation of the NHS as an issue on which there is perhaps no longer a consensus between the main political parties. However, it is important to distinguish between substantive differences and political rhetoric. This in turn necessitates consideration of actual measures and policy statements within the context of previous changes.

The first major structural change to the NHS was implemented in 1974 by means of the NHS Reorganisation Act 1973. This brought together hospital and community health services which were to be provided by Area Health Authorities (AHAs) directly or through their Districts where appropriate. Regional Health Authorities (RHAs) were also established with responsibility for regional planning and monitoring as well as for the provision of certain central services. In addition, Family Practitioner Committees (FPCs) were established to administer general practitioner services and although they operated autonomously, each was linked with an AHA sharing the same boundaries. Finally Community Health Councils (CHCs) were created, one for each District, in order to represent the views of the consumer and act as a local pressure group.

The aims of the 1973 Reorganisation Act were commendable in that it sought to integrate more fully healthcare provision by bringing together the hospital and community health sectors and by promoting comprehensive strategic planning in preference to disaggregated hospital planning. This restructuring was quickly followed by the constitution of a Resource Allocation Working Party (RAWP) in 1975 to address the issue of inequalities in the system for distributing health resources throughout the country.

However, despite these developments critics of the reorganisation argued that there were too many tiers of management for efficient decision-making and the report of the Royal Commission on the NHS (Command 7615 1979) accepted the need to eradicate one tier. In addition, the Conservative election victory in 1979 meant that attention would be focused on levels of public expenditure. For the NHS this meant assessing the use to which resources were put and how they might be supplemented. The Conservatives stated they would 'make better use of what resources are available' and would 'simplify and decentralise the service and cut back bureaucracy' (Conservative Party 1979 p26).

The Health Services Act 1980 eliminated the AHAs and their functions were transferred to newly-established District Health Authorities (DHAs). These were held accountable for managing their own hospital and community health services and encouraged to delegate responsibility for decision-making to units of management, usually hospitals, wherever possible. The Act also sought to encourage private sector health care provision by reducing restrictions on private medicine. It also legalised lotteries and voluntary fund raising by health authorities.

During the early 1980s central government placed the emphasis on accountability and value for money. This led to the introduction of annual performance reviews supported by the publication of the first set of performance indicators for the NHS in 1983 and initiatives were launched aimed at securing the most efficient utilisation of scarce resources.

In 1983 the Griffiths Inquiry was commissioned whose subsequent report (Griffiths 1983) proposed another restructuring of the NHS to promote speedier decision-making and enhanced accountability. Consensus decision-making at Unit, District and Regional level was to be abolished and replaced by general managers at all levels who were to be given clear responsibility for implementing policy directives and meeting targets. The management structure of the NHS was revised and two Boards were established: a Health Services Supervisory Board, chaired by the Secretary of State, with responsibility, *inter alia*, for formulating strategic objectives; second, a Management Board, chaired by a Chief Executive responsible for the execution of policy decisions and the control of strategic performance. Tangentially, the idea of delegation to the lowest practical level was developed through the introduction of management budgeting, a concept whereby individual responsibility for the consumption of resources is identified and incorporated into the budgeting process. This meant clinicians became budget holders thereby making them more accountable for their decisions.

This focus on accountability and control of resources was reinforced throughout the 1980s with initiatives such as the contracting-out of support services, the introduction of limited prescription lists for general practitioners, the establishment of cost improvement pro-grammes for health authorities and new income generation plans for the NHS. At the same time a debate arose about the government's alleged underfunding of the service. This debate continued until the launch of the NHS Review, announced in 1988, culminating in the publication of the White Papers *Working for Patients* (Command 555 1989) and *Caring for People: Community Care in the Next Decade and Beyond* (Command 849 1989). The proposals contained in these reports were embodied in the NHS and Community Care Act 1990. This has been followed by a Green Paper, *The Health of the Nation* (Command 1523

1991), proposing a long-term strategy to bring the best balance of health benefits to the nation; *The Patients Charter* (Dept of Health 1991) which sets out the key rights every citizen has in respect of the NHS; and nine National Charter Standards which the NHS is expected to achieve. The NHS and Community Care Act affects both the NHS and local authorities and represents a watershed in the history of health care in the UK. To understand why this is the case requires consideration of the main features of Conservative policy post 1989 and its underlying rationale.

Conservative policy: a rationale
The Conservatives believe that the way the NHS is organised is ill-suited to the present-day; it represents a 1940s organisation attempting to meet the needs of the 1990s and beyond. The kernel of the problem is not the total level of resources but rather the way those resources are used. Consistent with their belief in the efficacy of market forces as the most efficient mechanism for allocating resources, they advocated, in 1989, the introduction of market principles to the provision of health care. This was to be complemented by the use of private sector management techniques (combined with greater encouragement for private health provision). An indication of this was given in 1987: 'The NHS is a large and complex organisation. It needs good management. It is not a business, but it must be run in a business-like way . . . We will continue to ensure that the Health Service is as efficient as possible. But good management is not just a matter of efficiency. We value enterprise in the public service just as much as in the private sector.' (Conservative Party 1987 p15).

The recommendations of the White Papers of 1989 were logical extensions of this viewpoint and of the management arrangements introduced post-Griffiths. An underlying assumption seemed to be that establishing the most appropriate means of delivering services was paramount; ways of paying for them would be less of an issue given the improved efficiency which would naturally result from the implementation of their recommendations. The main thrust of the reforms rests on the introduction of an internal market. This means that the health authority function of financing hospital and community services is separated from that of actually supplying those services – the financing and supply functions are now called respectively the 'purchaser' and 'provider' functions. The internal market as a concept is based on the establishment of competition at the provider level whilst health authorities as purchasers continue to be financed from the Department of Health but in their new role have a duty to enter into contracts with a range of providers to secure the best and most efficient services possible for their resident populations.

In assessing the internal market, structural, funding and operational issues need to be considered.

Structure

A distinction is made between purchasers and providers within the market. The purchasers are the RHAs, DHAs, GP fundholders and private patients. The focus here is on the role of GP fundholders as purchasers, an innovation which is perhaps the greatest area of controversy, and NHS trusts as providers.

The introduction of GP fundholding reflects a recognition of the fundamental importance of the GP as the gatekeeper to healthcare for the majority of patients. The initiative is designed to complement the other reforms in *Working for Patients* and to give GPs an incentive to improve the services they offer and enable money to follow the patient from the GP practice itself. The essence of the proposals means that the GP enters the contracting process as a purchaser of health care for his/her patients. Practices can opt to become fundholders providing certain conditions, mainly relating to the size of the practice and its ability to manage budgets, are met. Once granted fundholding status a GP practice receives a budget from its RHA intended to cover the cost of purchasing certain services. The budget is determined by the practice list size and previous referral patterns and, once set, the practice may enter into contracts with a range of providers – Trusts, DMUs (Directly Managed Units -please see below), private hospitals – to purchase a defined range of services for its patients.

The first GP fundholders were established on 1 April 1991 with 306 practices granted fundholding status (the average practice comprises just over 5 GPs). The Conservatives anticipate that in total over 5500 GPs will be fundholders by April 1993 (Conservative Party 1992 p58). Furthermore, the former Secretary of State for Health, William Waldergrave, announced early in 1992 that the scheme is to be extended from April 1993 to allow GP fundholders to purchase additional services such as district nursing and health visiting if required.

With regard to providers, the reforms involve significant change for hospital and community units in that they are now able to apply for

NHS trust status and thereby become self- governing. Each Trust is run by a Board of Directors whose chairman is appointed by the Secretary of State and is statutorily entitled: to employ staff and to determine their pay and conditions; to enter into contracts as providers of services, thereby earning revenue, and to buy in services and supplies from others; to borrow money from the government or from the private sector subject to government external financing limits; and to raise income within the scope set by the Health and Medicines Act 1988. The first set ('wave') of NHS Trusts came into being on 1 April 1991 (57 in total); the second set (99 in total) became Trusts with effect from 1 April 1992. By September 1992 153 units gained approval for Trust status from 1 April 1993.

Units which do not seek Trust status, known as Directly Managed Units (DMUs), will continue to be managed by and accountable to their District Health Authority. However, as provider units they are obliged to enter into contracts with purchasers to cover the volume of patient services they will supply and as such they will compete with NHS Trusts, other DMUs, GP fundholders and the private sector for income from service contracts.

In considering the structure of the market and the participants within it, it is important to highlight a further and fundamental element of change *ie* that relating to community care. Prior to 1989, the fragmentation of community care provision was a function of the number of parties involved, including family and friends, voluntary bodies, health authorities, local authorities etc. This plurality of input was complicated by the diversity of needs which had to be addressed – from the elderly, the mentally ill, and the mentally and physically handicapped – involving widely-varied combinations of professional skills and durations of treatment. The funding of community services also became more problematic in that social security expenditure – which is one element of funding, others being local and health authorities' budgets and contributions from individuals themselves – rose rapidly from 1979 to the mid-1980s. This increase reflected the growth and cost of private sector nursing and residential homes.

Fragmentation of provision and escalating cost of funding, combined with criticisms from bodies such as the Audit Commission, the National Audit Office and the Public Accounts Committee, led the Government to instigate a review, undertaken by Sir Roy Griffiths. His report (Griffiths 1988) led to the White Paper *Caring for People*.

Initially, Griffiths' recommendations were unpopular to certain ministers because he believed the primary responsibility for coordinating community services should be assigned to local authorities. The unpopularity of this recommendation was not the result of practical objections but rather a political aversion to enhancing the role of local authorities in any sphere, combined with concern over the implications for levels of public expenditure.

Nonetheless, the government has accepted that local authority social services departments should have responsibility for assessing needs and ensuring they are met, within the constraint of a finite level of resources. However, consistent with Griffiths, their role is to be that of enabler rather than provider. In other words, social service managers are expected to demonstrate value for money in the purchase of services from competing bodies in the public, private and voluntary sectors.

Funding

The Conservatives strenuously deny accusations that they have underfunded the NHS or sought to privatise it. On the contrary, they are proud of the increased resources they have devoted to it. From 1979–80 to 1990–91, expenditure increased in real terms by 39.2% (from £19.9bn to £27.7bn at 1990-91 price levels – see Command 1920 1992 Table 2.3). These resources have enabled more doctors and nurses to be employed and more patients to be treated.

Despite these increased resources there have been periods of acute pressure brought to bear on the Government when shortages of beds, staff etc have been extensively publicised. In particular, the winter of 1987–88 was embarassing for the government when the heads of three royal colleges of medicine complained that the NHS was 'in crisis' and close to breaking point and which led to a non-recurring injection of cash by the Government to meet expenditure. The problem was, and remains, that demands on the service are insatiable. Demographic factors, medical advances, expensive technology and the need to comply with Governmental objectives all meant that increased resources when measured against the Retail Prices Index were never likely to be adequate.

In addition to the problem of determining the total level of resources to be devoted to health care, there is the secondary problem of deciding how resources are to be allocated, both geographically and clinically. An important change was the replacement of the existing resource allocation system (RAWP), the formula for which had been the subject of much debate and criticism (Jones & Prowle 1987; Perry 1986; Birch

& Maynard 1986; NHS Management Board 1986 & 1988). The revised allocation system means that all hospitals and community units, whether self-governing or DMUs, earn revenue on the basis of work undertaken; district health authorities and GP fundholders, as purchasers of health care, are funded by central government by reference to their resident populations adjusted for factors such as population structure *ie* a weighted capitation basis.

An additional feature of the funding and allocation process is the impact on the flow of funds of the introduction of capital charging. Accounting arrangements in the NHS in respect of capital expenditure differed substantially from those of commercial organisations in that expenditure on capital items was written off in the year of purchase and health authorities did not need to include a charge for the depreciation of fixed assets in their accounts nor record the cumulative value of fixed assets in the balance sheet. These arrangements were the subject of much discussion and debate (see AHST 1985; Lapsley 1986; Mellet 1988) but a new system of charging for capital (Dept of Health 1989) was introduced from 1 April 1991.

Health authorities now incur an interest and depreciation charge for the use of existing capital assets and new capital investment. Simultaneously, a new definition of capital has been introduced to cover all tangible assets, with minor exceptions, with a life of one year or more (£1,000 lower limit). These revised arrangements have an impact on the funding and allocation systems in that capital charges are now paid by DMUs to the RHAs which then reallocate these funds to purchasers on a weighted capitation basis. The newly formed NHS Trusts are subject to differing arrangements whereby depreciation is retained within the Trusts and provides a source of funds for capital expenditure. Interest charges are not payable but instead Trusts are required to earn a rate of return (6%) on the current value of their net assets. The target rate of return set for NHS Trusts is identical to the interest charges payable by DMUs to reflect the need to ensure that contract prices for services are calculated on a common basis.

Operation
The market requires providers to enter into contracts with purchasers in which the volume, quality and cost of services are specified. Prices are to be based on full-cost recovery with marginal costing only being the basis of price where there is spare capacity for a short period, and there should be no cross-subsidisation between services. Contracts may

be one of three types: block; cost and volume; cost per case. In a block contract the provider is paid an annual sum in return for which the purchaser's residents gain access to a defined range of services, with limitations in respect of volume. A cost and volume contract requires the purchaser to pay for the treatment of a specified number of cases. In a cost per case contract, the purchaser agrees the price of treatment of individual patients. In practice, the prevalent contract has been that which was envisaged *ie* block.

An important requirement for the successful operation of the market is the availability of relevant, accurate and timely information. This issue actually acquired more urgency as a result of NHS developments in the 1970s and 1980s. In the 1970s, the idea of specialty costing was proposed, a specialty cost being the average cost of treating patients in the same clinical specialty. Whilst these costs were imprecise mainly because of the lack of appropriate supporting software, they did provide useful management information on which to make comparisons and base resource allocation decisions. In 1983 the sixth in a series of reports chaired by E Körner (NHS/DHSS Steering Group 1983) was produced addressing specifically the collection and use of financial information in the NHS. Its main recommendations were that basic work units be associated with a departmental analysis of expenditure for each hospital site and that specialty costs be produced as a minimum for all health authorities. These proposals were adopted by the DHSS and included as statutory returns in the annual reporting framework. However the information produced was relatively crude and not integrated with health authorities' management information systems. Management budgeting, as advocated by Griffiths, provided an incentive for further development work on clinical budgeting but as a concept it did not succeed. This was mainly because of uninterest on the part of clinicians combined with poor information technology support. It was succeeded by the Resource Management Initiative (RMI) launched by the NHS Management Board in 1986 which has a broader perspective than management budgeting and focuses on the participation of clinicians and other staff in the development of management information. Experimental work on the RMI began in 1986 on 6 hospital sites. This was followed by the announcement, in *Working for Patients*, of a further 50 hospital sites to be included in the initiative from 1989 with the remainder of the large acute hospitals in England expected to commence development work on the project by the end of 1992. Within the White Paper, the Government expressed its commitment to the RMI as a means of producing the information needed to support its proposals. The development of the RMI has been supported by the NHS Management Executive (Scott 1991) and products and services are available providing guidance on information technology procurement for example. Further work is in progress to develop more sophisticated information systems to ensure the success of all aspects of the NHS reforms.

All the policy areas considered above were enacted in the NHS and Community Care Act 1990. Whilst many of the reforms were introduced on 1 April 1991, others continue to be implemented gradually and research into their impact and effectiveness is ongoing (see, for example, NHS Reforms Bulletin 1991; NHS Management Executive 1992). However, it is possible to make certain preliminary comments concerning the policy programme implemented by the Conservatives.

Conservative policy: a critique
The controversy resulting from Conservative policy reflects genuine objections and not simply political posturing. To understand the debate it is necessary to evaluate the policy; this will also be based on structure, funding and operation.

Structure
It may be argued that Conservative policy would have engendered less opposition and public mistrust had it excluded GP fundholding. The introduction of overt budgetary constraints may lead to increased anxiety that medical decisions concerning appropriate treatment are being compromised by financial considerations. There is a real possibility that the treatment prescribed or purchased may be the cheapest rather than the most appropriate. This is not to impugn the medical integrity of GPs but simply to point out that, in the interests of all their patients, a GP practice may, of necessity, seek to economise on treatment. There is also the problem of establishing realistic budgets for practices given variations in size (subject to a limit of 9000 patients), location, fluctuations in demand for care and referral patterns. Also relevant is the unsophisticated nature of information technology and management accounting systems prevalent in GP practices.

Another major criticism of GP fundholding is that it will result in a two-tier system whereby patients of fundholding practices will be treated preferentially. This was in fact recognised by the Government and the Secretary of State issued a directive prohibiting hospitals from disadvantaging non-fundholder patients. The effectiveness of this will need to be monitored. The creation of NHS Trusts is designed to increase competition within the health service. Their ability to determine their own staffing levels and pay and conditions of service is also consistent with the Government's aim of reducing trade union influence and bargaining strength. Their success or failure will depend on their performance in the market and, theoretically, should a hospital have to close as a result of failure to compete then this could be attributed to market forces rather than arbitrary political decisions. Beyond this, however, they appear to solve little. Flynn (1990 p65) states: '[NHS Trusts] are not a solution to the problem of the distribution of resources to patients, nor to the uneven distribution of access to healthcare facilities. They provide a sort of solution to the problems of managing health districts, by taking the management of hospitals away from the district authorities and making them more like independent businesses in a competitive environment.' How far such an achievement justifies the creation of Trusts is debatable.

With regard to community care, most of the Griffiths proposals were welcomed by the relevant professionals. However, although the Government reluctantly accepted that the key role was to be played by local authorities, implementation was deferred from April 1991 to April 1993. The reason for the deferral was political and concerned the likely impact on poll tax bills.

Apprehensions remain as to the possibility that the level of funding will be simply insufficient to ensure the care in the community scheme actually works. This is extremely disturbing given the nature of the groups affected, including the mentally ill and the elderly. A recent report by Henwood (1992) accuses the NHS of divesting itself of the responsibility to provide long-term care for the elderly in the belief that the community care proposals will meet the need. Henwood identifies the 'demographic timebomb' of increasing numbers of the elderly and argues that many people are unaware of the implications of community care. The reduction in the numbers of helpers combined with changes in society (smaller families, more divorces, both partners working etc) mean that families will be less able to cope, placing greater reliance on local authorities. In turn, they may have to withdraw services (home helps, meals on wheels) in order to concentrate on those that need intensive care. However, the increased use of private nursing homes may mean that there are considerable shortfalls between fees and levels of income support. These shortfalls may have to be rectified, where it is an option, through sale of homes. Such a scenario is not unrealistic but, on a national scale, it is as yet unappreciated. It potentially involves a substantial financial shift from the social security budget to individuals and their families.

Funding

It is probably true to say that, given the nature of the health service, no amount of resources will be sufficient to meet the needs of the population. Political decisions have to be made to allocate finite resources to various programmes including education, defence, housing, transport etc; health must be considered alongside other priority areas. Decisions must also be taken as to how to allocate resources within the health service. These, too, are largely political though the marketisation of the NHS is partly concerned with improving allocative efficiency by allowing consumers to determine resource allocation, via the laws of supply and demand, rather than politicians or bureaucrats.

Political decisions, however, remain and the Conservatives point to their record as proof that they are committed to the NHS and the principles of universal healthcare free at the point of delivery. However, despite the increased resources, the NHS fares badly both relative to its existing needs and in international comparisons (see Chapter One).

The Office of Health Economics (OHE) (1992) has reported that the NHS needs an extra £10bn per year to lift UK expenditure on health to the level of the rest of the developed world. Definitive conclusions cannot be drawn from international comparisons (see Appleby 1992) and higher levels of expenditure are no guarantee of higher levels of service (they may, on the contrary, reflect inefficiency), but it is nonetheless worth noting that amongst the 20 industrialised countries of the Organisation for Economic Cooperation and Development (OECD) only Greece spends a smaller share of its national wealth (Gross Domestic Product or GDP) on health care than the UK. The UK devotes 6.1% of GDP to health compared with over 8% for countries including France, Germany and Holland. The OHE also reported that the NHS is underfunded even to achieve the Government's own targets and quantifies a cumulative underfunding of £1.6bn since 1981–82. In addition, although total health spending is estimated to reach a record £35bn in 1992, the annual rate of growth, adjusting for inflation, has reduced from 5.5% in the 1960s and 1970s to 3% in the 1980s.

Against this, private health care expenditure doubled between 1973 and 1990, almost certainly resulting from the inadequate levels of service provided by the NHS and the fiscal incentives to acquire private health insurance. This now covers one in six households, a record 7.5m people (13% of UK population). These figures partly reflect Conservative policy towards public expenditure (see Chapter One). Since 1981 public expenditure has been planned in cash terms and this means that should pay and price inflation exceed the Treasury forecast there is no guarantee that the excess will be funded by the Government. This has been the source of much controversy given the high proportion of the health programme which is subject to cash control. The debate has been heightened by research from a number of sources (see, for example, Social Services Committee 1986; Command 1913 1992) which suggests that the NHS requires 1% additional real growth per annum just to meet the demands generated by demographic change and the ageing population. In addition it is estimated that an additional 1% real growth per annum is needed to cope with the impact of advances in medical technology and to fund governmental reforms.

The allegations of underfunding have centred around these claims about required annual growth and the government practice of not always funding shortfalls in pay and price inflation which has meant that in some years the excess has had to be funded out of planned real growth for the year or out of planned efficiency savings. There has also been some debate about the inflation index which ought to be applied to the NHS. The government uses a measure of inflation for the economy as a whole, the Gross Domestic Product deflator, to arrive at cash limits. Critics of this approach argue that indices more specific to the NHS should be used to reflect more accurately the real incidence of spending on health.

The principle that funds follow patients can be said to be an improvement on the former system in that hospitals which treated additional patients were financially penalised given the absence of an automatic link between demand for health care and funding. However, the practical limitations of the market mechanism when applied to health, the lack of knowledge on the part of consumers, the potential for reductions in the numbers of purchasers in that several may combine to form a large consortium, the perhaps unrealistic assumption that patients will travel to receive treatment (conversely, there may be no point in doing so if there is no contract between a health manager and a distant hospital), the problems of determining accurate costs of treatment *etc* all 'distort' the market. Such problems lead to legitimate doubts as to the internal market being inherently more likely to achieve optimal resource allocation than RAWP.

An area where reform was needed is that of charging for capital. This is a major innovation for the NHS and should ensure greater efficiency in the use of capital stock. However, there is potentially a problem for hospitals occupying expensive sites and for districts purchasing their services given that the cost of capital will be a component part of the prices charged. Such hospitals are at an immediate competitive disadvantage in the market. To address this, revenue adjustments were made in 1991–92 to ensure that district purchasers had the cash necessary to meet the capital component of their bills but, in the longer term, the system is not intended to be neutral. However, even in 1991 research (NAHAT 1991; Robinson & Appleby 1992) has shown that the original objective of neutrality was not fulfilled and that whilst 1992–93 is also supposed to be capital charge neutral, the problems of compensating purchasers who have to buy from providers with above average capital charges will need to be addressed.

Operation
There are profound criticisms of the principle of an internal market when applied to health care. The market mechanism may be sound as a theoretical model but the existence of the prerequisites of perfect competition is confined to textbooks. Increasingly the state has intervened to address the failings of the market place and to regulate its activity. These failings apply *a fortiori* to health care. The consumer (patient) is hardly in a position to express a demand in the market place for a specific drug or form of treatment; rather, he/she relies on the supplier to specify what he or she needs. However, it can also be said that demand is not expressed by the patient but rather by his/her agent in the market, *ie* the GP. However, the GP also, as a non-specialist, is largely reliant on the supplier to specify the service required.

The result is not so much a market but a *quasi*-market (see Chapter Two). However, the term internal market is also misleading as Prowse (1990 p155) points out: 'The government wants to create a health care market but not one that is internal to the NHS. One of its main objectives is to blur the boundaries between the public and private sectors. There will be three kinds of purchaser – DHAs, budget-holding GPs, and privately-insured patients; and three kinds of provider – NHS trusts, directly-managed units and private hospitals. The intention is that contracts between purchasers and providers will be based on quality and value for money considerations, rather than on public or private status.' It is this scenario of blurred boundaries which critics believe deliberately undermines and ultimately threatens the existence of the NHS.

It is also important to appreciate that markets mean winners and losers on the part, in particular, of suppliers. Losing may mean ceasing to exist. In the case of hospitals this would mean closure. The theory is that patients would choose, say, a hospital for treatment in the way that they choose, for instance, a supermarket for shopping. Those offering the highest standards of service, efficiency and value for money will prosper because they will attract custom and, concomitantly, funding. The incentive is there for suppliers to maximise efficiency and competitiveness. Again, however, the consumer is not in a position to judge and insofar as his/her agent, the GP, is in such a position, the choice made may depend less on the suitability of treatment and more on the cost of one type of treatment relative to another. This may be the case given that GPs also are constrained by their budget. Finally, it remains to be seen whether the ultimate sanction of the market – closure – is politically feasible given that the organisation in question may be a hospital, providing essential services in a given locality, and not a supermarket branch.

There are also costs associated with the internal market. Prowse (1990 p156) states: 'Trading in health care will be possible only after heavy investment in information technology, billing systems and financially-trained staff such as accountants. Proportionately, more money is likely to be spent on administration and less on care for patients'. Though *Working for Patients* anticipates that any extra costs associated with the reforms should be offset by improved efficiency, it remains to be seen whether this is actually the case.

Finally, to operate efficiently, markets need prices which reflect the true cost of supplying any particular product or service. In the NHS, patient costing represents the most accurate basis on which to gather information about treatment costs, but it is also the most expensive and difficult to develop. In the first year of operation of the internal market prices were usually based on estimates using relatively crude average specialty costs. Also, because of the prevalence of block contracts, providers have had little control over the volume of services provided. For the future, providers are keen to develop more accurate and relevant costs so that contracts can be established on a cost per case or cost and volume basis. This will facilitate more effective monitoring of the contract on the part of the provider. The issue certainly needs to be addressed. CIMA (1992) has recently reported that the costing and pricing data currently available to NHS managers are inadequate to meet the needs of the internal market.

Health care: the future

The Conservatives are committed, *inter alia*, to: increasing each year the level of real resources to the NHS; developing a comprehensive research and development strategy; continuing the NHS Trust movement; continuing to encourage the involvement of doctors and other medical staff in the management of services and to extending the scope of GP fundholding as the scheme develops; implementing the *Patient's Charter*; implementing a strategy for health and complete implementation of the community care proposals (Conservative Party 1992 pp59–61).

However, there is also evidence that policies have been modified in the past and may well be in the future. This, of course, is to the Conservatives' credit but against that it can be said that the need for modifications may have been less had they experimented on the basis of pilot schemes, particularly in the case of the internal market. Robinson (1992 p96) states: '. . . many of the details have been developed as implementation has taken place. One noticeable feature of this process has been the modification and refinement of particular aspects of policy as the year has progressed. In particular, the degree of regulation that will be placed upon the market has been extended some way beyond that envisaged originally, with the result that the system is now often described as an example of *managed competition*.' [Emphasis in original]

An illustration of managed competition provided by Robinson relates to NHS Trusts. They may have believed they would be allowed to operate in an autonomous manner but in a number of important respects they are unable to do so. For instance, their freedom to borrow, and therefore their ability to undertake capital programmes, is strictly controlled by the Department of Health. Despite the increasing evidence of a more pragmatic approach, the general direction of Conservative policy will remain the same.

However, ironically, a significant impediment to the achievement of their objectives is their commitment to three others – reducing public expenditure as a percentage of GDP; reducing direct taxation; adherence to European convergence criteria (see Chapters One and

Two). These policies, combined with the current state of public finances, mean that legitimate questions can be asked about their manifesto spending commitments on areas such as health.

All of this means that accusations of underfunding, combined with fundamental objections to many of the principles upon which Conservative policy is based, will ensure that health remains prominent as an area of political disagreement.

By the next election, there will have been a considerable change in the structure of the NHS. It is clear that some form of intermediary tier of management will be required to act on behalf of the Management Executive to implement national policies, agree targets, monitor performance and, perhaps most importantly, regulate the market. There is likely to be a fundamental change concerning RHAs, perhaps involving their abolition although the Health Secretary, Virginia Bottomley, speaking at a National Association of Health Authorities and Trusts conference in February 1993 proposed that RHA's continue to be responsible for delivering NHS objectives in their region but with a streamlined role. There will be a significant impact on the purchasing function as the number of GP fundholding practices increases whilst the number of DHA purchasers diminishes. With regard to provision, the self-governing trust is the Conservative's model and it will be exceptional for a provider unit not to be a trust. It is also likely that there will be a rationalisation of the number of providers and, consequently, availability of beds. This will vary across the country but London is almost certain to be disproportionately affected as evidenced by the proposals of the Tomlinson Report (1992). In summary, the NHS will have been considerably altered after a full-term of the Conservative Government.

The Labour Party will have to refine its policy to meet the changed circumstances but it is unlikely that the principles upon which its policy is based will have changed. Labour's policy on health (see Labour Party 1989, 1990, 1991, 1992) is in contrast to that of the Conservatives and, essentially, involves the abolition of the market. Labour stressed its commitment to increased investment in the NHS from proceeds of economic growth rather than prioritise in favour of cuts in direct taxation. Their policy also involved: negotiation of Performance Agreements with each health authority, backed by an Incentive Fund, which would set local targets reflecting local priorities; establishment of a Health Quality Commission; halting the reduction in NHS services for long-term care and community health services; finally, creation of community health authorities, representative of local people (Labour Party 1992 p16).

Liberal Democrats (1992 pp35–36) were committed to: replacing the internal market with service agreements between authorities and hospitals and other health units; replacing GP fundholding with a system which guarantees GPs freedom to refer patients outside service agreements negotiated by health authorities; creating a common structure of Local Management of Hospitals and community units and ending the ability of NHS Trusts to dispose of their capital assets, to set their own terms and conditions of service for staff and to withdraw from local planning of health services.

Party policies may change but it remains likely that health is one issue on which there will continue to be fundamental, not simply rhetorical, disagreement.

Conclusion
It is too early to reach conclusions about the success or otherwise of Conservative policy. Increases in activity have been observed but, according to John Appleby, Policy Unit Director of the National Association of Health Authorities and Trusts (NAHAT) this does not mean that the reforms have led to the increased activity; there was even an outside possibility that activity could have increased even more without the reforms (see *Public Finance and Accountancy*, 24 July 1992, p8). He was commenting on the result of a survey by the NAHAT (1992a) which concluded that it is impossible at this stage to judge whether the reforms have been a success. However, a further survey by the NAHAT (1992b) revealed at best an ambivalent attitude to the reforms by the people expected to be most enthusiastic towards them – health authority managers. For instance, only 44% of those surveyed believed that opted-out trust hospitals were necessary to produce the benefits of the purchaser/provider split and 69% believed that underfunding was a fundamental problem confronting the NHS (though this had reduced from 86% in a survey published in October 1990). It will take several years before meaningful conclusions can be drawn, though there could also be a change in direction. The future structure of the NHS will be determined by developments up to the next general election and the result of it. It remains to be seen whether Conservative policy towards the delivery of health care proves as enduring as that of the Labour Government in 1948.

References

Appleby, J (1992) *Financing Health Care In The 1990s* Open University Press

Association of Health Service Treasurers (1985), *Managing Capital Assets in the National Health Service* CIPFA

Birch, S and Maynard, A (1986), *The RAWP Review : Rawping Primary Care, Rawping the United Kingdom*, University of York, Centre for Health Economics

Chartered Institute of Management Accountants (CIMA) (1992) *Cost methods for NHS healthcare contracts* CIMA

Command 555 (1989) *Working for Patients* Department of Health

Command 849 (1989) *Caring for People : Community Care in the Next Decade and Beyond* HMSO

Command 1523 (1991) *The Health of the Nation* HMSO

Command 1913 (1992) *The Government's Executive Plans 1992–93 to 1994–95, Department of Health and Office for Population, Censuses and Surveys* HMSO

Command 1920 (1992) *The Government's Expenditure Plans 1992–3 to 1994–5 Statistical Supplement to the Autumn Statement* HMSO

Command 7615 (1979) *Report of the Royal Commission on the National Health Service* HMSO

Conservative Party (1979) (1987) (1992) *The Conservative Manifesto* Conservative Central Office

Department of Health (1989), *Capital Charges, Working for Patients*, Working Paper 5, HMSO

Department of Health (1991) *The Patients Charter* HMSO

Flynn, N (1990) *Public Sector Management* Harvester Wheatsheaf

Griffiths, R (1983) *Report of the NHS Management Inquiry* DHSS

Griffiths, R (1988) *Community Care: Agenda for Action* HMSO

Henwood, M (1992) *Through a glass darkly: community care and elderly people* Kings Fund Institute

Jones, T and Prowle, M (1987) *Health Service Finance: An Introduction.* The Certified Accountants Education Trust

Labour Party (1989) *Meet the challenge, Make the Change: a new agenda for Britain* Labour Party

Labour Party (1990) *A fresh start for health* Labour Party

Labour Party (1991) *Your good health: A White Paper for a Labour Government* Labour Party

Labour Party (1992) *Labour's election manifesto* Labour Party

Lapsley, I (1986) 'Managing Capital Assets in the National Health

Service: A Critique' *Financial Accountability and Management* Vol No 2 (3) pp227–232

Liberal Democrats (1992) *The Liberal Democrat Manifesto* Liberal Democrat Publications

Mellet, H (1988) 'One Transplant the NHS Doesn't Need' *Accountancy*, January 1988 pp118–119

National Association of Health Authorities and Trusts (1991) *A Review of Capital and Capital Charges: Cutting Through the Confusion* NAHAT

National Association of Health Authorities and Trusts (NAHAT) (1992a) *Financial survey of health authorities and provider units* NAHAT

National Association of Health Authorities and Trusts (NAHAT) (1992b) *Implementing the Reforms: A Second Survey of District General Managers* NAHAT

NHS/DHSS Steering Group on Health Services Information (1983), *A Report on the Collection and Use of Financial Information in the NHS* HMSO

NHS Management Board (1986) *Review of the Resource Allocation Working Party Formula* DHSS

NHS Management Board (1988) *Review of the Resource Allocation Working Party Formula – Final Report* DHSS

NHS Management Executive (1992) *NHS Reforms: the first six months* Department of Health

NHS Reforms Bulletin (1991) *Monitoring and Evaluating the NHS Reforms*, Kings Fund Institute

Office of Health Economics (1992) *Compendium of Health Economics* HMSO

Perry, B (1986) 'Social Deprivation and NHS Funding – Time for a change?' *Public Finance and Accountancy*, 18 April 1986 pp17–18

Prowse, M (1990) 'The National Health Service' in *Public Domain: a yearbook for the public services*, Jackson, P & Terry, F (Eds) Public Finance Foundation pp 153–161

Robinson, R (1992) 'Health Policy in 1991' in *Public Domain: The Public Services Yearbook*, Terry F & Jackson P (Eds), Public Finance Foundation pp95–109

Robinson, R & Appleby, J (1992) 'Hard Cash' *Health Service Journal* 27 February 1992 p24

Scott, T (1991) 'Health Resources' *Public Finance and Accountancy* 22 November 1991 pp12–14

Social Services Committee Fourth Report (1986) *Public Expenditure on the Social Services* HMSO

Tomlinson B (1992) Report of the Inquiry into London's Health Service, Medical Education and Research HMSO

INDEX